NGO and Global Policy : Current Issue and New Challenges

NGO and Global Policy : Current Issue and New Challenges

V. Mathur

CYBER TECH PUBLICATIONS
4264/3, Ansari Road, Daryaganj, New Delhi-110002 (India)
Ph.: 011-23244078, 011-43559448 Fax: 011-23280028
E-Mail: cyberpublicationsdelhi@yahoo.com
Website: www.cybertechpublications.com

NGO AND GLOBAL POLICY : CURRENT ISSUE AND NEW CHALLENGES

V. Mathur

First Edition 2010

Published by : Asian Offset Printers

G.S. Rawat for **Cyber Tech Publications**
4264/3, Ansari Road, Daryaganj, New Delhi-110002 (India)
Ph.: 011-23244078, 011-43559448 Fax: 011-23280028
E-Mail: cyberpublicationsdelhi@yahoo.com
Website: www.cybertechpublications.com

Preface

Today good governance needs support of NGOs. Different NGOs have different mission and their management challenges need different kind of approach. Another issue of significance attached with functioning NGOs is related to finances. Donors are funding agencies are liberal in their approach but policies need to focus in the fact that funds are channeled in right direction and their utilisation brings in the benefits to those for whom they are mentioned. NGO colleagues, delegates in the diplomatic missions, international civil servants, and all others who care about the future of global policy making. GPF has devoted considerable research and resources to this project. In an effort to do justice to the issues, the report speaks more frankly than is common in most United Nations discourse. It seeks to plainly identify problems and find useful solutions. Those who wish further information should consult the Global Policy Forum web site, where they can find more than 150 documents and analytical articles on NGOs and the UN system.

A number of NGO colleagues read drafts of this report and provided helpful comments, corrections and additional information. We have learned much from them and from others in the UN community who believe in NGOs. In particular, we want to thank the many delegations and Secretariat staff who have offered us their generous and wholehearted support and cooperation over the years. Their help and encouragement are greatly appreciated. The book is aimed at being useful to NGOs, policy-planners, social activists and others concerned with social work.

—*Author*

CONTENTS

Preface

1. Introduction 1
2. NGOs Role in Ecological Decision-making 39
3. Positive and Negative Aspects of NGOs Activities 85
4. NGOs and the World Bank 122
5. NGOs and the Transnational Finance 214
6. Promises and Actions of the NGOs 279

Bibliography 302

Index 303

1

Introduction

A new stage of activity of nongovernmental organizations has appeared. It is characterized by use of the Internet. Public movements cannot do without the Global Network. The Internet forms its own virtual environment where people look for new forms of communication. The goal of the research carried out at the Faculty of Journalism of Moscow State University is to trace interrelations between the nongovernmental sector and new communication technologies and to discover characteristics and differences of the new electronic information environment in comparison with the conventional one. Other tasks are data collection and analysis of current newspapers, digests, and bulletins issued by NGOs and aimed at other NGOs.

COMPONENTS OF SUCCESS

Since the UN Conference on Environment and Development (Rio de Janeiro, 1992), NGOs have had key positions in establishing democratic structures with public participation for sustainable development and conservation of the Earth's ecosystem. Their high prestige results from their responsible and constructive role in society. Both official and informal organizations, as well as local movements, are recognized as valuable partners in realization of Agenda 21. Nowadays, as the world community tries to walk away from impractical development patterns and chooses the way of ecological security and sustainable development, NGOs have the task to increase the membership of their structures for recognition of common goals by people in all layers of society. NGOs cannot realize their opportunities without modern information technologies.

Electronic media, particularly the Internet, play a significant role in data expansion, the search for partners, and creation of positive images of these organizations. The Internet is a powerful channel to solve difficult problems, including:

- o Increasing professional competence
- o Participation in decision-making
- o Access to data
- o Broadening scientific opportunities during assessments of ecological and economic aspects of specific problems

In spite of its novelty, the Internet in Russia gives the following opportunities for Russian NGOs:

- o Increasing data receipt and access to data for NGOs
- o Distributing information on NGOs and NGO projects
- o Organizing integrated information databases

The main problem now is providing easier access to the network by both electronic users and by creators of their own sites.

ACCESS TO THE INTERNET

The necessity of new information technology is now evident all over the world. Every day the news industry uses Internet pages with more confidence. For a long time, leading western newspapers and magazines have been creating electronic versions. Many American and European radio stations broadcast not only at conventional radio frequencies but on-line also. Every fifth inhabitant of the planet could have access to the resources concentrated in the global computer networks, including Russian ecological databases. The Internet is gradually turning into a global version of mass media.

As to Russian experience, a new tendency from conventional forms of data to new progressive techniques is taking place, similar to developments in the West. Nevertheless, many Russian researchers consider the Internet not as an independent means of information, but as a channel for conventional mass media. Many Russian papers and magazines have their own sites in the computer network. On the one hand, Internet-journalism leaps forward, and, on the other hand, different political parties with certain ecological agendas as well as other organizations use the network space successfully. At numerous sites of leading Russian political parties-Union of Right Forces, Yabloko, Fatherland All Russia, KEDR-one can find answers to many questions, such as appropriate use of natural resources, support of ecological principles, and effectiveness of environmental education.

Such sites increased during the last election for the State Duma when people realized the possibilities of the new technologies reaching large audiences. Russian statistics recorded approximately 350,000 computer units with unique identification numbers that were connected with political informational sites each week. According to Novaya Gazeta (May 17-23, 1999), the section Politics was in fourth place for average daily entries with more than 300,000 hits. The first place always belongs to the section Entertainment, the second one to the section Business, and the third one to Mass Media. If we unite the thematically similar sections Politics and Mass Media, we have approximately 800,000 hits. This number corresponds to the level of Entertainment.

The number of Russian-language users interested in ecology is nearly equal to that of Business. There is an opportunity for NGOs to use the Internet seriously in order to accomplish their tasks. It became possible just recently when many public movements were supported by western funds. As a rule, grants were given for specific projects to certain ecological groups. One of the priorities was purchase of computing equipment for scientific research, databases, newspaper or bulletin publishing, and opening of individual sites. That is why, nowadays, NGOs have rather good opportunities for network access and use.

INTERNET-JOURNALISM

Public organizations and movements began to develop the new information field as users of mass media sites present on the Russian Internet. Moreover, active members of these movements became authors. They expected that a lack of publicity in the society would be one of the most serious problems of the green movement. Publicity can result not only from successful actions but also from their frequent mention in the press. The Internet gave ecologists a real chance to come into contact with an audience as often as necessary. For this purpose, they use the entire media spectrum offered by the Internet. It includes electronic versions of publications, network news agencies, and bulletins. Of course, electronic versions are used by the general press as well as the ecological news. In order to bolster their image, NGOs can send information on themselves to any periodical. But experience shows that their own green press is preferable. An analysis of electronic issues of Zelyony Mir (Green World) proves this. The Russian ecological paper offers internet sections like Eco-press, Ecoglobe, ZM Mailbag, and others. This paper is also true to its credo that "pages of the paper are open to nongovernmental, state, and industrial organizations and private persons who are active participants of the Russian ecological movement." Front page information about the Azov-Black Sea region and opposition against an oil port that threatens preserves of the Black Sea coast illustrates this. The positive aspects of ecological journalism on the Internet are the following:

- There is the possibility of watching ecological topics in progress. As an example, Ecoline deals with the Lagonaki-Dagomys road through the Caucasus State Biosphere Reserve. One can find documents, photos, maps, and a list of broken laws. The actions concerning the project are illustrated in detail at the page "Doroga Lagonaki-Dagomys" (Lagonaki-Dagomys Road) at www.ecolain.ru.
- An electronic newspaper has no volume limits. That is why a problem can be covered completely with many facts necessary for understanding the problem.
- Professionals prepare these publications. According to survey data, representatives of ecological organizations and nongovernmental funds, i.e. journalists-ecologists, prepare them. They are not looking for sensations. They try to show ecological improvement because that is their little victory too.

- o Accuracy of the information is important. Journalists and members of ecological organizations know how to find necessary sources of data. Even if a source of information gives incorrect data, an experienced journalist- ecologist will not be misled.
- o A regional approach is emphasized. Electronic communication facilities give an advantage to the local press in coverage for a mass audience. Public organizations work better at the regional level. They are well informed about ecological problems of the region, they establish relations with local authorities, and they can watch the problems with their own eyes. Hence, journalists-ecologists of the regional press have easier access to local information. This has resulted in an abundance of regional ecological papers, such as Tabiat (Tajikistan), Ekovesti iz Luganska (Econews from Lugansk), Most-Silta (the Northwestern region), and others.
- o There is a wide audience. A mass audience benefits from many regional organs in the network because they help to form a complete ecological picture.
- o Accessibility is easy. Subscription to the electronic media is usually free. In order to subscribe one can send a letter to a subscription address. If you subscribe, you will receive informational messages from several paragraphs to dozens of pages, with various frequency from less than a week to a month.
- o There is a possibility to vary the information volume. Sometimes only a part of a bulletin may be of interest. This problem can be solved by means of e- mail. Due to a special procedure, every subscriber can receive only a brief annotation of an issue and then has an opportunity to receive the full report of interest. The service is named "What is new?"
- o Databases are preserved. Almost all periodicals provide archives. You can look through any interesting issue of any year since the beginning of publication.

- There are different ways of reading the text-an electronic version and hard copy. Also, one can obtain an electronic newspaper in a printed form, as it is not difficult to print the text from a monitor. So, as active Internet users, NGOs in many respects stimulated Internet-Journalism. They evaluated the advantages of electronic mass media. That is why many periodicals are located at NGO servers.

SERVERS OF PUBLIC ORGANIZATIONS

At present Internet servers of NGOs are the main ecological information carriers in Russia. Hence, the experience of the Socio-Ecological Union (SEU), the largest public ecological organization within the former USSR, is interesting. Public nonprofit organizations usually have difficulties in establishing continuous connections with the mass media, so this might be the most important task of a press service. For easier access of journalists to data obtained by NGOs, their press services publish bulletins and press releases.

The SEU was the first with its own server on the Internet network: "Internet for ecological movement, www:server Ecoline." In 1996 it began providing information about the public ecological movement. All the time, information at the server is routinely increased. Ecoline aims to make the server as a specific "open tribune" of the nature protection movement by allowing various ecological organizations to put their information there. A number of public organizations opened their pages on the server. Their task is to help each other work better in the present situation. Opening of the server appeared to be the next stage in development of this NGO that made ecological data available to the general public and also provided a good image both for itself and nature protection. Since 1993, the press service based at the Center of Coordination and Information of SEU has dealt with information campaigns and press conferences-essential information for the Russian mass media. Present tasks of the press service are the following:

- Providing information about the activity of SEU and improving the SEU image as an active public organization protecting human and nature rights.

- o Assistance in increasing ecologically competent publications in the mass media.
- o Assistance in training journalists in problems of protection of the environment and public health.

About once a month the press service organizes press conferences devoted to ecological problems, such as deforestation in Karelia, construction of new nuclear reactors in the country, and budgets for preserves. Press releases and press packages are prepared before the press conferences.

Press service tasks are much wider than only collaboration with mass media. It is a department of public relations. Journalists know it as an original source of fast, reliable, and interesting ecological information, while many members of SEU and other public organizations appreciate the opportunity to publish local ecologically essential information. Journalists who used to consider any NGO representative as incompetent in journalism now regard the press service workers as their colleagues, not rivals. Experts and scientists, who expect journalists to always distort data, unhesitatingly permit the press service to process and prepare results of their research for publishing.

Since January 1997 the SEU's CCI press service has issued the weekly bulletin Ekosvodka, intended primarily for journalists. Its electronic addresses are seupress@glasnet.ru and press@ecoline.ru. Bulletin materials give popular information about the most significant ecological problems known to SEU members and to other ecological NGOs. The bulletin announces actions, press conferences, and other events of interest to journalists. Ekosvodka is interesting to journalists and is routinely used by approximately fifty Russian central and foreign periodicals. Ekosvodka is more of an instrument of SEU than an independent source. Every item is supplied with a contact person for additional information, such as Ecological Watch of Sakhalin, Ecojuris institute, and the ecological fund Chernomorye. SEU also issues Ekosvodka-obozrenie (Ekosvodka-Review). Unlike the weekly Ekosvodka, this bulletin is issued bimonthly as a record of actions. One can get additional information according to the problem. Besides Ekosvodka and Ekosvodka-obozrenie, SEU publishes an ecological electronic newspaper. It differs from the bulletins mainly as being more analytical than news. The newspaper's goal is to create interest of a wide audience.

REGIONAL ECOLOGICAL ELECTRONIC BULLETINS

Review of Internet-materials shows that regional NGOs can use the ecological press to reach a wider audience than earlier when they had only printed media. As a rule, electronic bulletins are devoted to the problems of a certain region. For example, Transboundary Ecological News deals with problems of the Northwestern region (information from vika@lake-peipus.net), Ecostan-news (information from catena@glasnet.ru) informs about events in Central Asia, and Kislotny Dozhd (Acid Rain) root@green.lipetsk.su publishes materials about ecological problems of Lipetsk. These bulletins are free.

It is possible to subscribe to open networks. The participants can distribute their messages to each other by means of the network. An example of an active network is Ecological North West Line (ENWL), redproj@sci.mail.iephb.ru. An advantage of such networks is that an addressee receives not only the information itself, but almost immediately responses of other members and sometimes experts. So, there is an opportunity to find a mistake or gather more data. ENWL, which has two mailing lists, ENWL and ENWL-inf, was organized in 1997. The first list is for message exchange on regional problems. Debates are permitted. At present the list contains 120 addresses of different ecological organizations mainly from the northwest of Russia and the Baltic States: Estonia, Finland, Sweden, and Denmark. Important messages pass through the network on http://spb.org.ru/enwl.

The second teleconference, ENWL-inf, deals with information messages and short digests only. At the same time it is not limited to regional themes, so it unites 250 subscribers all over the world. Most network periodicals of the former Soviet states are routinely distributed by this mailing list. Both lists publish short reports, conference announcements, and scientific and ecological news. They often distribute information received from international ecological servers. Besides these mailing lists, the ecological network of northwest Russia has EcoNews at http://solar.rtd.utk.edu/~valery/econews/econews.html. It publishes thematic reports on key problems of ecology. Russian and English are official languages of both. In November 1998, every ENWL subscriber received more than 1300 KB of information in text format, while ENWL-inf subscribers received more than 900 KB. ENWL subscription is free. Send your address to n jordomo@spb.org.ru in order to subscribe for ENWL or ENWL-inf. The total number of subscribers for all the above lists is about 750. One can obtain detailed information from the network moderator Vladimir Levchenko: vflew@lew.spb.org (http://www.iephb.ru/labs/lab38/). A year was enough for a rather significant ecological network of northwest Russia to appear. There is a great interest in ecological problems of the northwest region.

One more project of interest is Most-Silta, a newspaper also devoted to the problems of the northwest region. The server spb.org.ru contains three electronic papers: Green World Baltic News, Baltic Region-Our Habitat (analytical bulletin), and Most-Silta, the only Russian-language paper. It is the result of collaboration of two Finnish and two Russian public ecological organizations. The project began in St. Petersburg at a Russia-Finland forum "Our Common Environment." The newspaper is aimed at cooperation between Russian and Finnish ecological public organizations. It is to become a permanent discussion forum concerning the environment and nature protection. The first issue is devoted to a review of the present state of northwest Russian and Finnish ecological movements. The newspaper publishes opinions of representatives of the state nature protection departments and public organizations. Community participation in decision-making is also discussed. Cooperation between public organizations and authorities in Finland has been in place for decades, while in Russia this cooperation has taken its first steps.

Interviews have an important place in the newspaper. Although they are rare in electronic periodicals, Most-Silta routinely publishes interviews on the first page, introducing representatives of northwest Russian ecological organizations. Let us examine an interview of V.A.Gushchin, a representative of the All-Russian Society of Nature Protection. He talks about a bloc of organizations engaged in wildlife protection and environmental training and education on the base of this old organization.

The interview of E.B.Popov, a leader of the public association Biocenter, is a continuation of the previous article. He speaks not only about his organization, which was established in 1991, but also about the newspaper Yuny Biolog (Young Biologist) and the annual Ecological Holiday in Moscow's Park of Victory. The Association of Young Journalists-Ecologists attached to Biocenter is of special interest.

Other items of the newspaper are interesting too, especially those informing about public organizations of the region. For example, Green Cross of the Northwest, established in 1993, unites more than 70 collective members such as industrial factories, firms, scientific groups, and public organizations. In Murmansk Oblast, one can now find about 50 registered organizations connected with nature protection. To some extent, publication of this newspaper stimulated new sites of public organizations. The Kola Informational Ecological Center ECONORD (econord@ksc.inep.ru.) is among them. It is one of the first ecological organizations, formed in 1991 by a group of scientists from the Institute of Problems of Industrial Ecology of the North of the Russian Academy of Sciences. The Center's main task is informational and educational activity. Since its foundation, more than 10 issues of a magazine have been published, and annual youth ecological camps and scientific conferences have been organized. The youth scientific ecological society EcoAS within ECONORD gives pupils an opportunity to carry out scientific projects under the leadership of scientists from the Kola Scientific Center.

This site also informs about the main activities and active projects of the coordinating ecological center Geya, which has been operating since 1991. To contact another ecological movement in Murmansk Oblast is also possible by the addresses gaia@mstu.edu.ru in Murmask and krugl@aprec.ru in Apatity. Geya publishes the almanac Zhivaya Arktika (Living Arctic). It gives information about the Karelia Republic Council of the All-Russian Society for Nature Protection, which is celebrating its fortieth anniversary, and about propagation of Agenda 21 ideas among different groups.

It is interesting to know about the Green Association of Karelia, which established the first national parks of Karelia Vodlozero and Paanjärvi. One can also be acquainted with the association Priroda (Nature) in Medvezhegorsk, which protects the beautiful place Zaonezhye, known all over the world with its pearl, Kizhi.

The regional eco-bulletin Dikoye Polye (Wild Field) is devoted to ecological news of the Donbass. It is distributed by the ecological and cultural center Bakhmat at: berezin@bahmat.donetsk.ua. The two last letters of the address show that it is in Ukraine. The bulletin Kislotny Dozhd (root@green.lipetsk.ru) is a sort of "branch establishment" of the Lipetsk department of SEU. Thus, it publishes materials on environmental problems of Lipetsk. Journalists have enough information because the Lipetsk ecological committee's activity is highly rated. The Lipetsk department of SEU belongs to the top five Russian ecological committees. Lipetsk itself may be characterized as "the cleanest city among the dirtiest ones." This city takes sixth place according to its air pollution, twenty-fifth place according to general pollution, and thirtieth place according to degree of hazardous pollutants. Due to efforts of professional ecologists, Lipetsk is known as the cleanest of the metallurgical cities.

The bulletin deals with ecological education and the pluses and minuses of gold mining in the region. A little item from one of the issues tells about car owners who used to drive from their garages through connecting courtyards of apartment houses right by a kindergarten. This simple item illustrates a state of ecological thinking of ordinary people that is very difficult to change. The author introduces a real person into the text, and it shows that one ought to think globally while acting locally.

The news agency Kislotny Dozhd, which exists along with the bulletin, offers short informational reports. For example, ecologists are outraged with the cutting of supposedly harmful poplars, in the center of Lipetsk. Poplar was once selected as the most resistant tree against pollution with increased foliage coverage and ability of air purification. In spite of this, its total destruction is taking place. Both the Bulletin and the news agency Kislotny Dozhd publish information on the activity of the local club Ekolog (Ecologist). Due to new information technologies, ecological problems are discussed without boundaries. The Internet now keeps a united information field of the former USSR. One example is the bulletin Zelyonoye Spaseniye ("Green Rescue") (mailserv@cci.glasnet.ru), which has appeared since 1995 registered in Kazakhstan. One of its issues, for example, is devoted to sustainable development after the UN Conference on Environment and Development.

It includes materials concerning resource status, economies based on raw material resources, role of transnational corporations, their influence on different aspects of social development, and a search for indicators of sustainable development.

The bulletin is meant for professors and students of the humanities, active green workers, and people engaged in sustainable development. As far as one can see, electronic bulletins play an intermediate role in NGO activity. They promote people's knowledge on sustainable development, and they disseminate information about NGOs.

SERVERS OF STATE STRUCTURES

NGOs consolidate their positions on the Internet by opening their own servers. They display legislation texts and other governmental information. For example, every Internet user can obtain minutes of U.S. Congressional sessions for recent years. The U.S. EPA server www.epa.gov is also informative. Recently Russian state bodies began to pay attention to placing their information on the Internet. The server of Goskomekologia (the State Committee on Environmental Protection), for example, contains electronic versions of the Report of

Environmental Status from 1992 to 1994. Servers of regional state bodies appear to be more interesting such as the one of Komprirody (Nature Committee) of Tomsk, with a review of the environment status of Tomsk Oblast (green.tsu.ru). The server of the authorities of St. Petersburg and Leningrad Oblast, base.dux.ru, contains a review of environmental status and legislation of the region. The interdepartmental server www.priroda.ru has been opened by the Ministry of Natural Resources with assistance of other departments. Its goal is to support the State's activity in coordination of natural resource management. Official reports on environmental status and certain types of pollution located on the server are very useful for NGOs. Recently these reports have been difficult to access due to limited editions. Now they are accessible to a greater number of readers on the Internet server. They are important for the official positions on different problems concerning environmental protection.

The tasks of the agency are the following:

- Informational and analytical support of the state structures in natural resources management.
- On-line distribution of management information and normative documents of natural resource departments.
- Establishment of an interdepartmental system of information exchange of the natural resource departments.
- Distribution of periodicals for natural resource departments.
- Interconnection of mass media with press services of governmental bodies.
- Informational and publishing support of federal executive authorities.
- Introduction of modern means of collection, storage, analysis, processing and distribution of information on problems of natural resources and development of data bases.
- Complex analysis of natural resource information.
- Preparation of analytical reports and references.

Short information reports of the agency reflect the state interests, first of all. This is very important for NGOs, which often have no guidance for their activity and have difficulty in choosing priorities.

For example, the item "Days of Protection of the Amur-2000" appeared on the routinely updated server. Ecological action on protection of the river was announced by the Far East Public Nature Protection Committee, established nine years ago. It includes ecologists, physicians, lawyers, and representatives of local authorities of Primorye and Khabarovsk territories, Chita Oblast, and the Jewish Autonomous Region. The goal of the action is to attract attention of Chinese authorities to the problem of preservation of the great river. The second item of the same issue is entitled "Contaminated Waters Reach Ukraine." In Romania, waters poisoned with cyanide entered the Danube, and the level of river water contamination in Ukraine increased also. Similar to the previous report, this an international problem which can be solved only by united efforts both of governments and NGOs of these countries.

Public activity should force the state structures to pay more attention to their image as well as organization of their own news departments. At the first All-Russian conference "Information Dissemination of Nature Protection Activity in the Russian Federation" (November 1997), with participation of representatives of nature protection bodies of 29 administrative units, a decision was made about a fundamentally new approach to information. For the first time, a serious analysis of the legislation base and state information systems was carried out at the conference. Participants of the conference, including numerous members of public movements, analyzed information support of nature protection activity and determined its priorities.

The conference discussed "Main Statements of a National Strategy of Development of Information Support for Nature Protection Activity." This formed a basis for improvement of the work and development of programs in this sphere. A permanent topic at the interdepartmental server was the discussion of ways of improvement of information support for state and industrial monitoring. This information is very important to NGOs, and they use it in their routine practice. The main achievement is the establishment of both interdepartmental servers and those of NGOs. So, a user has an opportunity to compare information. Then we can make more deliberate choices to support nature preservation.

ECOLOGICAL ELECTRONIC BULLETINS

Electronic mass media analysis shows that only a few organizations can afford to design and support then own servers. In order to make access to information obtained by NGOs easier for journalists, press services of the organizations publish bulletins and press releases and distribute them by electronic mail. For example, SEU sponsors development of e-mail networks among participants of ecological movements. The greater part of nongovernmental ecological associations publish bulletins and distribute them by e-mail. The advantages of e-mail are evident. They include free subscription, high information rate, and as a result, wider audience coverage.

Electronic mail now is comfortable, relatively cheap, and quick. Many ecological organizations all over the world use it. Many different electronic bulletins are published by ecological organizations, for example, Anti-atom Press (Antinuclear campaign of SEU), Problems of Chemical Security (Movement For Chemical Security of SEU), Kislotny Dozhd and Lesnye Novosti (Forest News and Forest Clubs) E-mail is used in large educational projects with many participants in different towns of the country. Program ICLEI, aimed at the improvement of city environmental management, is an example of such a project. It is appreciated by its participants who are representatives of nongovernmental ecological organizations in Russia and Ukraine.

The ecological press can be divided as follows:

- o According to coverage: regional (territorial, regional, district) and interregional.
- o According to information content: thematic (concerning only one or a few ecological problems, such as biological

diversity, chemical security) and general (dealing with all branches of ecology).

- o According to informational difficulty: popular and specialized, aimed for experts in a certain branch.
- o According to kind of publisher: political parties, governmental structures, international ecological organizations and funds, public ecological organizations, and private persons.

TECHNICAL AND FINANCIAL PROBLEMS

In spite of the foregoing optimism, NGOs do not completely use the advantages of the Internet. The main reasons are technical and financial problems. Many movements and organizations do not have direct access to the Internet. In big cities they can find Internet providers. If a group of enthusiasts lives in a little town or village, it is rather difficult to find a provider. Financial problems are difficult, as the quantity of grants from foreign funds has rapidly decreased in recent years. For many public organizations, searching for money to pay for access to computer networks has become a serious obstacle.

As a rule, NGOs try either to find allies in research institutes and colleges, which receive special funds for electronic communication facilities, or appeal to businessmen. Some of them try to find grants. In this case they are interested in updated databases of funding sources located at the ecological server Ecoline (http://cci.glasnet.ru). Let us take some examples of collaboration between NGOs in Russia and other countries of the former Soviet Union. The organization Children of the Baltic offers children's groups without Internet access the opportunity to use its website to publicize their activities. In Crimea, the Institute of Biology of the Southern Seas of the Ukraine Academy of Science provides opportunities for the public to use its Internet server at low cost. According to its director, providing access by the general public, and especially by NGOs, to world informational resources is one of the tasks of the scientists and administration of the institute.

Information should be interesting, systematic, and routinely updated. It is necessary to choose a list of connections and references to other pages devoted to the same topic. In its turn, this step is connected with new expenses. One more problem is to find proper specialists. As a rule, the majority of public organization participants are not trained to work on the Internet. Many are not experienced in journalism. If nobody is ready to undertake this work on a voluntary basis, the organization needs money for the necessary specialists.

As a result, many organizations do not think about the recipients and include random names into their lists of addresses. While preparing the material, it seems not too difficult to think about the following:

- o Whether the information would be interesting to the receiver.
- o Whether the facts are reported briefly.
- o Whether the report includes contact information and how to subscribe.
- o Whether there is an apology for possible duplication.

RESULTS

Only joint efforts of NGOs can solve technical and financial problems. In order to realize the potential impact of NGOs, collaboration is necessary. Public movements can improve their effectiveness in sustainable development activity. The informational level of every NGO participant can increase due to new possibilities of obtaining information. The Internet already promotes on-line distribution of information concerning public movements, their active workers, and the projects they suggest.

EMERGING TOOLS FOR DEVELOPING, INTEGRATING, AND DISTRIBUTING CONSERVATION INFORMATION

Both the United States and Russia face a range of challenges related to environmental protection and natural resource conservation.

Urban sprawl, loss of biodiversity, air and water pollution, hazardous waste disposal, and global climate change are among the problems our nations are working to address. Science is the foundation upon which effective solutions to these problems must be built, and geospatial data are fundamental components of that foundation. Key geospatial data sets include satellite and aerial imagery of the landscape, critical wildlife habitat and rare species, point sources of pollution, waste disposal sites, and carbon sources and sinks.

The Association for Biodiversity Information (ABI) coordinates a network of organizations dedicated to building knowledge about the diversity of life, primarily in the Western Hemisphere.

ABI is comprised of 85 components called natural heritage programs in the United States and conservation data centers in Canada, the Caribbean area, and Latin America. The natural heritage network was built gradually over a 25-year period. A central office in Arlington, Virginia, houses 75 staff that work to advance the network by developing data standards and methodologies, database management software, and tools to support conservation decision-making.

We specialize in generating information on the location and status of rare and imperiled species and ecological communities. This fall, ABI released NatureServe, an on-line encyclopedia of life containing information on the location and status of 50,000 plants, animals, and ecological communities in North America. This will be expanded to Latin America early next year. ABI also develops tools that encourage the use of biological information in the decision-making process. ABI's basic approach to informing conservation decision-making can be applied anywhere in the world. We are happy to share the lessons we have learned in building and operating our organization.

THE POWER OF GEOGRAPHIC INFORMATION SYSTEMS

A geographic information system (GIS) is a powerful tool for organizing, displaying, and analyzing geospatial data. As the technology has advanced, it has become increasingly accessible. Just five years ago GIS software was expensive, ran on high-end computers, and required significant technical training to operate. Today the software is relatively inexpensive, runs on personal computers, and requires little training to use. GIS is now used routinely in the United States at the federal, state, and local government levels and is used by most environmental NGOs that have scientific activities.

GIS is a powerful tool because it makes possible the integration of biological, physical, and socioeconomic information, allowing a more comprehensive depiction of data relevant to an issue. It is particularly helpful in land use planning as a tool that facilitates the organization of a wide variety of technical information and its depiction in a useful format.

The utility of GIS is advancing rapidly in parallel with development of related technologies. Inexpensive global positioning systems (GPS) allow one to quickly and accurately link data with a precise geographic location.

The Internet makes it possible to readily transfer data around the world. Wireless technologies allow the immediate entry of field data as well as its instant transfer to home research or to other laboratories. Advanced commercial aerial and satellite imagery makes it easy to incorporate high resolution images of the landscape into a GIS. The parallel development of technologies and capabilities such as these makes GIS a more powerful and sophisticated tool while broadening the range of users taking advantage of it.

FROM GIS TO DSS

Decision support systems (DSS) are now evolving. These systems couple GIS with analytical tools, models, and visualizations. The bulk of these systems are in the research and development phase and are being piloted in various locations around the world. Some are emerging for broader application. DSS's are particularly helpful in land use planning.

Models and visualizations can be used to help citizens and government officials develop alternative urban growth scenarios. For example, under one scenario an urban center might continue growing unconstrained as it has in the past. Under another, growth might be clustered around existing population centers and transportation systems. A third scenario might optimize opportunities to preserve ecologically sensitive areas as well as set aside open space for recreation uses. Each scenario can include detailed land use information, depending upon the needs of users. Land use resulting from a particular scenario can be depicted at intervals in the future, say 10, 20, or 50 years depending upon the model. Visualizations of this kind are particularly helpful in engaging citizens in the planning process.

Visualizations can also be useful in describing historical patterns of land use. LandSat imagery dating back to the 1970s can provide a 25-year depiction of landscape change. Aerial imagery sometimes allows visualizations as far back as the 1950s. And old maps make it possible to depict land use going back several hundred years.

When used for conservation purposes, historical visualizations allow descriptions of changes in vegetative cover and loss of habitat, as well as broader ecosystem decline.

BRIDGING THE CANYON BETWEEN MANAGEMENT AND SCIENCE

GIS and DSS are powerful tools for linking science and resource management, or more broadly, science and public policy. As such, they bridge the gap-and at times the canyon-between data and decision-making. They are especially helpful in organizing and integrating physical, biological, and socioeconomic information.

Coupled with visualizations these tools catalyze and enable citizen participation in the decision-making process. Since NGO activities often involve promoting public understanding of issues and contributions to their resolution, GIS and DSS are tools that these organizations should take full advantage of. These powerful technologies can significantly improve the effectiveness of NGOs by allowing them to readily make use of science to inform the public policy process.

EXPERIENCE IN COPING WITH EFFECTS OF RADIATION ACCIDENTS

Coping with the levels and severity of ecological problems on the threshold of the third millennium demands more effective measures. It is obvious that elaboration of such measures is more than a technical or economic task. It is also a problem of an adequate social response to the problems caused by previous development activities of society. Both lack of perception of ecological problems by Russian society and lack of readiness for effective efforts towards their resolution were characteristic less than ten years ago. Certainly, the main reason is the total social upheaval of recent years. However, the fact that ecological problems were often a screen for political and economic decisions is an important factor. Experience in overcoming the effects of the Chernobyl accident proves this point. This experience also shows the impact of information on public perceptions of ecological problems. A divergence between an artificial information image and the real problem may cause an incorrect base for decision-making. As a result, society appears to be facing new problems. So, it is necessary to emphasize the role of ecological organizations in informing and educating the society.

CHARACTERISTICS OF RADIATION HAZARD AWARENESS

Experience from radiation accidents, and especially the accident at the Chernobyl plant, has shown the impact of information on the population, both for individuals and for society, in comparison with the impact of radiation. On the one hand, the impact comes from perception of radiation hazard; and on the other, it is a result of a mechanism of social aggravation. Let us consider in brief the reasons and peculiarities of perceptions of radiation hazard. The starting point of radiation awareness as danger was the creation of nuclear weapons, the bombing of Japan, and large-scale nuclear weapons testing. One of the main reasons for formation and strengthening of extremely tense and unequal perceptions of radiation hazards has been the arms race, which for one-half a century has involved all nuclear countries (from the United States, Great Britain, and the USSR in the late forties to India and Pakistan at the end of the nineties). Still, opposition to nuclear activities in general is a reason too. Ionizing radiation is considered to be not only dangerous for health, but also an inevitable hazard for future generations.

Many factors have affected the perception of ionizing radiation. They are: secrecy, which has surrounded nuclear weapons production everywhere; international campaign drives for elimination of nuclear weapon testing; new types of production (H-bomb, N-bomb) in certain countries; international alarm over the danger of expansion of nuclear weapons; intensive attention to radiation effects on human health and the environment. Thus, a strong base exists for a special perception of radiation hazards in everyday life. It is seriously aggravated due to peculiarities of man-made accidents and catastrophes. Society more easily withstands natural disasters even if they have huge effects. This has been proven with quick revival of regions suffering from earthquakes, floods, hurricanes, and tornadoes, even if the danger of repeated disasters remains very high. In case of a man-made disaster, the first social reaction is to search for a reason and for culprits. The higher the level of responsibility, the harsher the social perception of the catastrophe. Thus, accidents and disasters at state-controlled factories appear to be the most serious for their social effects. Also, radiation accidents are certainly characterized with harsher social effects because it is the State which controls the use of radiation activities and especially nuclear energy activities.

We can see great differences in social attitudes to accidents and disasters. One is characterized by an adequate response including the following stages: defining the scope of a catastrophe and precise classification of victims; searching for reasons and culprits; paying compensatory damage, mainly, by insurance systems; punishing the responsible bodies (a producer, an operating organization); and identifying reasons (construction, organization, human factors) in order to prevent repetition of the accident. Such accidents include fires and traffic incidents. Society has adapted to traffic accidents in spite of the number of victims. Loss of life of dozens, hundreds, and thousands of people in train wrecks, car crashes, and shipwrecks does not cast doubt on their necessity. It means the society regards such hazards as socially acceptable.

The other extreme is rare man-made accidents. Social attitudes toward them are much more intricate and sharp. These include radiation and chemical accidents. The initial reaction of populations to information about such accidents, and first of all, those involving radiation, is concern about their own health and the health of their progeny. The circle of victims is uncertain. Soon the State is blamed for giving permission for the activity that caused the catastrophe. A mechanism of social aggravation starts to work. With the help of the mass media and organizations interested in public attention or recognition, the situation is dramatized. In its turn, the mass-media dramatization intensifies concern of the community and extends the circle of "victims." It can cause different social effects up to radical changes of public attitudes toward science and certain activities.

Let us briefly outline those people and organizations that can take an active part in this aggravation scheme. First are local authorities and political figures. They seem to be quite sincere and have different reasons (from a desire to increase state compensation to an interest in receiving public attention). Nevertheless, a lack of comprehension, a reluctance in obtaining official data from specialists, and a logic of opposition inevitably make them dramatize the post-accident situation. In conditions of high information capabilities of local authorities and greater public confidence in them in comparison with the State as a whole, their influence on the population is very profound. For example, in 1991 after adoption of both republic (Ukraine, Belarus, and Russia) and all-union laws, areas eligible for benefits and compensation increased. Authorities asked for their regions to be added to the list of radiation pollution areas. The only exception was Krasnodar Territory, where some resorts were polluted. The local authorities preferred to decontaminate polluted areas on their own rather than lose the image of the resorts.

The second group that is able and ready to take part in the social aggravation process includes ecological and anti-war organizations. The orientation of their reaction inevitably results from their usual stance because dramatization of accidents proves the correctness and significance of their previous activity. The movements of victims of radiation accidents play a certain role too. The members are inclined, on the one hand, to preserve their victim status and collect corresponding compensation and benefits and on the other hand, to mythologize about their participation in radiation accidents.

The third group of people that can play a very dramatic role in the aggravation of consequences includes cultural workers, artists, and intellectuals. A custom of identifying oneself as the nation's conscience together with the stereotype of the radiation impact can often increase the psychological after-effects. For example, after the Chernobyl accident cultural workers offered to discuss not only the danger of the burial of Chernobyl victims, but also the impossibility of burying them in "contaminated" land. Both problems (except in a few unique cases) had no sense at all, but they strongly influenced the community. The same problems with burial of radioactive accident victims took place in Goiania (Brazil, 1988) as the local population sharply protested. Cultural workers also try to change professional terms. For example, radiation pollution, which means appearance of harmful (in this case radioactive) substances in the soil, is changed to radioactive contamination (saturation with pathogens) or even more dramatically to health damage of the area.

In the case when a radiation accident takes place under conditions of economically successful activity, organizations and groups using alternative technologies can also participate in dramatizing the situation. It would be mistake to exaggerate the role of these factors after atomic plant accidents, but a number of cogent arguments are raised in arguing against atomic and for thermal power. The role and activity of the above mentioned groups can change at different stages after a radiation accident. Thus, cultural workers always deal with the problem for a short period. Ecological organizations usually act for a longer time, independent of any positive results of their activity. For example, campaigns conducted to collect money to send children for rest from the moderate climate conditions of central Russia to the south in the Crimea or Cuba give doubtful results. The reason for money collection is to support children who were exposed to radiation, but often healthy children benefit. So, information after the Chernobyl accident resulted in the following characteristics of radiation hazard awareness:

- o Radiation hazard is associated only with industrial business (power plant, defense industry), with all other sources of radiation hazard (natural sources, medicine) posing little hazard.

- o Radiation hazard is excessively high in comparison with other hazards.
- o Only the State is responsible for measures to decrease risk.
- o The current policy of risk reduction is insufficient.

None of these statements is true. Natural sources and medicine are the main part of radiation hazard (see Table 1). The share of radiation accidents and man- made sources in overall radioactivity is negligibly small even on territories with nuclear plants. But in dealing with problems of radiation hazard, the mass media say nothing or little about the facts. Proven ways to reduce risks, such as staying out of the sun or avoiding radon impacts, do not receive attention. As a result, the greater part of the population is not only ignorant of radiation hazard, but they also do not want to take even simple prevention measures. One can even state that the present Russian community is like a "zombie" on the whole problem of radiation hazard and the Chernobyl consequences. Most people repeat the mass media stereotype and equate radiation hazard to Chernobyl.

SCIENTIFIC VALIDITY OF DECISION-MAKING

Every large ecological problem, especially a radiation accident, is a unique event with a number of particular features. Therefore, scientific research and necessary scientific support take on special significance in the decision-making process that concerns safety measures and elimination of after-effects. Nevertheless, as shown later, many decisions have been made without scientific support or contrary to scientific recommendations.

Let us consider a number of examples showing the role of science in reduction of the Chernobyl consequences. Table 2 deals with dates of decisions (by the government or authorized ministry) on safety measures for the first five years after the accident and some characteristics of these measures, including their scientific validity.

They are divided into five groups according to the type of decision:

1. Sanitary code and regulations (S) approved by the Chief Sanitary Doctor of the Soviet Union or a republic
2. Executive decrees concerning certain settlements (ED), usually decrees of supreme public authorities
3. Government decrees and orders concerning recommendations and instructions on working procedures, departmental guides, and instructions (DG), usually dealing with regulations and instructions according to the characteristics of the radiation environment
4. Conceptual (C) decisions of Soviet National Committee on Radiation Protection (NCRP), later Russian NCRP, for the main intervention levels and their need in corresponding legislation and administrative decrees
5. Legislative decrees (L) on execution of certain measures by executive organs or determination of intervention levels.

The scientific and technical validity of the decisions is based on conclusions made by radiation safety specialists, which engender society's confidence. A number of actions inconsistent with the real danger made by political groups, the mass media, and others proved that a biased distrust of specialists appeared during the first month after the accident. The situation improved a little by the middle of summer 1986. Then the crucial decision-making process was completed, based on scientific and technical validity, while a number of incorrect decisions were revised. By the end of 1988, a large amount of data was collected for long-term radiation prognosis of polluted areas. Moreover, real opportunities for all safety measures were realized, as well as limiting negative consequences for the population that resulted in restrictions. The environment became better in some polluted areas. In these circumstances the Soviet NCRP suggested its 35-rem concept of total lifetime extra dose limit equal to 350 mSv (hereinafter, the concept of safe habitation). Practical realization of the concept provided for very limited resettlement of the most polluted settlements and significant lessening of restrictions in other areas. Nevertheless it did not work due to a number of social reasons. Beginning in 1988, a great number of articles on the Chernobyl problem were published simultaneously with the development of "glasnost" policies. The mass media adopted strictures on the concept of safe habitation. In 1989, taking into account the complex political situation in the country and in fact impeaching the credibility of its own specialists, the Government of the Soviet Union made an official request to the International Atomic Energy Agency (IAEA) for coordination of an "international examination of the concept of safe habitation in the areas contaminated with radioactivity after the Chernobyl accident developed in the USSR and an assessment of effectiveness of measures for public health protection within these areas."

As a result, the International Chernobyl Project (ICP) started in the spring of 1990. An independent international advisory commission of 19 members was organized under the chairmanship of the outstanding scientist Dr. I.Shigematsu, Director of the Radiation Effects Research Foundation in Hiroshima. Two hundred independent experts from 23 countries and seven international organizations took part in the project. Fifty scientific groups visited the USSR. Laboratories from several countries including Austria, France, and the USA helped to analyze and assess the data.

Initial information on the ICP was favorably reported. However, after the news that ICP members considered the measures in progress as quite adequate, the mass media changed their opinion on the project. Dozens of publications blamed the ICP members for trying to hide the radiological consequences of the accident for the sake of the international "nuclear Mafia." The resulting documents of ICP contained sharp criticism of both implemented and planned safety measures.

They were formulated as follows: "The International Advisory Commission noted that the adopted and planned long-term measures, though guided by good intentions, exceeded the strict requirements of radiation protection. Resettlement and foodstuff restriction measures are unsuitable from the standpoint of radiation safety. Nevertheless, any relaxation of the current policy almost certainly would give a negative effect due to the high level of stress and alarm of residents in contaminated areas and their current expectations. It is agreed, however, that social and political factors should be taken into account, so responsible and competent authorities should make the final decisions. In any case, future changes should not lead to stricter restriction criteria. "More specific criteria reducing foodstuff restrictions would be preferable to resettlement, taking into account all the social and economic factors connected with public health. Further application of the restrictions for use of local foodstuff products in the polluted areas means a significant worsening of quality of life for some people. The only way to avoid it is to resettle them to such regions where they could live in their previous manner if it is possible. Comparatively high criteria for foodstuff restrictions might have aggravated these problems..."

One could think the ICP results might close a debate concerning the possibility of habitation of polluted areas. In fact, the USSR Government planned a number of actions in June-August 1991, including meetings of socially active citizens with executive and legislative authorities. Large sections of the public should have been acquainted with the ICP results. However, the situation in the country became worse; events of August 1991 resulted in the USSR's collapse and prevented both practical realization and the acquaintance of the general public with the ICP advice. As a result, the governments of Belarus, Russia, and Ukraine in fact rejected both points: the NCRP suggestion of limited resettlement and the ICP view that rejected any resettlement.

Thus, neither the opinions of national specialists nor the views of leading international experts were taken into account. On the contrary, populist decisions resulted in significant economic and social waste.

ROLE OF POLITICAL FACTORS AND THEIR EFFECTS

Public discontent was stirred up by some persons who made a political, administrative, and public career based on the Chernobyl accident and incited the authorities to change their previous decisions. Since specialists did not support this revision, they were just excluded from the decision-making process.

Subsequent measures were realized according to soil pollution criteria instead of dose criteria, which are the only correct criteria for radiation safety. Just after the accident, soil pollution might be justified by lack of radiation data. Further, "territory pollution density" criteria should be used only for agriculture purposes. However, the adoption of dose principles is an important component of radiation accident reduction. This component was lost in the Chernobyl accident reduction effort.

By 1990 more than 500,000 people received different benefits because of the Chernobyl accident. By 1991 it turned out that many people were interested in further expanding the so-called radioactive contaminated zones. These circumstances caused problems in realizing rational ideas of developing a Unified Program of radiation accident reduction (as well as adopting the law on social protection of victims). The following persons insisted on using radiological principles in determination of radioactive contaminated zones:

- A few specialists in the radiation protection sphere, including those who had encountered public opposition.
- A number of outstanding scientists recognizing the role of radiation and other hazards in life.
- Some economists versed in the necessary costs.

Active supporters of maximum expansion of the radioactive contaminated zones were:

- Republic authorities of Ukraine and Belarus and Russian regional administrative elites interested in financial and material support from government funds.
- Numerous mistaken public figures who did not anticipate negative results of their activity, though they connected their political fortunes with the consequences of the accident.

Due to unclear positions of the politically weak Moscow Government, almost all demands of the Republics were completely fulfilled. They resulted in the broadest interpretation of radioactive contaminated zones. The so-called zone with privileged social-economic status with lower pollution density border at 1 Ci per sq. km. was of fundamental importance. This zone with its numerous benefits did not correspond to any radiological criteria. It should be mentioned that the authors of the decision concerning this zone did not know that more than 30 percent of the territory where the pollution density exceeded 1 Ci per sq. km. was situated outside the USSR. It is necessary to stress that there were no claims for damage nor indemnities for health injuries in the majority of foreign countries impacted by the Chernobyl accident.

Unfortunately, the price of incorrect decisions included more than money for benefits and compensations. The psychological health of many people was damaged because they were officially considered as accident victims. Strange as it may seem, health control based on the law played a significant role here.

Humane but abstract ideas gave negative results in specific circumstances during the last phase of the Chernobyl accident. Large resources were spent on health control using a list of possible health effects. First of all, it included thyroid gland cancers that were discovered during total screening. The law, in fact, required searches for any evidence of public health decline.

This surely was found in situations of decreasing living standards and unfavorable demographic trends. But inhabitants of polluted regions linked in their mind health problems due to many reasons with radioactive effects. Some of the health workers who dealt with increased death rates and other effects as the living standard declined were especially sure of this relationship. It is necessary in this regard to stress that the polluted areas and regions did not differ from other regions of Russia according to the main demographic criteria. Standards for participating in programs for eliminating accident after-effects were established in too simplified a manner. They caused an unjustified increase in the number of participants. By spring 1989, when the most extensive work was fulfilled, the number of participants was estimated as 250,000 people. It was a large but realistic number; but several years later it increased more than three times to 800,000 people.

A fundamental change of the basic structure of the Chernobyl law might be the only rational way out. But a serious change of public opinion toward radiation hazard and an increased ecological culture of the whole society is needed. It is possible only when there is societal confidence in scientists and specialists. One should stress the role of ecology organizations, which should base their activity on scientific arguments instead of propaganda stereotypes.

ROLE OF GREENPEACE OF RUSSIA AND OTHER PUBLIC ORGANIZATIONS IN THE CONSERVATION OF RUSSIAN FORESTS EVOLUTION OF ECOLOGICAL PROBLEMS

An extensive pattern of forest use exists in Russia dating back to the 1930s. It is characterized by exploiting more and more ancient forests instead of intensive forestry in developed regions. The best wood according to quality, supply, and accessibility is taken in the first cutting, with an absence of efficient reforestation. As a result, timber resources are disappearing quickly. Deforestation of the remaining ancient forestlands is inevitable. For example, only 6 percent of the taiga zone in European Russia has natural forests. Greenpeace of Russia made a map, "Last Remaining Forestlands of the European Taiga," based on space imagery and special nature studies.

Most of the forestlands may be destroyed in five to ten years. Gas and oil producing industries, gold mining, and other extractive industries are also responsible for deforestation. Enterprises and exploration activities of these industries are the main causes of fires. Forestland destroyed by fire is comparable with that destroyed as a result of felling.

The present pattern leads to the total destruction of natural forest ecological systems in a great part of the forest zone of Russia as well as to depletion of timber resources. It causes an avalanche of social problems. In the 1970s, the timber industry decline began in most taiga regions. It became especially evident in the end of the 1980s and in the 1990s. The main reason for the decrease is the depletion of woods in the vicinity of enterprises founded in the 1940s, 1950s, and earlier. Since the beginning of the 1990s, about one million employees here lost their jobs in the timber industry or will soon be unemployed. Several thousand "wood settlements" mainly in remote districts of the European North, Siberia, and Far East with four million residents are left without a livelihood. The pattern of depletion is stimulated by extremely low payments for forest exploration rights (forest tax). For example, standing wood has a token price of not more than one dollar for one cubic meter. That is about 2 to 5 percent of the commercial value of round lumber. As a result, the State has a lack of money for an efficient forest service. In 1999 the payment for forest exploration rights was about 15 percent of the total costs of the Federal Service of Forestry. The present pattern of forestry leads both to the total destruction of the last remaining ancient forests and to ecological disturbance of the forest zone (water balance, swamping, soil decay, biodiversity decrease). The whole state timber industry is unprofitable. Also, life in timber settlements is socially unstable due to a decrease of earnings and unemployment.

THE IMPACT OF GOVERNMENT DECREES

For the last decade, no government decrees for radical change of the situation and for stable forest exploitation have been adopted. The Forest Code of the Russian Federation requires timber owners to carry on multiple-purpose and sustainable forestry while promoting biological diversity. This requirement is not fulfilled because of the absence of appropriate laws. Even the existing nature protection legislation on forestry and forest exploration is not observed. For example, the Law "On Ecological Assessment" adopted in 1995 requires an ecological assessment of "schemes of protection and use of water, forest, land, and other nature resources," including organization and management projects for forestry and felling. Nevertheless, most projects are realized without any ecological assessment. Conservation of species under special protection is usually not addressed because these species are not identified within the scope of forest husbandry and planning. Forest husbandry, the base for forestry planning and management, is aimed entirely at accounting for timber resources.

"The Principles of Determination of Woodcutting Areas..." adopted in 1987 are still in force. They provide "a level of major harvest and regeneration felling for 20 to 30 years." Economically inaccessible woods are included into production reserves. As a result, forests located near roads in populated regions are subject to more intense cutting. The full use of woodcutting areas is impossible in the majority of regions due to a lack of economically accessible forest resources. Enterprises often try to solve this problem by disregarding ecological limits including those provided by legislation. "Criteria and Indicators of Sustainable Management of Russian Forests" adopted in 1998 does not have parameters of sustainable forest management and does not provide for any change in the present forest management system. Moreover, the majority of forestry employees know nothing about this document. The general type of felling is final harvesting on a large area (up to 50 hectares). This causes heavy soil erosion, swamping, and catastrophic changes of the forest environment, with an absence of reforestation and disappearance of many species of forest flora and fauna. The current Forest Legislation disregards international conventions for biodiversity conservation and does not include up-to-date scientific achievements for sustainable forest husbandry.

ROLE OF NONGOVERNMENTAL ORGANIZATIONS

A number of public organizations are involved in forest conservation. The most active ones have joined the Forest Club of Russian NGOs. It is an informal working group consisting of representatives of NGOs. Forest Club members are:

- Greenpeace Russia
- Socio-Ecological Union Forest Campaign
- Conservation Center for Wild Resources
- Druzhinas (Student Corps) for Nature Conservation Movement
- Information Center of Taiga Rescue Network-Russia
- Save Pechora Committee
- Individual activists

The main task of the Forest Club is to coordinate NGOs for forest conservation.

The Club's major activities are:

- Improvement of Russian forest legislation, forestry regulations, and technical standards

- o Inventory of natural old growth forests and other valuable forest areas
- o Monitoring of protected territories for illegal logging and poaching
- o Promotion of ecologically and socially responsible forestry and independent forest certification
- o Publication of the Forest Bulletin

The current state forest management system does not ensure participation of NGOs in forest management and development of forest policy. The overwhelming majority of Forest Service employees regard NGOs as hostile entities that should not interfere in forest affairs. Usually, the state bodies do not consider suggestions of residents and NGOs on changing felling practices, excluding some sites from exploitation, or changing the management system.

Consideration of public suggestions is not provided in the current forest legislation. Standard acts and forest legislation are usually developed in secret, excluding not only the general public, but also specialists outside the Forest Service.

The scientific and nature protection communities learn about a certain bill or project when it is introduced to the State Duma, registered at the Ministry of Justice, or confirmed with a department decree. As a rule, it is almost impossible to introduce any changes into the document at this stage. In those isolated instances when a project was open for discussion, specialist opinions outside the Forest Service were not taken into account. Since 1993, no representative from scientific or public organizations outside the Forest Service and other ministries and departments has managed to include any innovations in the documents. Efficient collaboration between the government and the public at the federal level is almost impossible. The only effective participation of the general public is open protest against certain state activities and projects.

RESULTS OF ACTIVITIES OF NONGOVERNMENT ORGANIZATIONS

NGO activities are diverse. The Forest Club has the following activities:

1. Improvement of Russian forest legislation; promotion of ecologically and socially responsible forestry; and independent forest certification. Detailed analysis of illegal felling shows the weakness of the current Forest Code, with 20 percent of timber being felled illegally. Greenpeace proposed a forest program of sustainable forest management that would provide timber settlements with regular work. In a clear manner, a reference book describes the current forestry structure, as well as felling standards and rules. It suggests possibilities of public participation in forest management in Russia.

   Greenpeace prepared standards for assessment of the less disturbed forest areas. These standards were published in a number of issues of the Forest Bulletin and were repeatedly discussed at conferences of environmental activists and forestry workers, including two conferences in 1998, devoted to problems of forest management and protection in Karelia and Sakhalin.

2. Inventory of natural old growth forests and other valuable forest areas. Since 1996, Greenpeace in cooperation with the Biodiversity Conservation Center, the Socio-Ecological Union, and other NGOs carried out an inventory of ancient taiga areas in the European and Ural areas of Russia. The work was based on 1999-2000 space images of middle and high resolution. The work included more than one hundred expeditions of NGOs; specialists of Moscow, Pushkin, Tambov, and other state universities; and reserve workers. The NGOs use updated sources of information on the condition of forestlands and more up-to-date technologies in comparison with the state nature resource departments. The inventory of ancient taiga areas all over Russia is now carried out within the project "The Forest Watch of Russia." Russian research and production institutions, the technical center Skaneks, the International Institute of Forestry, and regional organizations, such as Altai-21 Century Foundation, Friends of Siberian Forests (Krasnoyarsk), and the Bureau of Regional Public

Campaigns (Vladivostok) participate in the project. Undisturbed forest assessment criteria are used, research techniques are improved at model sites (usually they are reserves), and the basis for new reserves and national parks are developed. Identification Atlas of Taiga Plants cf European Russia was published to assist field investigations.

3. Monitoring protected territories to detect illegal logging and poaching. Since 1997, Greenpeace workers have actively participated in revisions of forest management and forest husbandry in several regions, such as Moscow Oblast, Leningrad Oblast, Sakhalin Oblast, Republic of Buryatia, and Primorye Territory. In a few regions, the revisions were informal without participation of state bodies. In Moscow and Leningrad Oblasts the revisions resulted in improvement of forest management and observance of current legislation. In Primorye Territory, a protest was carried out against the export to Japan of illegally cut timber, bought and "legalized" by official wood exporters. As a result, the business activity of some companies was suspended for some time. Unfortunately, the situation has now returned to the original pattern. Demonstrations to attract public attention are important for NGOs. For example, in Moscow Oblast illegal felling took place in the immediate vicinity of a forestry office, but forest guards never reacted to these acts. This action was described in the press and shown on TV. As a result, the Board of the Moscow Forest Department organized the Public Council of Forest Management to solve such problems. As a result of protests of NGOs, Scandinavian companies and Russian wood importers declared a moratorium on purchase of timber from forestlands in Karelia in 1997. Due to this moratorium, the most valuable remaining timber stands were saved in Kalevala Forestland, which is as an official reserve. At present, an advisory panel is discussing the future of these forestlands.

4. Public participation in forest management. Opportunities for teamwork with local authorities in a few regions are

wider than opportunities at the federal level. For example, for the last five years in Moscow Oblast reviews of environmental legislation compliance were carried out with participation of NGOs (in fact, the reviews were completed thanks to the efforts of the NGOs themselves). One such example is the "Summary of the Results of the Interagency Commission on Assessing the Status of Forestry in Vyborg, Priozersk, and Vsevolozhsk Regions of Leningrad Oblast." According to the results of the revisions, rather strong sanctions were often applied to law violations. For example, commercial "clear cutting" in strictly protected nature reserves practically stopped in Moscow Oblast. State ecological examinations are now carried out for projects of forest management and felling plans. "Hot" problems may be discussed with forest department officials. Nevertheless some problems remain. In August 2000, the state reserve Atleka in Vologda Oblast was established as a result of a discussion among representatives of local authorities, forest industry companies, NGOs, and the scientific community. It is the first case of a strictly protected national reserve established by a logging enterprise. The Vostochny Reserve in Sakhalin Oblast is one more example of constructive collaboration between public and State structures. Unfortunately, examples of similar understanding by the authorities of the actions and demands of the "greens" are still very rare and in the majority of regions completely absent.

5. Educational activity, including education of members of environmental organizations and education of the general public. To improve professional qualifications of environmental organization members and forest officers, the Forest Club publishes the periodical Forest Bulletin as well as other materials, for example the book European Taiga on the Verge of the Millennium by A.Yu Yaroshenko. Booklets, calendars, and posters are published for the general public, such as the calendar for 1999 and a booklet devoted to Lake Baikal.

6. Lobbying of nature protection initiatives and attraction of public attention to regional and federal ecological problems. Organizing support for an environmental referendum was a main activity in 2000. The current legislation requires two million signatures. More than 2.5 million signatures were collected, so the referendum depends on the Russian Government. It may avoid the referendum by declaring signatures to be "faulty" or "inaccurate."

2

NGOs Role in Ecological Decision-making

It is necessary to develop a legislative mechanism providing for participation of NGOs in ecological decision-making. A way for information about government decrees and actions to reach NGOs and the general public is needed along with a way for ensuring responsiveness to suggestions from NGOs. Up to now, important decrees are usually prepared, unknown to the general public. Even if NGOs learn about a decree and put forward proposals, they are disregarded without discussion. To solve these problems it is necessary:

- To distribute information for the general public about the substance of new draft laws and departmental and interdepartmental regulations if they are not connected with state secrets. The simplest way could be publishing the texts on the Internet and in the central mass media. The information should be published not less than a month before the date of their official consideration or, in the case of a federal law or interdepartmental standard, not less than three months before the date.
- To develop a way to ensure responsiveness to suggestions from the public on the substance of new laws and standards, natural resource policies, and other problems concerning interests of different population groups. An obligation of a reasonable answer on such proposals from the state bodies within a limited time period is important. o To have a mechanism for monitoring ministries and departments that are active in

environmental protection and natural resource use. In particular, regular restructuring of the departments in the regions with participation of public organizations in this restructuring is important. Public councils with participation of NGOs should be established and linked to federal ministries and departments and their regional divisions. Participation of fictitious "public" organizations should be avoided.

- To make obligatory the participation of interested NGOs in commissions of experts conducting federal and regional ecological examinations. It is necessary to publish information on projects and territories that have already undergone ecological examinations.
- To require public monitoring of large investment projects, including those with foreign investments. The easiest means of doing this appears to be the establishment of a public council for every project with participation of NGOs. The council must have access to non-commercial data concerning the projects and all information about the current legislation.
- To provide free access for the general public and NGOs to data concerning implementation of projects for use of natural resources and for environmental protection. It is necessary to remove unreasonable obstacles for access to ecological data, including costs, particularly if they are already paid from budgetary funds.

PROBLEMS OF WASTE MANAGEMENT IN THE MOSCOW REGION

The scientific and technological revolution of the twentieth century has turned the world over, transformed it, and presented humankind with new knowledge and innovative technologies that previously seemed to be fantasies. Man, made in the Creator's own image, has indeed become in many respects similar to the Creator. Primitive thinking and consumerism as to nature and natural resources seem to be in contrast to this background. Drastic deterioration of the environment has become the other side of the coin that gave the possibility, so pleasant for the average person, to buy practically everything that is needed. A vivid example of man's impact as "a geological force" (as Academician V. I. Vernadsky described contemporary mankind) is poisoning of the soil, surface and underground waters, and atmosphere with floods of waste that threaten to sweep over the Earth. Ecosystems of our planet are no longer capable of "digesting" everincreasing volumes of waste and new synthetic chemicals alien to nature. One of the most important principles in achieving sustainable development is to limit the appetite of public consumption. A logical corollary of this principle suggests that the notion "waste" or "refuse" should be excluded not only from professional terminology, but also from the minds of people, with "secondary material resources" as a substitute concept for them. In my presentation I would like to dwell on a number of aspects of waste disposal. It is an ecological, economic, and social problem for the Moscow megalopolis in present-day conditions.

PRESENT SITUATION WITH WASTE IN MOSCOW

Tens of thousand of enterprises and research organizations of practically all branches of the economy are amassed over the territory of 100,000 hectares: facilities of energy, chemistry and petrochemistry; metallurgical and machine- building works; and light industrial and food processing plants. Moscow is occupying one of the leading places in the Russian Federation for the level of industrial production. The city is the greatest traffic center and bears a heavy load in a broad spectrum of responsibilities as capital of the State. The burden of technogenesis on the environment of the city of Moscow and the Moscow region is very considerable, and it is caused by all those factors mentioned above. One of the most acute problems is the adverse effect of the huge volumes of industrial and consumer wastes. Industrial waste has a great variety of chemical components.

For the last ten years we witnessed mainly negative trends in industrial production in Moscow due to the economic crisis in the country. In Moscow the largest industrial works came practically to a standstill, and production of manufactured goods declined sharply. At the same time, a comparative analysis in 1998-99 of the indexes of goods and services output and of resource potential showed that the coefficient of the practical use of natural resources per unit of product, which had been by all means rather low in previous years, proceeded gradually to decrease further. At present we have only 25 percent of the industrial output that we had in 1990, but the volume of water intake remains at the same level. Fuel consumption has come down only by 18 percent, and the amassed production waste diminished by only 50 percent. These figures indicate the growing indexes of resource consumption and increases in wastes from industrial production.

Every year about 13 million tons of different kinds of waste are accumulated in Moscow: 42 percent from water preparation and sewage treatment, 25 percent from industry, 13 percent from the construction sector, and 20 percent from the municipal economy.

The main problem of waste management in Moscow city comes from the existing situation whereby a number of sites for recycling and disposal of certain types of industrial waste and facilities for storage of inert industrial and building wastes are situated outside the city in Moscow Region, which is subject to other laws of the Russian Federation. Management of inert industrial and building wastes, which make up the largest part of the general volume of wastes and of solid domestic wastes (SDW), simply means in everyday practice their disposal at 46 sites (polygons) in Moscow Region and at 200 disposal locations that are completely unsuitable from the ecological point of view.

The volume of recycled waste is less than 10-15 percent of the volume that is needed. Only 8 percent of solid domestic refuse is destroyed (by incineration). If we group industrial waste according to risk factor classes, refuse that is not dangerous makes up 80 percent of the total volume, 4th class low-hazard wastes 14 percent, and 1st-3rd classes of dangerous wastes amount to 3.5 percent.

The largest part of the waste is not dangerous-up to 32 percent. Construction refuse, iron and steel scrap, and non-ferrous metal scrap are 15 percent. Paper is 12 percent, and scrap lumber is 4 percent. Metal scrap under the 4th class of risk factor makes up 37 percent; wood, paper, and polymers more than 8 percent; and all-rubber scrap 15 percent. So, most refuse can be successfully recycled and brought back into manufacturing. This is related to SDW too. The morphological composition of SDW in Moscow is characterized by a high proportion of utilizable waste: 37.6 percent in paper refuse, 35.2 percent in food waste, 10 percent in polymeric materials, 7 percent in glass scrap, and about 5 percent in iron, steel, and non-ferrous metal scrap. The paper portion in commercial wastes amounts to 70 percent of the SDW volume.

A number of programs initiated by the Government of Moscow are underway for the collection and utilization of refuse and for neutralization of industrial and domestic waste. A waste-recycling industry is being developed in the city of Moscow, mostly for manufacturing recycled products and goods. One of the most important ecological problems is the establishment in the region of ecologically safe facilities for the disposal of dangerous wastes of 1st and 2nd class risk factors. Pre-planned industrial capacities for thermal neutralization of SDW will be able to take 30 percent of domestic waste and dangerous industrial waste. Construction of rubbish-burning works according to the old traditional approach is not worthwhile and should come to an end. Waste-handling stations have been under construction in the city for the last five years. In two years there will be six such stations which will make it possible to reduce the number of garbage trucks from 1,156 to 379 and to reduce the amount of atmospheric pollution they produce. In addition the switch to building stations with capacity of briquetting one ton of waste into a cubic meter will decrease the burden on waste disposal sites and prolong their life span by 4-5 fold. Trash hauling enterprises will also make profit because of lower transportation costs.

Putting into operation waste-segregation complexes (10-12 sites) would reduce volumes of refuse to disposal sites by 40 percent-that is 1,200,000 tons per year. The total volume of burned or recycled SDW would reach 2,770,000 tons a year. A total of 210,000 tons of waste per year would be buried. So, in the course of a five year period, full industrial recycling of SDW could be achieved in practice. Collection of segregated waste is one of the important elements in effective disposal and utilization of SDW. It facilitates recycling of waste and return of secondary material into the manufacturing process. Future trends in segregation and collection of SDW will demand wide popularization and improvement of the ecological culture and everyday behavior of people.

In recent years the high increase in the number of cars in Moscow has brought about not only higher pollution of the atmosphere, but also an avalanche-like accumulation of refuse from vehicles. Besides littering residential and recreation areas, cars represent a source for toxic pollution of land and reservoirs. At the same time, automobile wastes are a good source for recycled products. In the short-term outlook, Moscow has to resolve the problem of collection and utilization of decommissioned vehicles and automobile wastes with particular emphasis on activities of the private sector. Setting up a system for collection and utilization of bulky domestic waste and electronic equipment refuse is also on the priority list. In 1999 in Moscow the following volumes of secondary raw materials were produced or used in the city or were recycled: 300,000 tons of construction waste, 296,000 tons of metal scrap, 265 tons of car battery lead, 21,000 tons of glass, 62,500 tons of paper waste, 4,328 tons of oil-bearing waste, and 306 tons of refuse from galvanizing plants.

Such traditional secondary materials as metal scrap and paper waste are not recycled in Moscow but are shipped to other regions of Russia. The worldwide practice of sorting and recycling industrial and domestic wastes demands the establishment of an industry for secondary recycling. Otherwise segregation of waste becomes ineffective. There are restraining factors for the development of an effective system of assorted selection, segregation, and use of secondary raw resources, namely lack of sufficient manufacturing capacities and of suitable technologies for secondary recycling.

The problem of utilization of wastes is closely linked with the problem of modernization and sometimes even demands fundamental restructuring of industries. The practical use of equipment for less energy consumption and a smaller volume of wastes and a transition to the use of alternative raw materials are needed. Large enterprises-the main producers of dangerous wastes-are in a difficult financial situation now, which is an impediment for proceeding along these lines.

Private and medium-size enterprises are becoming gradually aware of the economic profitability in rational use of waste. For example, the firm Satory started as a transportation organization specialized in removal of scrap from demolished buildings and those undergoing reconstruction. It now benefits from recycling of waste, having developed an appropriate technology for the dismantling of buildings with segregation of building waste. So, as it has been already mentioned above, the first task for Moscow is to establish a basis for waste recycling.

HOW TO CHANGE THE SITUATION WITH WASTE

Transition to modern technologies in the utilization of wastes requires either sufficient investments or a considerable increase in repayment for waste on the part of the population. Obviously, these two approaches are not likely to be realized in the near future. The recovery of one ton of SDW with the use of ecologically acceptable technology requires not less than $70-100. Given the average per capita income in 1999 and the likely increase up to the year of 2005, in 2005 it will be possible to receive from a citizen not more than $14 per year. This means that the cost of technology should not exceed $40 per ton of recycled waste. Unfortunately, this requirement can fit only unsegregated waste disposal at the polygons (taking into account an increase in transportation costs by the year 2005).

Such being the case, it looks like there is only one acceptable solution for Russia to solve the problem of waste in an up-to-date manner: to introduce trade-in value on packaging and on some manufactured articles. In recent years domestic waste includes more and more beverage containers. Plastic and glass bottles, aluminium cans, and packs like Tetrapak stockpiled at disposal sites will soon reach the same volumes as in western countries. In Canada, for example, this kind of waste amounts to one-third of all domestic waste. A characteristic feature of this kind of waste is that the packaging for beverages is extremely durable and expensive. Manufactured from polyethylene terephthalate (PTA) and aluminum, it is sometimes more expensive than the beverage it contains. What are the ways for solving the problem? Practically all of them are well-known, but most will not work in Russia in present conditions. The first problem relates to collection of segregated waste in the urban sector and in the services sector. A number of reasons make this system unrealistic, specifically in large cities. Sorting of waste at waste-briquetting sites and at polygons is possible. But if we take into account the present cost of secondary resources, this system turns out to be economically unprofitable and cannot be widely introduced. The introduction of deposits on containers for beverages is at present the most acceptable option for Russia. This system turned out to be most effective in a number of countries that have much in common with Russia. In fact this option is not at all new for us. Surely, all people remember the price of beer or kefir bottles. A system of deposit for glass bottles was in operation in the USSR, and waste sites were free from hundreds of millions of glass bottles and jars. We simply need to reinstate this system at present in the new economic conditions according to new types and modes of packaging. Deposits could be introduced also on glass bottles and jars, PTA and other plastic bottles, aluminium cans, and Tetrapak packing. Let us investigate several non-ecological aspects of this problem, because the ecological impact of secondary recycling of billions of bottles, cans, and packs is quite obvious.

Most of the population in Russia lives below the poverty line. When people buy bottles of vodka, beer, or soft drinks, they will have to pay a deposit value (10- 20 kopeks for a bottle). The poorest people will carry the bottles to receiving points. A system of collection of packaging will function by itself. Only receiving points are needed. Millions of rubles that are collected will be redistributed among the poorest people for their benefit, and a social problem of the poor will be solved to a certain extent not by charity, but with normal economic means.

A second point is also well-known. In a market economy one of the most important problems is that of employment. What happens when the trade-in value is introduced? Thousands of new jobs are created at receiving points and at enterprises that recycle glass, plastics, etc. And we don't need a single penny from the state budget. More than that, these enterprises will pay taxes and consume products of other branches of industry, thus yielding a return to the budget, not to mention income tax from new jobs.

There is another aspect of the matter. Considerable funding is needed from budgets of local governments, including communal repayments for waste collection and disposal at polygons and incinerators. Reduction of expenses for utilization of waste can be significant support for housing and communal reform in general. It is practically impossible to evaluate in general an ecological effect when thousands of tons of waste will cease to occupy plots of land near cities as long-term disposal sites. Operation costs of receiving points and transportation costs could be covered by funds obtained from manufacturers and from returned packaging. Besides, when a waste recycling industry develops and becomes profitable, recycling factories will be able to render partial support to receiving points. Trade-in value can be introduced on all types of packaging except milk products and products for children. It could amount to 15 or 30 kopecks per container, depending on its size. If all plastic bottles with water and beer are sold with trade-in value only in Moscow, the total sum will reach 450 million rubles a year. If we include glass bottles, aluminum cans, and packets, the sum will be one billion rubles. This sum will be redistributed at receiving points among people with scanty means when they receive the money for used packaging and jobs at receiving points and at recycling factories.

The bottleneck of the problem now is the absence in Russia of high technology industries for waste recycling. It can be resolved rather easily. At the first stage, used packaging can be sold as raw material for enterprises, including those overseas. There is unrestricted demand for PTA and aluminum on the part of foreign firms. When waste collection mechanisms are established, there will be limited investments in this branch of industry.

With regard to the inexhaustible source of free raw material, this recycling industry will become one of the most reliable from the point of view of recoupment of investments. The Government, regional authorities, the population, and of course ecologists should all be interested in having such a law. The same should be done with sales of cars, tires, and car batteries. Prices of every tire or battery should be higher by 30-50 rubles. These sums of money should be returned back to a buyer or credited when he buys a new tire or a new battery. For sure, such being the case we will not find used batteries thrown about the city dumps. In this case the task is even simpler because there are already a number of facilities for the recycling of tires and batteries. In fact, a law of trade-in value can change the situation with waste in Russia in a fundamental way. Russian legislation has already been prepared, and the concept of an ecological tax has been introduced in the new Internal Revenue Code. Now it needs to be competently introduced. The outlay for waste recycling has to become a type of ecological tax. To realize this task much work has to be done among the deputies and with the Government. Public ecological organizations, including international ones, should play a leading role.

ACTIVITY OF PUBLIC ORGANIZATIONS IN THE SPHERE OF WASTE MANAGEMENT IN THE MOSCOW REGION

We know examples of the ever increasing role of the general public in the solution of the problem of waste utilization, first of all in those countries that have well-developed democratic institutions. "Fight Against Waste" is one of the popular slogans of public organizations abroad. Public opinion has brought about measures of sanitary cleaning in cities, secured better work by municipal services, shut down hazardous industries, and restricted and prohibited incineration facilities. Nevertheless, the struggle against wastes in the economically developed countries, being a manifestation of an advanced attitude towards the environment, has in the long run brought about a paradoxical result. Transfer of hazardous industries to countries with lower environmental standards and inadequate public support- Russia, as an example-has made the world even more dangerous from the ecological point of view.

Russia has just embarked on the path of formation of environmental public movements by the establishment of nongovernmental organizations. Representatives of nongovernmental organizations from Russia took part in the international gathering in Bonn in March 2000 of nongovernmental organizations that are members of the International Persistent Organic Pollutants (POPs) Elimination Network. A declaration against incineration was adopted in Bonn by nongovernmental organizations, which called for elaboration of effective alternative technologies for utilization of waste and safe technologies for elimination of existing stockpiles of POP.

Quite a number of environmental organizations are operating now in Moscow. First to be mentioned is the All-Russia Society for the Conservation of Nature, which was established in Soviet times. There are other nongovernmental organizations: Ecosoglasiye, Ecolain, Ecological Union, and the Russian branches of Green Cross and Greenpeace. All these organizations collect and popularize environmental information and organize protest actions against policies of the Government or local administrations on ecological matters. A new political party- Russia's Movement of the Greens-is being formed. Laws currently in force in the Russian Federation ("On Protection of the Environment," "On State Ecological Examination by Experts," "On Production and Consumption of Waste") declare the right of the public to participate in environmental examination of projects that are to be implemented, including those on the establishment of facilities for elimination and disposition of waste. Public examinations can be organized by the initiative of citizens and public associations. For example, under the law of Moscow "On Protection of the Rights of Citizens while Implementing Decisions on Construction Projects in Moscow," public hearings are organized by the city's boards. Decisions taken by local authorities, at referenda and public meetings, may be the very reason for carrying out public examinations. Such examinations are conducted mainly by commissions, collectives, or ad hoc groups of experts. Members of public examination panels are responsible for the accuracy and validity of their expert evaluations in accordance with the legislation of the Russian Federation. A decision of a public environmental panel has an informative nature as a recommendation, but it becomes legally mandatory after its approval by the appropriate body of the State. Besides, the opinion of the public is taken into account when a project submitted for state environmental review has undergone public examinations and there are supporting materials.

Public environmental examination is supposed to draw the attention of state bodies to a definite site or facility and to disseminate well-grounded information about potential ecological risks. This important facet of public environmental organizations in Moscow and in Russia is very weak. To a large extent, it can be explained by an insufficient level of specific and general knowledge of ecology even on the part of the environmentalists themselves. Lack of knowledge on the part of ordinary citizens and public groups and inadequate information (for various reasons) produce alarm-motivated behavior by those who harm the organization of environmental activity in general and waste management in particular. There are nevertheless positive examples of public participation in designing policies of local authorities in the waste management sphere.

Speaking about the Moscow region we can point to the very productive work of the Public Ecological Commission attached to the Council of Deputies in Pushchino, in Moscow Oblast. The population of Pushchino is 21,000. The polygon for solid biological wastes (SBW) has practically exhausted its capacities. In 1996, in order to find a way out, the Administration of the town showed an interest in a proposal made by the Austrian firm FMW to support financially the construction of an electric power station in the vicinity of the town that would operate using both fuel briquettes and SBW of the town.

The briquettes would be manufactured in Turkey and would contain 70 percent Austrian industrial waste with added oil sludge. It was also envisaged that during the construction period of the electric power station, 300,000 tons of briquettes would be shipped and stockpiled. The original positive decision was annulled due to an independent evaluation of the project organized by the Public Ecological Commission.

The general public of Puschino put forward a counter proposal before the Administration in order to reduce volumes of SBW disposal at the polygon and to prolong its operation- segregation of SBW (food waste, paper refuse, fabrics, metal, glass, used car batteries). As a result, a new scheme for sanitary measures in the town was worked out in 1998, which on the basis of segregation of waste provided for a considerable decrease in refuse flow to the polygon. Unfortunately, for lack of finances in the town budget, the scheme has not been introduced to the full extent. But in spite of severe shortages of special containers for segregated wastes, a network of receiving points for secondary materials was set up. One of the pressing tasks for greater public activity is wide popularization of environmental knowledge on waste management, especially among the young generation.

There is a very important role for public organizations to play in this domain when enlightenment and education are becoming a primary concern of nongovernmental organizations. Referring again to the example of the Public Ecological Commission in Pushchino, I have to underline that this organization is taking an active part in the enlightenment of the population through organizing exhibitions, placing publications in the press, and spurring school children into action to encourage cleaning of the town by means of environmental contests, seminars, and conferences. Children help the Commission organize mobile receiving points for secondary material. They even prepare announcements and post them around the town calling on the citizens to take valuable amounts of domestic wastes and car batteries to receiving points.

There are other examples of a growing influence of public organizations on the policy of administration in the sphere of waste management in the Moscow region. The Moscow Children's Ecological Center has worked out the Program "You, He, She and I-All Together Make Moscow Clean," which is being introduced with the support of the Moscow Government. In the framework of this program, children collect waste paper at schools, and they are taught how to be careful about the environment and material resources. The storage facilities agreed to support the initiative. They buy waste paper at a special price for school children. Then, the schools spend the earned money for excursions, laboratory equipment, books, and plant greenery.

Another example of an enlightened activity is a project realized in 1999 by the firm Ecoconcord on producing video-clips for TV about the adverse effects of waste incineration and the illegality of unauthorized storage of waste.

The name Ecoconcord speaks for the main purpose of this organization-to achieve mutual understanding between the general public and governmental organizations, to encourage public involvement in decision-making, and to promote the formation of policy bodies that would not let public opinion be ignored.

Proceeding from the global task of integrating the activities of interested parties in lessening adverse waste pollution, public organizations have to cooperate with authorities and not stand against them. Cooperation and consensus between governmental and nongovernmental organizations in working out strategies and tactics in waste management should become a prerequisite in successful realization of state policy in this sphere in the Russian Federation.

EMISSIONS OF POLLUTANTS INTO THE ATMOSPHERE AND HYDROSPHERE OF THE KUZNETSK COAL BASIN

The Kuznetsk coal basin (Kuzbass) is located largely on the left bank of the Tom River, the most urbanized part of Kemerovo Oblast. The main industries in this part of the Kuzbass territory are ferrous and nonferrous metallurgy, power engineering, machine building, construction, and chemical enterprises. Therefore, the general ecological condition of the Kuznetsk coal basin is determined not by the coal industry alone, with restructuring calling for liquidation of 35 coal mines by flooding, but also by other industries.

Given the geographical variance in environmental conditions and industrial impacts, several ecological-geographic districts can be distinguished. These are first of all the territories that have undergone the most intense industry-induced impacts: destruction and degradation of soil cover, disturbance of hydrogeologic conditions, pollution of surface and subsurface waters, atmospheric pollution from industrial emissions, and degradation of natural flora and fauna. These territories are in the Kemerovo and South Kuzbass ecological-geographic districts. Boundaries of the maximum industry-induced pressure on the biosphere coincide with the boundaries of these districts.

This pressure is present in about 30 percent of the territory within the limits of Kemerovo Oblast, where about 70 percent of the population lives and practically the entire coal industry of the Kuzbass is concentrated. The second group of districts (about 40 percent of the territory, 20-25 percent of the population) is subjected to a rather heavy industry-induced load from enterprises and from pollutant transport from adjacent territories, but the abundance of forests stabilizes to a large measure the ecological environment. And, finally, the third group of ecological-geographic districts (about 30 percent of the regional territory with 5-10 percent of the population) may be regarded as ecologically satisfactory. The atmospheric condition is an important ecological characteristic of the region. Air pollution still remains one of the most pressing ecological problems because the bulk of people live in districts where pollutant concentrations are often in excess of maximum permissible levels. The most polluted cities are Kemerovo and Novokuznetsk.

Air pollution in Kemerovo Oblast results from an extremely high concentration of various industries. Of 1,472 enterprises with pollutant emissions under the control of Goskomekologiya (State Committee on Ecology) of Kemerovo Oblast, the following are located on a small territory of 95,700 square kilometers: 21 enterprises of ferrous and nonferrous metallurgy, 126 coal-mining and coal- processing enterprises, 18 thermal-power engineering facilities, 10 chemical enterprises, 83 machine-building and metal-working plants, 184 construction- industry enterprises, and 308 enterprises of rail and motor transport and road services, as well as agricultural, food, light industry, and furniture enterprises and numerous steam heating plants.

The total pollutant emissions into the atmosphere in the populated areas of the region in 1999, including stationary and mobile (motor, rail, and air transport) sources, were 1,358,573 tons, including solid substances-235,899, sulfur dioxide-138,875, carbon dioxide-610,018, nitrogen oxides-143,282, hydrocarbons-211,916, other gases-18,486. Most of the total emissions are from pollutants from combustion of various fuels.

Emissions from mobile sources are 260,032 tons (19.14 percent), including the following: motor transport-239,595 tons, railroad transport-19,867 tons, and air transport-570 tons. The majority of emissions from mobile sources are exhaust emissions from motor transport amounting to 92.14 percent. The motor transport contribution to pollution is 19.14 percent in the region as a whole, while it is much higher in some towns, such as Anzhero-Sudzhensk-38.4 percent, Mezhdurechensk-40.1 percent, Kemerovo-44.1 percent. The exhaust emissions from motor transport have increased by 6.0 percent (or by 14,479 tons) as compared with 1998.

The stationary sources accounted for 1,098,541 tons of pollutants emitted into the atmosphere (the emission limit being 1,127,547 tons). Incomplete data indicate that around 200 substances enter the atmosphere. The majority are highly toxic and carcinogenic (3,4-benz(a)pyrene, various metal and silicon compounds, cyanides, fluorides, and a broad spectrum of hydrocarbons, including volatile organic compounds that enter into photochemical reactions in the atmosphere to produce ozone and other oxidants).

Enterprises of the following sectors are the main contributors to air pollution: metallurgy-421,706 tons, power engineering-206,170 tons, fuel-233,459 tons, chemical industry-5,209 tons, and other sectors-231,708 tons. The volume of recorded emissions into the atmosphere in comparison with 1998 has increased as follows: in the fuel industry-by 60,275 tons due to the more accurate accounting of methane emission sources; in electric power engineering-by 6,911 tons due to increased amount of burned fuel; in the chemical industry-by 1,952 tons due to a production increase; in metallurgy-by 29,346 tons due to a production increase. In 1999, 80 new enterprises were registered, while 115 enterprises were either liquidated or merged. The increase of emissions into the atmosphere throughout the region has totaled 98,309 tons. During the last five years (1995-1999), pollutant emissions from stationary sources have decreased by 7,004 tons, or by 6 percent, as a result of recession in the main sectors of the economy. Four million tons (79.4 percent) of pollutants were removed at the enterprises of the region in 1999. The highest level of removal was in the power engineering (92.3 percent) and chemical (87.4 percent) industries. A low level of pollutant removal was in housing-communal services-33.9 percent, at transport and road-service enterprises-30.5 percent, at trading enterprises-24.4 percent, and in public health services-6.6 percent. Noxious substances from the communication, educational, material, and technical supply enterprises go to the atmosphere without cleaning. The greatest volume of emissions is registered in the towns of Novokuznetsk, Kemerovo, Belovo, Leninsk-Kuznetsky, Myski, Prokopyevsk, Kiselevsk, Kaltan, and Mezhdurechensk. A great number of industrial enterprises are situated near residential districts. Recurrent weather conditions unfavorable for dissipation of emissions cause the high level of air pollution. This is confirmed by observations at the hydrometeorology and environment monitoring centers located in Kemerovo, Novokuznetsk, and Prokopyevsk. The pollution level in Kemerovo and Novokuznetsk, according to a generalized index developed by Rosgidromet (Russian Hydrometeorological Service), is estimated to be high.

Pollutant emissions into the city atmosphere in 1999, including stationary and mobile (motor, railroad, and air transport) sources, amounted to 117,777 tons. The main contributors to emissions from stationary sources are the enterprises of: power engineering-71.26 percent, ferrous metallurgy-7.15 percent, chemical processing-7.65 percent, housing-communal services-4.06 percent, and fuel industry-3.69 percent. Pollutants removed at city enterprises amount to 588,245 tons, which comprise 90 percent. The level of removal is the highest in the power engineering industry-91.7 percent, in chemical industry-87.7 percent. It is low at the enterprises of housing-communal services-29.1 percent, machine building and metal plants-26.6 percent, transport and road services-4.3 percent. Emissions from trading and from material and technical supply enterprises go to the atmosphere without cleaning.

As compared to 1998, emissions from stationary sources have increased by 2,004 tons due to the production increase at city enterprises (Azot, Khimprom, Kemerovo State Regional Power Plant). Statistical accounts have been submitted by 140 enterprises for which MPE (maximum permissible emission) standards are established. In Kemerovo, regular observations of air pollution are performed using a network of eight stationary points of the state hydrometeorology and environmental monitoring committee.

Staff members of the Kemerovo scientific center have carried out work on the ecological zoning of the city territory based on investigations of sulfur accumulation by leaves of plants. Based on inventory data and the distribution of weather conditions (wind velocity, wind direction, and atmosphere stability), the average annual near-ground concentrations of the sum of sulfur-containing impurities have been calculated. Industrial processes associated with coal mining are sources of man-induced impacts on the environment. These sources are power plants, coal transportation, storage and loading, degassing and ventilating, burning spoil banks, maintenance- technological services, and motor transport. All possible sources of emissions and an assessment of their impact on the atmospheric pollution should be described in the design of a newly opened mine. Mine methane at operating enterprises goes to the atmosphere mainly from degassing and ventilating units.

According to the presently accepted documents, methane is one of the least harmful pollutants (maximum permissible concentration=50 milligrams per cubic meter). Today, the payment for one ton of methane emission is approximately 1,000 times less than for one ton of sulfurous anhydride. Therefore, the economic and administrative sanctions on methane emissions on the part of Russian territorial nature-preservation authorities are quite insignificant. However, the worldwide tendencies of recent years toward the limitation of greenhouse gases lead to greater attention to methane emissions. It is not unlikely, therefore, that the standards of payment for atmospheric pollution with methane will significantly increase in the near future, which, in view of the large emissions of this gas in the Kuzbass coal mines, may result in a substantial increase of nature-preservation payments and in a decrease of coal mining profitability.

A generalization of inventory data on the sources of harmful substance emissions into the atmosphere at the Kuzbass mines provides the ranges of total emissions per mine. Under the most unfavorable conditions, the payment of fines for methane emissions into the atmosphere does not exceed 6,450 rubles per year. A review of inventory data also shows that at Kuzbass mines, ventilation unit emissions at a height of 5-6 meters typically have a relatively high vertical velocity of gas-air mixture discharge (8-19 meters/second). This condition substantially increases the effective flare height and leads to a decrease in the near-ground concentrations at short distances from the source. With the indicated source parameters and the emissions at the upper boundary level, the maximum near-ground concentration is achieved at wind velocities of 3-5 meters/second at a distance of 50-300 meters and may be equal to 3-4 MPC (maximum permissible concentration). When a coal-mining enterprise closes, most sources providing loads on the atmosphere disappear. At the same time, state environmental control over the sources of pollutant emissions is terminated. But this does not mean that the closed mine completely ceases its negative influence on the atmosphere. Products of incomplete burning of spontaneously ignited coals and of mine equipment in the fire zone may be emitted. Spreading of dust from poorly controlled spoil banks also persists.

As to methane, after a mine is closed its ventilation ceases, and emissions of methane-air mixture are significantly reduced. But, as pumping of water also ceases, the water table rises, with the result that pressure in the mine grows and methane begins to escape to the surface and into the atmosphere. The rivers of the Kuzbass are polluted with waste waters disposed from numerous enterprises of different branches of industry. The quality of water bodies continues to be below standard specifications.

The most widespread pollutants of surface waters in the region are petroleum products, phenols, metal compounds, ammonium, and nitrites. The principal source is waste waters of industrial enterprises and housing-communal services. Four main water basins are in the region: the Tom, Inya, Chulym, and Chumysh Rivers basins. More than 32,000 rivers with a combined length exceeding 76,478 kilometers flow over the territory. Depending on local characteristics and relief, the rivers of the region are subdivided into plain- and mountain-type rivers. All of the rivers flowing over the territory of the region link to the Ob River basin and are tributaries of its upper reaches.

The main reasons for the increase in water consumption were an increase in output at some enterprises (West-Siberian Metallurgical Complex and Kuznetsk Metallurgical Complex in Novokuznetsk, Azot and Khimprom in Kemerovo, Yurga Machine-building Plant in Yurga) and an increased use of water at coal-mining enterprises. The shrinkage of the irrigated land areas and the reduction of livestock populations have resulted in a decrease of water consumption for irrigation and agricultural needs.

Rivers of the Tom basin, where the main industrial potential of the Kuzbass is concentrated, are the most used and most subject to industry-induced impacts. According to the pH value, the Tom's waters are usually neutral or weakly alkaline. The contents of biogenic substances (Si, Fe, and compounds of N and P) show enhanced amounts of iron and ammonium ions, occasionally also of NO2. The concentrations of trace elements vary over quite a wide range, but the average level of their contents is not high. An examination of data has shown that the Tom's waters are polluted most with organic substances, with enhanced concentrations of petroleum products and phenols being most often registered throughout the length of the river. Identified in the Tom's waters (in the framework of experimental investigations) is an extensive list of various organic substances falling into the following classes of compounds: saturated and aromatic hydrocarbons (including those of petroleum origin), alkyl phenols, fatty organic acids and their ethers, alcohols, organic phosphates, and chlorine-organic compounds. Thus, based on the results of investigations in 1990-1993 along the

Tom River on the Kuzbass territory, the three most heavily polluted areas have been delineated: in the zones of influence of Novokuznetsk, Kemerovo, and Yurga. Among the most characteristic pollutants in surface waters of the Tom River, for which values exceeding MPC have been continuously or occasionally registered, are suspended solids, ammonium nitrate, heavy metals (Pb, Zn, Ni, Fe, Mn, Cr, Cd), petroleum products, highly volatile phenols, and other organic substances of different classes of hazard. The mode of distribution of hydrocarbons suggests their man-induced origin.

The presence of SAH (surface-active hydrocarbons) in nanogram quantities of lighter aromatic hydrocarbons (naphthalene and its derivatives anthracene, fluorene, fluorenthene, and pyrene) suggests that the enhanced concentrations of SAH in the Tom River are caused by the discharge of mine and subsurface waters contacting with coal rocks enriched in these compounds. The Inya River basin is second in importance and ecological loading. Sixteen million cubic meters of water were taken from water bodies of the basin in 1999, mainly for the needs of production (10 million cubic meters). Discharged into the basin's surface water bodies were 116 million cubic meters of waste waters from the towns of Belovo, Leninsk-Kuznetsky, and Guryevsk and from the Promyshlennov, Leninsk-Kuznetsky, Guryevsk, and Belovo districts. Of 115 million cubic meters of waste waters needing purification, 104 million cubic meters (89.8 percent) have been treated, of which .01 million cubic meters have been purified to meet specified standards. Together with waste waters, 125,000 tons of pollutants are discharged into the rivers of the basin, including 249 tons of toxics and 20,562 tons of pollutants with reduced toxicity.

The source of the Inya River is located on the Taradanov ridge. The Inya is the right tributary of the Ob and flows through industrial and agricultural areas in the central part of Kemerovo Oblast. The river is 663 kilometers long, extending for 433 kilometers over the Kemerovo Oblast territory. The drainage basin area is 17,600 square kilometers. Within the region, the river is regulated by means of the Belovo Reservoir. The Inya is polluted mainly with waste waters from coal-mining enterprises and communal services, which is reflected in the chemical composition of water. A

total of 66 million cubic meters of waste waters have been discharged into the river, including 3,800 cubic meters without treatment. Together with waste waters, 81,000 tons of pollutants have been discharged.

The main pollutants of the Inya River and its tributaries are petroleum products, phenols, nitrogen- containing substances, and ions of heavy metals. Phenol pollution of the river averages 6-9 MPC. The one-time maximum concentration was registered in 1999:18 MPC in the summer low-water period. Average concentrations of petroleum products varied within a 3-6 MPC range. While the concentrations of petroleum products in the monitored section downstream from Leninsk-Kuznetsky remain within a 4.5-5.5 MPC range, in the section upstream from the town a decrease from 6 MPC in 1997 to 3 MPC in 1999 has been registered. In 1999, as compared with two previous years, the average concentrations of ammonium nitrates and nitrites decreased both upstream and downstream from the town.

Pollution of the Inya with organic substances, as judged from BOD5 (biochemical oxygen demand) and COD (chemical oxygen demand) indicators, is stable within a 1.5-2 MPC range, while average concentrations of total iron and zinc increased a little in 1999 (to 1-1.5 MPC) as compared with two previous years (0.5-1.0 MPC). The Chulym River basin includes the Yaya River and its tributaries, the Kiya and its tributaries, the Itatka, and others. About 33 million cubic meters of water were taken from water bodies of the basin in 1999, mainly for the needs of production.

Discharged into the surface water bodies of the basin were 61 million cubic meters. Of 55 million cubic meters of waste waters requiring purification, 49 million cubic meters (81.3 percent) were treated. Twelve million cubic meters (19.7 percent) were treated in accord with specified standards. Together with waste waters, 28,000 tons of pollutants were discharged into the rivers of the basin, including 87 tons of toxic substances and 4,400 tons of toxic sewage wastes.

The Chumysh River basin includes the Chumysh and its tributaries: Kara- Chumysh, Yegos, and others. Some 95 million cubic meters of water were taken from bodies of water in the basin, largely for the needs of production. Discharged into the rivers of the basin are waste waters from enterprises of Novokuznetsk Region and Prokopyevsk. A total of 23 million cubic meters of waste waters were discharged, including nine million cubic meters (40 percent) without treatment. Together with waste waters, 9,050 tons of pollutants were discharged, of which 21 tons were toxic and 1,600 tons were toxic sewage wastes.

Mining exerts an adverse effect on the water regime of Kemerovo Oblast. Dehydration of mining areas occurs and cones of depression form, with sizes depending on the geologic and hydrogeologic conditions and on the length of the mining period. An area of depression cones in the Kuzbass exceeds two thousand square kilometers.

The effect of mining on the river discharge is reflected in a decrease in the subsurface water discharge into the river due to drainage pumping in mines or quarries, by an increase in the river sedimentation caused by the same factors, and by a decrease in the subsurface water reserves. The daily flow from Kuzbass mines and open pits exceeds one million cubic meters. Drainage of deposits results in a decrease of water reserves in surface water bodies, drying up of wells and water supply wells, and exhausting of springs, streams, and small rivers. In the zone of mining, more than 200 rivers have disappeared or diminished, and a general degradation of the territories continues, which results in the destruction of habitat conditions and degradation of vegetation.

The coal industry is the second in importance for pollution of Kuzbass water bodies after power engineering, which discharges into the rivers 58.9 percent (1,515 million cubic meters/year) of untreated waters. The coal industry accounts for 14.6 percent (384 million cubic meters/year) of untreated waters. Coal enterprises discharge 34.4 percent of all suspended solids and 10 percent of petroleum products. Mines, per unit of output, discharge into water bodies 3.6 times more suspended solids, 5.2 times more chlorides, 2.6 times more easily oxidized organic substances, and 3.72 times more petroleum products than open pits. Suspended substances are the main pollutant of mine waters. Waste waters of some mines contain phenol, which forms as a result of pyrogenic decomposition of coal. Mine waters show strong bacterial pollution.

Closure of coal mines by means of flooding will lead to the contraction of their depression cones and to a change in the discharge directions of mine-polluted subsurface waters. The result may be that the subsurface waters previously discharged into mines will begin to discharge into surface water streams with pollutants from dumping grounds of various waste products (including dangerous chemical waste). The influence of waste waters on the surface water quality can be observed near the following mines: Pionerka-the Big Bachat River, Bungurskaya-the Bungurska River, Dimitrova-the Aba River, Shevyakov-the Olzheras River, Shushtalepskaya-the Kondoma River, Baidaevskaya-the Garshina River, Vakhrushev-the Aba River. An analysis of mine waters after they have passed treatment plants shows that the majority of solids analyzed exceed MPC. Thus, suspended substances in all of the mines analyzed exceed MPC from 2 to 34 times, BOD from 1.6 to 20.8 times, ammonia from 1.3 to 18 times, and so on. The discharges of waste waters from mines being closed have resulted in an increase of MPC in surface waters by a factor of 2 to 7 for a number of components.

The subsurface waters of the Kuzbass are of the infiltration type, with reserves formed due to atmospheric precipitation. The infiltration in the upper part of the geologic section varies, according to G.M.Rogov, from 200 mm (25 percent of precipitation) in the mountain-taiga zone to 85 mm (14 percent) in the low- mountain-taiga zone and to 35 mm per year (7-8 percent of precipitation) in the steppe zone.

According to Zapsibgeologiya (West-Siberian Production-Geological Association), traces of industry-induced pollution of subsurface waters have been recognized west of Myski and in the vicinity of Novokuznetsk. Pollution by a number of components (phenols, formaldehyde, COD, BOD) ranges up to 150 MPC. Much of the explored reserves in the Myski and Kiyzak areas are not exploited now because of the pollution with waste saline waters from a district steam heating plant over an area of four sq. km. and the liquidation of reservoir gravel by the Kiyzak building material quarry. On the territories of large livestock complexes and poultry plants the contamination of soil has resulted in the pollution of subsurface waters with nitrogen compounds and heavy metals. In some cases the subsurface waters under farming lands were found to have enhanced contents of pesticides (Kemerovo Region), nitrates-from 2 to 30 MPC (swine-breeding complexes in Chistogor and Tal), and organic compounds-phenols up to 3000

MPC (Kemerovo: Azot, Tokem). Observations of the subsurface water regime under natural conditions conducted for many years show that the mode of ground and subsurface water table fluctuations depends most of all on the amount of precipitation and on the regime type. The wells under the riverside and terrace regime conditions clearly show a spring and autumn rise of the water table and its smooth recession in the course of winter. The minimum levels of summer-autumn low-water periods differ from those of winter low-water periods in both directions, but are most often lower or close to them.

The annual amplitude of water table fluctuations varies from 0.2 to 4 meters. Only the spring water table rise is registered (lagging in time, as a rule, in comparison with the riverside regime) followed by a smooth recession. Minimal levels in the summer-autumn low-water period are close to those in the winter low- water period. Annual amplitudes are insignificant, rarely exceeding one meter. The effect of the coal-mining complex on the hydrosphere causes a change of water regime of the territory-pollution of ground and waste waters with products of physical and chemical weathering of subsurface rocks. In every case, the zone of mining and the territories adjacent to it are drained by means of tunnels, pumping, and disposal of subsurface waters into the hydrological network beyond the mining area. The natural regime of subsurface waters becomes disturbed and their reserves diminish. In the process of both subsurface and open-pit mining, the lowering of the ground water table forms a cone of depression whose size depends on the geologic and hydrogeologic conditions of the mining area and on the duration of mining. One of the most adverse aspects of mine flooding is the possibility of polluting the subsurface waters, which are a source of drinking water. This will necessitate an urgent solution of the water supply problem for the populations of Novokuznetsk, Belovo, Kemerovo, and Anzhero-Sudzhensk.

Pollution of mine waters with metals is registered for zinc (up to 14 times background levels), copper (up to 270 times), lead (up to two times), manganese (up to 325 times), molybdenum (up to four times), arsenic (up to 100 times), vanadium (up to five times), fluorine (up to 5.9 times), and aluminum (up to 2.3 times). As is evident from an analysis of mine water pollution dynamics, the contents of nitrogen group compounds and petroleum products increase in spring, summer, and autumn and sharply decrease in the winter period. This means that an important role in the pollution of mine waters with these substances, particularly when water levels are extremely high, is played by snow-melt and storm waters bringing to the mines pollutants from petroleum products and household refuse accumulated on the territory allocated for mining.

To help solve the large- scale problems of natural resource monitoring and environment protection in Kemerovo Oblast, an integrated information system based on the use of geoinformation technologies has been developed. Ecological Atlas of Kemerovo Oblast (ATLAS) is designed for the collection and storage of graphical and semantic information on the state of the environment and natural resources in Kemerovo Oblast, as well as for processing this information. The system provides support for the solution of a wide range of problems concerning monitoring, accounting, planning, distribution, and financial regulation in the field of natural resources usage and payment for environment disturbances and pollution. Besides, ATLAS can be used in higher and post-graduate ecological education. The system based on GIS-technologies is used as follows:

- o To form electronic maps of localities using a base of graphic layers with a summary map of all semantic descriptions of objects available in each layer.
- o To establish relationships between individual objects with semantic information stored in databases of the dBASE and PARADOX format.
- o To create and/or attach cartographic-mathematical models of technical- natural phenomena with the visualization and saving of their results in a separate graphic base layer.
- o To process and edit semantic and graphical data (in compliance with information security).
- o To form, browse, and print out normative-reference information.

The aggravation of the ecological situation in Kemerovo Oblast in recent years is connected not only with the activation of production in heavy industry sectors, but also with the lack of ecological culture among the great majority of managers of all levels. At present, 12 public ecological organizations work in the Kuzbass. Among the most active of them are the following: Kemerovo Department of the All-Russian Society for Nature Preservation, Information Ecological Agency, Ecological Parliament of Children and Young People, Kemerovo Regional Society Social Health, Kemerovo Regional Department of the Russian National Organization Green Cross, and Ecological Movement Kuzbass. Scientists of the Kemerovo Scientific Center of the Siberian Branch of the Russian Academy of Sciences take an active part in the work of the majority of these organizations. The principal lines of activity of public ecological organizations are the following:

- Publication of Information Ecological Bulletin
- Ecological audit and consulting
- Public ecological expert examination
- Informational support and service in the environmental field

The regional Ecological Parliament of Children and Young People has adopted its own ecological code for children and young people in February 2000 on the basis of the recommendations of the UN Conference on the Environment and Development (Rio de Janeiro, 1992). Its fundamental principles are as follows:

- Destruction of the environment is a consequence of the destruction of personality, of a person's inner life, of his values.
- There is but one step from ecological ignorance to a crime against humanity.
- We have no right to enrich ourselves at the expense of nature; we must live in harmony with it.
- To preserve man as a species, we should preserve the natural environment; in order to preserve the environment, man should change himself, his attitude to it.

The Ecological Parliament of Children and Young people has concluded an agreement on cooperation to participate in the solution of regionally significant ecological problems with the Kemerovo Oblast administration in an effort to strengthen the interaction between the authorities and the ecological movement The Information Ecological Agency (IEA) may now be called a professional public organization. The agency collects and systematizes ecological information with special attention to regional ecological problems. The main emphasis is on involving the general public in the process of significant decisions and regulations in the field of environmental protection in the Kuzbass.

Information Ecological Bulletin is a monthly 24-page monthly publication with a circulation of 950 copies. The bulletin is intended for specialists, industry personnel, teachers, and representatives of public organizations. It covers the following issues: regional problems, projects, and public actions in the field of environment; ecological legislation, ecological audit, and ecological management; the environment, public health conditions, and the ecological rights of citizens; technologies in the field of environment; and ecological education. The IEA provides services for ecological audits, environmental impact assessments, ecological substantiation of business activity, valuation of maximum permissible pollutant emissions, waste disposition, permissible levels of environmental impact, and confirmation of limits on the use of natural resources. The IEA has appropriate licenses for all of the above-listed types of activity.

To realize these activities, the Agency forms temporary groups of specialists in different fields from IEA members. Since February 1998, the IEA has been affiliated with the Russian Network of Regional Centers of public ecological expertise in the context of a program realized by the Moscow public organization Ecoline and supported by the Institute for Sustainable Communities (USA). The Agency supports development of information and exchange of information. The scientists of the Kemerovo Scientific Center of the Russian Academy of Sciences take an active part in the popularization of ecological knowledge and of the problems of stable regional development by publishing popular scientific papers in the mass media and in the Information Ecological Bulletin. They participate in expert appraisals of regional legislative acts aimed at nature preservation and of regionally significant business projects.

Currently special attention is paid to the problems of ecological education and training. An analysis of the present situation shows an absence of multilevel ecological education as a system. The number of ecological schools in the region is far from sufficient. This is connected with the absence of ecological education programs, the lack of personnel, the complexity of curricula, and the lack of textbooks and training aids.

In schools of the region (mainly in the innovative educational institutions), attention is given to the scientific-research work of students in ecology. Their work is presented at scientific conferences, in the ecology sections. The Kuznetsk department of the Geographical Society together with the tourist station of Novokuznetsk has organized training on practical ecology for groups of students. Students become acquainted with methods for the observation and study of birds, with determination of water quality, and with the world of plants. They carry out ecological games and walking tours.

Additional ecological-biological education in Kemerovo Oblast involves the regional station of young naturalists as a coordination center of uninterrupted ecological education and ecological culture formation among pre-school children and among elementary and middle school students.

There are 15 scientific associations of pupils and students in the region established on the basis of young naturalist stations, ecological-biological centers, and children's and young people's centers. They include "Genetics of Animals," "Ecology of Plants," and "Biochemistry and Cytology" in Novokuznetsk; "Microbiology," "Young Forester," and "Fauna" in Kemerovo; and "Young Ecologist and Biologist" in Anzhero-Sudzhensk, and Myski.

Stations of young naturalists in Mezhdurechensk, Novokuznetsk, Anzhero- Sudzhensk, Topki, Kiselevsk,

Prokopyevsk, Kemerovo, Yurga, and other towns, together with schools, are engaged in an integrated study of the ecological conditions of their towns, in the examination of large and small rivers, and in the investigation of flora and fauna of their native land. Various methods used in this study include ecological monitoring; bioindication of water bodies and air basins; and hydrobiological, zoological, and botanical investigations. It has become a tradition that the regional station of young naturalists, together with the regional Goskomekologiya and Kemerovo State University, conducts rallies/competitions of young ecologists, including defense of research works by the rally participants, and their demonstrations of ability to use the main methods of field ecology.

With active support from the regional Committee of Young Naturalists, the groups of young ecologists of the Kemerovo region participate in the realization of several Federal educational-research projects: "Phenology of Birds," "Life to Russian Waters," "Crane, the Bird of Peace," "Water on the Earth," and others. Ecological shifts at the stations of young naturalists continue in Kemerovo, Novokuznetsk, Mezhdurechensk, Yurga, Anzhero-Sudzhensk, and Myski. Pupils of School No. 62 in Kemerovo are engaged in the problem of potable water under the program "Clean Water of the Taydon-to the Kuzbass Towns." They report the results of their expeditions at Russian conferences and receive well-deserved diplomas and certificates.

The Kemerovo Scientific Center, with the participation of institutes of higher education and public ecological organizations, has conducted a number of international, all-Russian, and regional scientific-practical conferences and seminars. The most significant were the All-Russian scientific-practical conference "Ecology and Economy: Regional Problems of Transition to Stable Development. A Look into the Twenty-First Century," the international scientific-practical conference "Ecological Problems of the Regional Coal-mining Sector Under the Transition to Stable Development," the second international conference "Reduction of Methane Emission," and the scientific-practical seminar "Regional Problems in the Economical

Education on the Eve of the Twenty-First Century." The aforementioned seminar discussed methodological approaches, standards, and training aids for a system of multi-level ecological education and training. The discussion demonstrated experience in the ecological education and training of the people. In the system of general secondary education, ecology is being introduced as an independent subject. In the higher schools, special courses of ecology, nature preservation, engineering ecology, and rational use of natural resources are being introduced. Several centers of ecological education work within the system of post- graduate professional development.

At the same time, the process of ecological education and training has not become continuous and obligatory, as is required by the Environmental Protection Law. A scientifically based system of ecological education and training is absent in the region, and the legal and normative foundation has not been formed. There are great difficulties in providing the material-technical and educational-pedagogical basis for carrying out practical expeditions. The difficulties in the dissemination of ideas and experience of Russian and foreign ecological education are aggravated by the absence of available information systems and periodicals.

To raise the level of ecological education, the following should be done:

- It is necessary to pass the law "On the Ecological Education and Training of Population in Kemerovo Oblast."
- A regional target program should be developed "Perfection of Ecological Education and Training in Kemerovo Oblast for the Years 2001-2005," with the specification of financial resources from the regional budget (via the Education Department and the Science and Higher School Department) and the regional ecological fund budget.
- A system of centers of ecological education and training should be established. They should have the following tasks: development of regional standards of different-level ecological education; assessment of the effectiveness

of ecological education, expert appraisal, and certification of training aids; development of retraining and professional development programs for teachers in the ecological education system of the Kemerovo region; and assistance in the preparation and publication of training and methodology aids, including tutorial computer programs.

- o The role of public organizations and the mass media in the process of ecological education should be increased. A standing seminar (school) for journalists and public activists is needed, together with a cycle of broadcasts and telecasts.
- o Ethical and aesthetic education at each educational level should be improved and extended.

RUSSIAN FAR EAST ENVIRONMENTAL PROBLEMS

The Far East Region includes ten eastern entities of the Russian Republic: the Republic of Sakha; Primorye and Khabarovsk Territories; Amur, Kamchatka, Magadan, and Sakhalin Oblasts; the Jewish Autonomous Region; and Koryak and Chukot Autonomous Districts. It occupies a sizable territory of 6.215 million square kilometers or 36.4 percent of Russia. As of January 1, 1997, the region was inhabited by 7.421 million people or only 5.03 percent of the nation's population. The average density of the population is 1.19 persons per square kilometers or one- seventh the national average. A recent downward trend in the population has developed as migration to other regions increases.

Strangely enough, development of the region began from the north. Russian expeditions initially explored Chukotka and Kamchatka in the first half of the eighteenth century. Exploration of the southern part of the region began only in the second half of the nineteenth century. Slow development of the region was related to its remoteness and unfavorable climatic conditions. Yet the region enjoys an important geopolitical location, for it provides access to the Pacific Ocean and to the frontiers with Japan, Korea, China, and the United States. Industrial, economic, and cultural development of the region was carried out by military forces, by newly arrived workers, and by prisoners-all perceived as temporary residents. Historically, genealogically, and culturally, most of the region has been linked to Central Russia and Siberia. The region is rich in natural resources-fish, timber, oil, gas, and minerals such as gold, diamonds, coal, and non-ferrous metals. With 5.03 percent of the population, the region produces 9.0 percent of the nation's timber and 67.1 percent of the fish catch. Industrial output reached 4.7 percent in 1990 and 4.6 percent in 1996, while farming was 3.2 percent and 2.9 percent, respectively. During the period of reforms, the share of these industries was on the rise, although the share declined considerably in other sectors. Consequently, recent trends are toward increased resource-extraction industries with growing pressure on the environment. The main environmental problems in the region relate to preservation of biodiversity, use of marine resources, pollution of rivers and lakes, preservation of forests, and urban development.

PRESERVATION OF BIODIVERSITY

The huge region spreads over several climatic zones from the polar area in the north to the subtropical areas of Primorye Territory, including continental, coastal, and island areas. It has unique biological diversity-vegetation, animal, and marine. The southern areas of the region were not exposed to ice formation during the glacial period, which resulted in preservation of ancient biospecies. The southern area of Primorye and Khabarovsk Territories exemplifies a unique coexistence of both northern (e.g., larch, stone birch) and southern (e.g. liana, lotus) plants. Such a unique mix is also typical for the animal world.

There are more than 5,000 vascular plant species and more than 1,500 types of mushrooms. In the south of Primorye territory there are more than 1,200 types of plants, 120 mammal species, 50,000 insects, and 550 birds. There are 104 types of fish in the Amur River alone. Diversity was preserved to a great extent due to the low level of development of the region as compared with other regions of Central Russia. There are many ancient plants in the area. For example, in the Sikhot Alin mountains, among the 800 plants 200 fall into the class of ancient relics. Three groups stand out among the relics of vegetative and possibly animal origin: relics well adapted to current conditions and renewable by nature, mobile relics, and relics that are being reduced by natural and anthropogenic forces. A distinguishing feature of the region is the availability of unique endemic plants and animals. Many of the over 250 endemic plants are on the verge of disappearance and are now in the Rare Species Book. The principal challenges to biodiversity are:

- o Natural and anthropogenic disasters.
- o Reduction of growth areas due to impacts such as deforestation and industrial development.
- o Predatory and poaching extermination of tigers, musk deer, ginseng, lemon trees, and the Amur sturgeon.
- o Lack of proper resource management.

Reduction of biodiversity in the Far East is inevitable due to a weakening of governmental control over resource-related activities, curtailment of funds for nature protection, poaching, and a sharp growth of smuggled exports. Different measures could counter biodiversity reduction. Among such steps are an increase in the size and number of protected areas, environmental education- particularly for school children-control of poaching and smuggling, and better resource management.

PROBLEMS IN THE USE OF THE PACIFIC SEAS

Problems arising from man's marine activities include loss of biodiversity, impacts of shipping, pollution from the Navy's activities, wastes from off-shore oil and gas production, and industrial and household dump sites. Ocean problems are often of an international character. Loss of biodiversity is often associated with fishing on the high seas as well as in coastal waters. Problems arise with international quotas and harvesting methods. It is not easy to implement an agreement when on frequent occasions each party tries to attain an excessive share of the resources and to hide its catch. Even though there is recognition of the importance of observing the agreement by the government, it is hard to persuade businessmen, sailors, and fishermen to comply. In recent years, poaching for illegal export has reach an industrial scale. The process from fishing to payment involves many activities on the sea. Government control is complicated, although the state is trying to use fishing inspectors and Coast Guard capabilities. The poaching of mollusks and trepangs (sea cucumbers) is taking on a massive scale in coastal waters. Trepangs are widely used in Chinese medicine and are therefore bought and smuggled out of the country in volumes that threaten the disappearance of the species. Artificial cultivation of seafood could be an alternative to reduce poaching. But this activity has not been developed due to a lack of investment funds and the mentality of the population, which prefers to rely on nature rather than cultivation. The negative environmental impact of marine industries is associated with the fact that the Russian fleet is aging. In the past 15 years there have been practically no new ships. Privatization and creation of joint-stock companies have resulted in small shipping companies that violate all the rules and regulations concerning marine ecology and navigation safety. The sinking of the Russian tanker Nadezhda with a resulting oil spill not far from Japanese islands is an example of the problems. Many ships are even banned from entering foreign ports. The Navy's activities, including cruises of nuclear-powered vessels, also damage the marine ecology. Apart from technical problems connected with the Navy's operations that impact the coastal areas, the military mentality is in principle unfriendly toward the environment. This is true in any country, not only Russia. Graveyards of decommissioned warships are a threat to coastal waters, although recently some problems were solved by the dismantling of vessels.

Off-shore oil and gas production has begun near Sakhalin Island under a Russian-American-Japanese project. But due to the novel character of the program, there is a serious risk of negative environmental consequences. There is a problem associated with industrial and domestic waste disposal in the seas. Vladivostok provides a typical negative example. Poorly processed wastes have been discharged for over one hundred years into Amur Bay. As a result, the bay is polluted and swimming is unsafe. To solve this problem there is a need to build wastewater treatment facilities and to control their operations. Unfortunately, economic and political chaos has slowed down such activity. The environmentally oriented world community is greatly concerned about the dumping of liquid radioactive waste from nuclear power plants into the seas. A new facility should be built to clean up such waste. One inadequate facility exists in Bolshoi Kamen.

AMUR RIVER CHARACTERISTICS AND CHALLENGES

The Amur River is among the ten largest in the world, with the following characteristics: length of 4,444 kilometers, annual runoff of 350 cubic kilometers, delta runoff of 10,900 cubic meters per second, and a runoff area of 10,900 square kilometers. A 10,000-kilometer stretch serves as the border between China and Russia, with the source of the Amur River lying in Mongolia. A main characteristic of the Amur River is biodiversity. In the northern hemisphere it is second to only the Mississippi River in this respect. The Amur has over 100 fish species, with two-thirds of them being food fish. There are relic species in the river, since its watershed was formed in ancient times. The watershed was not affected by ice during the glacial period, which led to the preservation of species.

With respect to the ichthyological diversity in Russia, the Amur is comparable to Lake Baikal. The Amur sturgeon is well known for its large size and weight of over one ton. It is similar to white sturgeon in the Volga River and American white sturgeon in the Columbia River. There are specific features of the Amur River, particularly the international aspects involving a number of disputes over the border despite treaties that date back one and one-half centuries. Problems also arise concerning engineering structures, fish catches, environmental monitoring, and industrial and municipal waste discharges.

In the judgment of specialists, poaching has been the main problem with regard to disappearing fish resources. Poaching now exceeds legal fishing, with 1,500 tons of Siberian fall salmon taken legally in 1997 but 10,000 tons taken illegally. In Khabarovsk, endangered species are sold openly while enforcement measures are ineffective. Poaching is growing due to unemployment, and the situation cannot be returned to normal without solving the social problems. Legislation seems incomplete and even ridiculous. For example, selling of all types of fish nets is authorized despite a ban on the use of certain types of nets. In practice the poachers are allowed to sell their catch. At the same time sport fishing is growing, and it too is not controlled. The public needs to take a more active stand on poaching. In the United States an organization in Oregon, the Wild Salmon Center, provides an example of effective activity to protect rare fish species. They are involved not only in the United States, but also in the Russian Far East. The Amur River also faces the "phenol" smell problem. This permeates the fish and prevents the sale of fish. It is similar to the smell of the chemical phenol. The first response of the public was that it was linked to industrial spills. However, tests and investigations showed that the problem was more complex. Most of the course of the river is fed by marsh runoff saturated with organic substances of vegetative origin. As a result of the biochemical interactions with the flora and fauna of the river, xenobiotics are released and penetrate the fish through respiratory and trophic channels.

Although the origin of this problem is mainly nature, anthropogenic discharges, particularly waste dumps, can trigger the process. Also, man-caused discharges into the river may create additional toxic xenobiotics, and efforts to reduce discharges should not slacken. At present the problem cannot be immediately solved, but investigations can provide information about the timing and places of the problem. Specialists of the Khabarovsk Research Center have been of considerable assistance in addressing this problem. As for public environmental organizations, they have not been helpful. Initially they simply cast blame on those directly involved in industrial production and on the authorities. Then they relied on scientists who were not competent to investigate the problem.

FOREST FIRES

The Far East region has considerable timber resources. They are of great importance in the formation of the planet's atmosphere. Woods are concentrated primarily in the southern areas, i.e., in Khabarovsk and Primorye Territories and in Amur and Sakhalin Oblasts. Severe fires occur there on the average of once every 22 years, with the last spate of large fires in 1998. The periodicity is apparently related to cyclic arid conditions and to the build-up of combustible material during the periods between fires. Also, in the eastern areas of the region there are frequent fires. Overall, probably 85 percent of the fires of the region are triggered by human activities. The 1998 fires occurred in the spring and lasted six months. Over 2.5 million hectares burned completely, although the fire area was much larger. Each burned hectare released 100 tons of particulate containing 55 percent tar and water, 25 percent soot, and 20 percent ash. These particles are harmful when inhaled by humans or animals. In addition, 10 to 12 tons of nitrogen, sulfur, and carbon oxides were discharged, including oxides with toxic effects. In sum, the fires resulted in the discharge of 250 million tons of particulates and 25 million tons of harmful gases with widespread impacts. For example, in Khabarovsk, located 200 kilometers from the fires, cars used headlights during the day. Pollution lasted for a few months and increased death rates. The impact on newborn children was particularly harmful. The UN Council on Humanitarian Issues reported that the fires had caused a large- scale problem of international concern.

Fires have many negative impacts. They destroy animal habitats. They change the flora composition of the forests. They change the insect population and may cause sudden outbreaks of some species. Runoff may pollute reservoir. And of course fires hamper reforestation efforts.

Prevention and elimination of forest fires should be of a comprehensive character including legislative, administrative, environmental protection, educational, and social programs. One factor responsible for the extent of the fires is the lack of agreement between the federal government and entities in the territories with regard to forests. Forests are federal property with regard to timber exploitation areas and timber sales. However, forest protection, fire fighting, and reduction of the consequences of fires are under the authority of the region. Unfortunately, lengthy discussions on these topics between the federal and Khabarovsk authorities in 1998 were largely a waste of time as the fires ignited.

RADIATION SITUATION

In the region there are a few sources of possible radioactive contamination- natural, household, industrial, military, energy supply facilities, and radioactive waste storage facilities. Natural sources are associated with specific geological structures that give off radon that results in the background levels. In Khabarovsk, the background from radon is 20 percent higher than the average for Russia. Particularly high background is associated with rocks containing uranium and thorium, with the levels dependent on porosity. Surveys indicate that 15 percent of city apartments using local building materials are moderately hazardous, 10 percent are hazardous, and 2 percent are particularly hazardous.

Other sources include radioisotopes used for research, production, and medical purposes and for standard measurements. Fifteen years ago, such sources in the Far East were in the tens of thousands, with 13,000 in Khabarovsk alone. The number has declined greatly due to curtailment of production and related activities. For example, in Khabarovsk the number has decreased by a factor of 22. Therefore, associated risks of contamination have also declined. In the meantime, however, there has been an increase in problems associated with waste disposal of radioactive sources. Quite often the sources are simply thrown out with ordinary waste rather than being delivered to appropriate waste storage sites.

Industrial sources include manufacturing and maintenance activities for nuclear submarines at Komsomolsk-on-Amur and Bolshoi Kamen. At present, production facilities at the former are closed, and decommissioned submarines are being dismantled at the latter. Also, at Bolshoi Kamen a plant for liquid radioactive waste processing is under construction. The state enterprise Radon has a storage facility for solid radioactive waste not far from Khabarovsk. It stores mainly household radiation sources from the entire Far East region. Neither the authorities nor environmentalists are concerned with the condition at the facility. The Bilibino nuclear power plant in Chukotka operates normally, according to the press. Additional military sources of radiation relate both to nuclear weapons and to the nuclear power units of submarines, but little information is available on relevant activities.

ENVIRONMENTALLY ORIENTED NGOS

There are many environmentally oriented NGOs, totaling a few hundred in the Far East region and over 50 in Khabarovsk alone. However, it is difficult to describe their activities as effective, meaningful, or discernible. NGOs may be divided into four groups: (1) opponents of the policies of the government, (2) "prisoners of conscience," (3) educational organizations, and (4) promoters of new technologies. The first group uses existing environmental problems as a basis for opposing the government. They appeared in large numbers in the mid-1980s, when environment was considered an area in which citizens could openly disagree with the state authorities. Many opponents intent on resolving political problems became involved in environmental activities. The opposition was of a radical character.

Subsequently, when they had other opportunities to become involved openly in political activities, they left the environmental movement. Also, as soon as some of them gained power, they changed their stand toward environmental problems. Thus, in the early 1990s deputies of the Primorye Territory Duma, who were members of NGOs, and other environmentalists opposed even conducting a feasibility study for the proposed construction of a nuclear power plant in the region, yet today they support such a project in view of the power crisis. Those who continue to join NGOs rely on the NGOs primarily as a channel for obtaining grants and fluids from other sources. The second group of NGOs, the "prisoners of conscience," represent organizations that unite people who are concerned over a safe environment and work for its improvement. The public Committee on the Protection of the Amur in Khabarovsk is such an NGO. However, despite their noble objectives and motivations, they lack the persistence and assertiveness characteristic of the first group. Often their activities are simply complaints in the press or emotional statements to limited audiences. These organizations need assistance from the local authorities and from the community. The third group includes organizations oriented to educational activities and advocacy of environmental protection and preservation, particularly among high school students and other young people. This is the most important trend, since it involves the education of a new generation of people and the future communities. The activities of these NGOs should be linked to work in youth and children's organizations including both the universities and the schools. But they also need the support of the authorities at all levels.

The fourth group of NGOs unites efforts of workers involved in production activities who try to promote the integration of "soft" or environmentally friendly technologies into existing production processes. Though the first three groups actually exist, the fourth group is still largely a dream that is urgently needed in reality. The solution of environmental problems should be considered within the framework of sustainable development of entire communities and the whole nation. Sustainable development implies the integration of social and environmental problems. Indeed, over the past ten years social conditions of the population, particularly indigenous populations, have become worse. It is difficult to convince people not to set fires in the taiga area or to stop poaching rare fish.

In a society there should be moral and psychological relationships between individuals and the environment. Unfortunately in Russia, during the period of economic reform-a period of wild capitalism-different approaches were in vogue aimed at generating material goods for individuals. Those shifty and energetic people who made a great deal of money felt indifferent to the needs of society and the environment. A substantial disparity in property status has made Russian society very unstable. Over the past decade, a young generation has grown up focused on solving their own financial problems with no glances at the surrounding world. To improve the situation the scientific community, first of all the Academy of Sciences and environmental NGOs, should be actively involved.

DYNAMICS OF RADIOACTIVE POLLUTION OF PRIMORYE TERRITORY AND THE NORTHERN SHELF OF THE SEA OF JAPAN

Investigations of the radioecological conditions in Primorye Territory and the Far-East region as a whole show that these conditions are closely connected to the radiation in the northern part of the Sea of Japan. Radiation contamination seems to be an acute problem in the Asia-Pacific region for three main reasons:

- o From almost the first years of the Soviet Union, this region has been completely closed to civilian organizations and individual researchers, inasmuch as intensive construction and development of military bases continued there for decades both before and after the Second World War.
- o The regional problem has caused public concern in the Russian Federation, Japan, Korea, the United States, and other states that have vital interests (fishery, aquaculture, recreation) that are potentially threatened by radioecological accidents and radioactive waste from Russia's Pacific Fleet.
- o The program of fleet reduction should have been completed in the region by 2000. During the last 10 years, 54 nuclear submarines have been taken out of commission, but only 10 were adequately salvaged with attention to wastes.

Governmental data and our own data were obtained and analyzed during long- term investigations of radiation conditions of the territories adjacent to submarine repair facilities and bases. Also, a study of radionuclide distribution in Peter the Great Bay was carried out. On the basis of these studies, we reached conclusions about the relatively insignificant contribution of anthropogenic sources of radionuclides to radiation background levels of our region as a whole. Such sources average less than one percent of the total.

Besides local pollution sources from the fleet, we also investigated global sources. A comparison of the effect of the last Chinese atmospheric nuclear test in 1980 with the consequences of the Chernobyl accident showed that the nuclear test effects were longer (more than one year) and had a higher level of total beta-activity of the lower atmosphere in Primorye Territory. However, total beta-activity levels of the two releases were comparable.

Concerning probable radioactive environmental pollution of the south of Primorye Territory (in the opinion of experts of the Fleet's chemical service), the coastal facilities along the bays of Bolshoi Kamen, Sysoyeva, and Chazhma are sources. These facilities deal with recharging nuclear reactors; replacement of filters; collection, temporary storage, and processing of radioactive waste; temporary storage of used nuclear assemblages; and repair and deactivation of contaminated equipment. Also potentially dangerous are the places where oil tankers with radioactive waste facilities were operating. The main components of radioactive waste are 137Cs, 90Sr, 60Co, and 144Ce. Until 1993, burial of liquid and solid radioactive waste had been carried out in deep-water regions of the northwestern part of the Sea of Japan, 200-300 kilometers from the coastline. The spontaneous chain reaction on a submarine in Bolshaya Chazhma in August 1985 has remained the most severe nuclear incident. It preceded the accident at Chernobyl and belongs to the following class of incidents:

- Uncontrolled reactor regime involving destruction of the active zone.
- Release of fission products into the environment-the atmosphere and the seawater in the bay.
- Wind transportation of aerosols of small dispersed particles through the industrial zone (the Navy ship repair works) and further, through the coastal part of the Dunai Peninsula with residential settlements. The difference between this nuclear incident and Chernobyl is that it took place with a reactor of a distinctly different design and with ten times less power. Its fuel assembly did not contain radioactive products accumulated during previous operation. Just before the accident, the reactor had been loaded with new fuel elements.

We have carried out the following studies as an independent expert examination of government activity in 1991-1994. We obtained the following data about the probable damage of the environment by the accident:

1. The amount of radioactivity, its radionuclide composition, and its explosion potential were developed.
2. Models of atmospheric transport and gradual redirection of radioactivity in Ussurisk Bay were developed.

3. Numerical estimates of turbulent transportation of radionuclides in water and their release into the atmosphere were carried out.
4. The dynamic processes of redeposition of high-level radioactive pollution in the upper layer of seafloor deposits directly in the zone of the accident were studied experimentally.
5. Estimates were made of future conditions of the bodies of water with attention to long-lived radionuclides. Investigations of Ussurisk Bay in 1990- 1992, using tritium tracers and numerical modeling, were evaluated.
6. Evaluations of doses received by the population of Dunai as a result of the accident in Chazhma Bay were carried out. The population received the heaviest radioactive doses during inhalation of iodine radioactive isotopes-131I, 132I, 133I, 134I, and 135I.
7. The coefficients of risk for the population of Dunai were evaluated. The population of Dunai is 20,000. Twenty-two additional deaths caused by all forms of cancer and the same number of non-lethal cancer cases were predicted in Dunai.

The inhabitants who were up to 150 meters distant from the explosion along the trace axis received significant doses of external gamma-irradiation and external beta-irradiation of the skin. The analysis of bottom samples from Chazhma Bay has shown that the distribution of radioactivity, which depends more than 95 percent on 60Co, is non- uniform over the area and along the vertical. A large part of activity in the epicenter zone is situated at a depth of 15-20 centimeters from the bottom. Some solid grains were extruded from the bottom samples with the help of magnetic separation of highly-active samples. These "hot" particles from the fuel assembly contribute 50 percent to the total radioactivity of the sample. The main processes influencing the space-time variations of radionuclides in bottom deposits in the region of the accident are radionuclide transport in water and radioactive decay. The flushing of radioactivity from the bay into Strelok Gulf reduces levels by about one percent annually. Radioactive decay of 60Co reduces levels each year by about 12 percent. This ratio is explained by the limited water dynamics, intensive sedimentation, concentration of most activity in larger "hot" particles with higher density, and low solubility of "hot" particles in seawater.

SOCIETY SHOULD BE PROTECTED FROM THE METAL THREAT

The Ecological Women's Assembly has been active since 1944, uniting within its membership women and youth of Russia and other former Soviet states. Among the many aspects of environmental protection of concern is the problem of chemical toxicants, including metals.

Listed in order of degree of human sensitivity to toxic metals, the metals are ranked as follows: Hg > Cu > Zn > Ni > Pb > Cd > Cr > Sn > Fe > Mn > Al. The sensitivity variations are not uniform.

Living organisms have special mechanisms of heavy metal detoxification. In response to the toxic action of Pb2+, Cd2+, and Hg2+, for example, the liver and kidneys increase the synthesis of low-molecular beta proteins, which contain cysteine in their structure. The high content of sulfhydryl groups in cysteine promotes the combination of metal ions into strong complexes, resulting in some level of detoxification.

But it is clear that we must protect ourselves from this "metal" threat. At one time the main anthropogenic sources of lead releases into the environment were lead-based paints, lead-containing pesticides (now forbidden), and lead in soils around some industrial enterprises. Now the main source of lead pollution is automobile fuel. Vehicle exhausts account for up to 80 percent of the total lead content in the atmosphere. Using ethylized gasoline with a high lead content results in widespread heavy metal pollution of the atmosphere. In cities overloaded by motor transport, lead concentration in the atmosphere exceeds background values by 20 to 30 times. Street dust sometimes contains up to 1,000 milligrams of lead per kilogram. Oxides and heavy metal salts are almost indestructible, and they gradually accumulate in the environment in areas where people live.

Entering the atmosphere from exhaust gases of automobiles and then accumulating in the top layers of the soil, lead enters the human body through the gastro-intestinal path, as well as by inhalation. Lead is delivered by the blood and accumulates in bones, the liver, the kidneys, and the brain. Lead irreversibly affects the nervous system, impedes functioning of the reproductive system, affects the kidneys, and causes mental and physical retardation in children. Especially dangerous is the effect of lead on children, who, when inhaling dust, receive approximately five times more lead for their body weight than adults.

Also, lead assimilates in children at a level several times higher than in adults. According to the World Bank, lead pollution of the air from motor transport has become one of the three main risk factors for health in Central and Eastern Europe. The UN Committee on Sustainable Development considers a general prohibition of ethylized gasoline a primary health protection task for the global population. The plan for complete cessation of leaded gasoline production was discussed at the Conference of the European Environmental Ministers in 1998 in Denmark. The parallel reduction of lead levels in human blood in the United States and the decreased use of leaded gasoline since the middle of the 1980s is clear. Also, it is interesting that in 1997, The Alliance to End Childhood Lead Poisoning (U.S.) issued a brochure entitled Myths and Realities of Phasing Out Lead Gasoline. The necessity and possibility of a complete change to unleaded gasoline are obvious.

When humans take in a combination of metals from the environment (during inhalation of polluted air, consumption of chemically contaminated food and water, and through the skin and mucous membranes), they are subjected to severe impacts of these toxicants. The combined effect of these toxicants is complicated because a living organism reacts to each toxicant differently: in some cases with adaptation (frequently temporary) and sometimes with sharp negative reactions. Frequently during medical examinations of people living in ecologically unfavorable regions, changes in the characteristics of blood are discovered. Also, the attributes of chemical intoxication are found (sometimes even exclusively) among children and older persons. Varying responses to the impact of chemical toxicants depending on sex differentiation have also been noted.

3

Positive and Negative Aspects of NGOs Activities

Environmentally sound decisions are reflected in legal actions adopted by state and local government bodies and constituent entities. Their execution has to do with individual sites and with the natural environment as a whole. The decisions must have an ecological basis and pass the environmental examination and public hearing process.

The following decisions on large-scale projects have been made by the Tomsk Oblast agencies taking into account public opinion:

- Stoppage of gravel extraction from the Tom River bed. (A public organization, the Committee for Conservation of the Tom)
- Ban on construction of a nutritional supplement biotechnology plant. (A public organization, the Ecological Initiative)
- Removal from service three of five reactors of the Siberian Chemical Complex. (A public organization, the Ecological Initiative)
- Ban on containers for storing fissile materials received from military units under the governmental decision on sharp reduction of nuclear warheads in Russia. (A public organization, the Ecological Initiative) The activity of NGOs made it possible to deepen public understanding of environmental problems and to exert pressure upon Tomsk Oblast agencies. One example is the public hearing held in September 2000 on the premises of the

Tomsk Oblast Administration. The public hearing or, to be more precise, a discussion on construction of the Seversk Nuclear Power Station (NHS-500), took place due to inquiries of public organizations and citizens under the federal law "On Using Atomic Energy" (Articles 11 and 14). Effective actions that had been carried out by public organizations of Tomsk, Moscow, and other towns forced the Tomsk Oblast government to conclude that the designers of the NHS-500 project must eliminate all shortcomings and violations of environmental legislation related to the project. The local authorities also decided that the NHS-500 project must be revised drastically in view of comments expressed at the public discussion.

The public discussion on construction of the Seversk Nuclear Power Station was the first large-scale public action in the region. All interested persons could take part. Those who were not able to make personal presentations could send their written proposals to the Tomsk Oblast government for consideration. Under the law, decisions of the government agencies must be officially published for the information of the general public, although this has not yet been done. A large number of Tomsk city and oblast public organizations and movements are involved in environmental problems. In 1999 there were more than ten public organizations working in the following areas:

- Free expression of opinion
- Participation in development of normative acts
- Referenda on problems of environmental protection
- Environmental examinations
- Construction projects and selection of sites
- Public environmental monitoring
- Ecological education

Let us briefly summarize achievements of the main local public organizations. The Tomsk Environmental Student Inspection (TESI) is a public organization created in October 1999. It has more than 200 members, primarily students of Tomsk. Much attention was given to TESI by the local mass media in 1999. Forty- seven articles were published in the regional newspapers; the town and regional radio stations broadcast 51 reports; and four local TV channels devoted 11 reports to its work. TESI is a major organizer of environmental demonstrations. The Tomsk Oblast Council of the All-Russian Nature Protection Society was founded in 1992. One of the main tasks of the Council is a TV program, "The Ecology Club," devoted to the environmental problems of Tomsk Oblast. A distinctive feature of TESI is its corps of inspectors.

Members have the status of non-staff inspectors of the State Committee for Protection of the Natural Environment. Under the law "On Non-Staff Environmental Inspection," TESI has the right to conduct inspections of different enterprises and plants and to make claims against inappropriate use of the natural environment. In 1999, TESI members carried out 165 inspections in the industrial zones of Tomsk and the oblast. In the course of inspections they prepared 81 claims, and they imposed 73 fines totaling 7,130 rubles.

In 1999, complex explorations of the Ob, the Tom, and the Ushaika rivers were conducted under the TESI environmental program "Clean Rivers." The Environmental Legal Center is a public organization founded in 1996 with the objectives of protecting citizens' rights to a safe environment and monitoring environmental legislation.

Its members are intellectuals, students of the Tomsk colleges, and farmers. The Center keeps in touch with prominent scientists. The Center deals with bans on environmentally hazardous activity and compensation for damage caused by abusing the right to a safe environment. The Center supports appeals against actions (or inactions) of state bodies violating citizens' non-property rights.

Recently the Supreme Court Judiciary Board overturned the Tomsk local court decision on a license for disposal of liquid radioactive wastes in the ground water areas of Seversk. The license was issued by the local administration to the Siberian Chemical Complex in 1996. The Environmental Initiative movement (EI) was founded in 1989 with the primary goal of providing a public focus for anti-nuclear activity. The main achievements are the following:

- o A 1989 ban on construction of a nutrition supplement biotechnology plant.
- o Support of the Krapivinsky water reservoir construction (1989-90).
- o Obtaining about 100,000 signatures to ban storage containers for fissile materials received from military units.

EI's primary goal is to counteract the plans of the Ministry of Atomic Energy to start construction of a nuclear-powered heating plant (AST-500) attached to the Siberian Chemical Complex. The goal is to be achieved by dissemination of reliable information about the hazardous impact of the complex on the environment and on the health of the population. EI also tries to expose "the nuclear myths" about the illusory low-price, ecological safety, and harmlessness of nuclear energy. A Tomsk Oblast public organization, the Wind Rose, was founded in 1992 with the purpose of attracting local attention to environmental problems, to ecologically safe commercial activity, and to ecological education. It has 10 members.

The organization has developed the following actions and publications: a training program of continuous ecological education for schoolchildren, a textbook, Education in Nature Protection: Elementary Course, and a textbook on ecology, Changing the World. It set up an ecological club, The Road to the Twenty-First Century, for pupils and students. It held an Internet conference, Environmental Security, and published materials of the conference.

A roundtable, The Tomsk Oblast's Pupils' and Students' Participation in Solving Regional Environment Problems, was held in November 1999. Teachers, lecturers, and local public organization representatives were among the participants. The subject was methods for informal ecological education such as tourism, clubs of ecologists, teenage environmental projects, Internet and e-mail, and cooperation with the mass media.

An ecological and ethnographical excursion called Elan was organized in September 1999. Twenty-four pupils and three teachers took part. A textbook on ecological-ethnographical excursions and games was developed. An information bulletin

EKObanderol [ECO Mailbag] is being published. If necessary it can include urgent information, such as developments in Yugoslavia (NATO strikes and the environmental consequences). A youth organization, Siberian House, was created in 1974 on the base of the Explorer tourist brigade. The team includes 20 youngsters and five tutors. The main activities are regional ethnography studies, summer camps, and sporting contests. One goal is exploration of rare sites of nature with visits to 19 sites. To clarify the formal status and legal base of the sites, appropriate documentation has been submitted to the Oblast Administration.

The Nature House is a children's ecological and tourist organization and has created reasonable attitudes to nature protection. The Aliom Club is an environmental educational society created to popularize ecologically safe technologies. Scientists, managers, engineers, and technologists are among its members.

The Tomsk Oblast Scout Center is an organization related to tourism and ecological education. Its activity stretches over seven regions. The number of scouts is about 500. In Chainsk district a school scout team cooperates with the local forest management authorities in the village of Podgornoye.

The tourist club Odyssey is a public organization created to organize tourism and ecological education. The Strezhevoi Ecological-Biological Center (the township of Strezhevoi) is a public organization dealing with ecological education and fostering. Summing up, the above public organizations are of great benefit to the community as well as to the region as a whole. In conclusion, let us make some recommendations on increasing the role of nongovernmental organizations in the environmental decision-making process. Is it difficult for state bodies to coordinate the activity of the public environmental organizations? Among the different laws currently in force, there are inconsistencies in regulations relating to public participation in managing state affairs. However, public environmental organizations must be able to make their own contributions. Adoption of appropriate normative acts is the only way out of the situation. It is these acts that provide for comprehensive and adequate public participation in environmentally sound decision-making. Also, it is necessary to carry out training courses on management and sustainable development for nongovernmental organizations. Problems of preventing environmental harm and compensation are of extreme concern for the population.

However, the solution is being implemented by "residual financing." Financial sources and the measures to prevent and compensate environmental harm should be determined by law. Nowadays it may be worthwhile to combine all financial payments to the local budget for utilization of natural resources in a joint natural resources restoration fund. The fund could allow for local government bodies to focus financial means on strategic directions. Payments for utilization of subsurface resources could form the principal part of the fund. Use of the funds for improvement and restoration of water resources, biological resources, and wild nature sites.

INTERACTION OF NONGOVERNMENTAL ORGANIZATIONS AND REGIONAL AUTHORITIES IN SOLVING PROBLEMS OF THE LAKE BAIKAL REGION

The UN Conference on Environment and Development (Rio de Janeiro, 1992) has proclaimed the concept of sustainable development as a basis for a new paradigm of future development of our civilization and has adopted a program of actions when entering the twenty-first century (The Agenda for the Twenty-First Century). Principle 4 of the adopted Declaration states: "In order to achieve sustainable development, environmental protection shall constitute an integral part of the development process and cannot be considered in isolation from it." The Lake Baikal region is an example of a territory that has not only national, but also international importance. It has an eternal value not only for Russians, but also for the whole of mankind. Lake Baikal is the most ancient lake on the planet. Its age is about 25-30 million years. It is the deepest lake, with a depth of 1,637 meters. It contains a tremendous volume of water-23,000 cubic kilometers or 23 percent of the world's resources of pure fresh water. It is also one of the largest in areal expanse.

According to present-day data, the genetic diversity of Baikal includes 2,565 species and subspecies of aquatic fauna and 1,000 species and subspecies of aquatic plants, of which two-thirds are endemic, meaning they are found nowhere else. To this number one should add many hundreds of species of water and bottom micro- organisms as well as viruses and microbes that have been little investigated. Thus, the diversity of Baikal has no equal in the world, and Lake Baikal is included in the UNESCO World Nature Heritage List of 1996.

What is the Baikal region? This is a region directly connected with the internationally known Lake Baikal and located in the center of Asia on the territory of two states, Russia and Mongolia. The territory of the Baikal region stretches from south to north for 1300 km, and from west to east for 1,000 km. Its total area is 800,000 sq. km. The unique combination of various landscapes in the center of Asia-from mountain-tundra and mountain-taiga to steppe and semi-desert along with the largest and most ancient freshwater reservoir-is of special significance and value in the biosphere structure of the planet as a whole. The Baikal watershed occupies territory in the southeast of Siberia and the northern part of Mongolia.

The largest part is located in Russia, where it has been divided without taking into account the lake's area over several administrative and territorial entities of the Russian Federation: Republic of Buryatia-73 percent, Chita Oblast-21 percent, Irkutsk Oblast-6 percent. The Baikal ecosystem has become better known just as its protection and rational use have become more complicated. New territories located outside the bounds of the lake's watershed have been included in the Baikal region, including that part of Irkutsk Oblast that adjoins the northwest boundary of the Baikal watershed. It is up to 200 km. wide and regarded as a zone from which atmospheric emissions of industrial installations may reach the watershed.

At present in accordance with the Law of the Russian Federation "On Protection of Lake Baikal," the Baikal region is divided into three zones:

- Central ecological zone ("the core")-territory that includes Lake Baikal and islands, a water protection zone adjacent to Lake Baikal, and protected natural territories adjacent to Lake Baikal;

- o Buffer ecological zone-territory outside the central ecological zone that includes the watershed of Lake Baikal within the bounds of the Russian Federation;
- o Ecological zone of atmospheric effect-territory outside the watershed of Lake Baikal within the bounds of the Russian Federation up to 200 km. wide to the north and northwest of the watershed where there are economic units with activity that has a negative influence on Lake Baikal. Such a division of the Baikal region is an important condition for preservation of Baikal as a part of the World Nature Heritage. At the same time, the Baikal region is characterized by considerable development of industry and agriculture, which cannot avoid affecting the condition of the lake. Therefore, the question of a balanced solution of ecological and socio-economic problems is especially acute here.

The following ecological problems of the Baikal region are priority issues:

- o The natural conditions of the geosystem components
- o Preservation of a large amount of biological diversity
- o Consequences of industrial and agricultural development
- o Use of reliable ecological information

The natural conditions of the Baikal region require accurate methods of investigations for measuring the parameters of water and ground ecosystems and the air basin. For the most part the region is still not polluted. While solving the questions of environmental protection in the Baikal region, particular attention must be paid to preservation of biological diversity which means, according to the Convention on Biological Diversity, variability of living organisms from all sources including soil, sea, and other water ecosystems as well as ecological complexes including these components. For addressing the questions of preservation of the Baikal region, the normative-legal basis includes both international documents and the laws of the Russian Federation:

- o Convention on Biological Diversity, Rio de Janeiro, 1992.

- o Convention on Protection of the World Cultural and Natural Heritage, 1972.
- o All-European Strategy of Preservation of Biological and Landscape Biodiversity, Sofia, 1995.
- o Convention on Assessment of Environmental Effects in a Transboundary Context, 1991.
- o Federal law "On Natural Environment Preservation," 1991.
- o Federal law "On Ecological Examination," 1995.
- o Federal law "On Especially Protected Territories," 1990.
- o Federal law "On Protection of Lake Baikal," 1999.
- o Water Code of the Russian Federation.
- o Forest Code of the Russian Federation.
- o "On State Strategy of the Russian Federation Regarding Environmental

Protection and Ensuring Sustainable Development," the Edict of the President of the Russian Federation of February 4, 1994, # 236.

- o "Conception of Transition of the Russian Federation to Sustainable Development," the Edict of the President of the Russian Federation of April 1, 1996, #440.
- o "National Plan of Action for Environmental Protection of the Russian Federation in 1999-2001." Approved at the meeting of the Government of the Russian Federation on November 12, 1998.
- o "Strategy of Sustainable Development of the Russian Federation." Approved at the meeting of the Government of the Russian Federation in December 1997.

Thus, in the Russian Federation there are a number of strategic planning documents in the field of environmental protection and Sustainable development that have not yet been put in a strict hierarchical order due to the fact that the legislation in this field is relatively new. However these documents can already be used as a legislative basis.

In the Baikal region a number of attempts have been made by state structures and public organizations to implement programs aimed at preservation. The state documents on Baikal preservation are as follows: o Resolution of the Central Committee of the Communist Party of the Soviet Union and the USSR Council of Ministers of April 13, 1987, # 434, "On Arrangements to Ensure Protection and Rational Use of Natural Resources of the Lake Baikal Basin in 1987-1995."

- o "Territorial Integrated Scheme of Protection of Nature in the Lake Baikal Basin," approved on April 14, 1990, by the Resolution of the Presidium of the Russian Federation Council of Ministers.
- o "Integrated Federal Program of Ensuring Lake Baikal Preservation and Rational Use of Natural Resources of Its Basin," 1994.

The role of nongovernmental public organizations in implementing the above decisions is difficult to overestimate. The destiny of "the sacred sea," as people living on the banks of Baikal call the lake, has worried both children and old people. This is evident from signatures for preservation of the unique Baikal, demonstrations, appearances on television, and unauthorized signs reading "Let us preserve Baikal" on the chimneys of the Baikal Pulp and Paper Plant. The most active supporters of environmental protection in the Baikal region are the following public organizations:

- o Baikal Ecological Wave, which has organized regular publication of the ecological magazine Wave.
- o Baikal Ecological Parliament, with prominent scientists from Irkutsk as its members.
- o Revival of the Land of Siberia.
- o Greenpeace.

The above public organizations are in continuous contact with local government institutions. They participate in all ecological decisions without exception. In particular, they put forward the idea of instituting Baikal Day, which since 1999 has been routinely conducted at the end of August-beginning of September in the form of various actions for the protection of the lake, thereby joining the efforts of local governing institutions and various ecological movements.

In March 1998, the Limnological Institute in Irkutsk and the Baikal Institute of Nature Management in Ulan-Ude, with the support of ecological organizations of Irkutsk Oblast and the Republic of Buryatia, started implementation of a TACIS project "Assistance in Gaining Ecological Information and Its Dissemination among the Population of the Baikal Region." The financial support was provided by the European Union and the technical support by the Society of Technical Assistance (Germany). The aim of the project is to distribute information among the population and organizations responsible for decision-making in the field of environmental protection. As a result of the joint work conducted by a large number of state and public ecological organization as well as institutions of basic and additional education, the Baikal Ecological Information Network has been established. Its participants are located in 12 towns of Irkutsk Oblast alone.

The inhabitants of the Baikal region realize that they are responsible to the whole of mankind and future generations for preservation of the world pearl, Lake Baikal. The ecological conditions in our region are very tense and complicated. Thus, realizing their personal responsibility, more and more people are standing up for environmental protection. People also realize that nothing will change if the way of thinking remains unchanged. But it can be changed only if there is reliable information. Ecological workers understand the importance and necessity of ecological education; but very often they have no possibility to obtain the information they need, even though such information is available at research institutes situated in the Baikal region. In Irkutsk alone there are nine institutes of the Russian Academy of Sciences conducting research on nature management. The organizers and those implementing the above mentioned project have identified the following problems:

- To collect and process ecological information and make it accessible to all those who need it.
- To establish a standing network of ecological organizations of Irkutsk Oblast and the Republic of Buryatia, including consumers and distributors of this information.

The project participants have defined the concept of providing the population of the Baikal region with information as a strategy of collecting, processing, and presenting data about natural resources of the territory based on the principles of integration and legal responsibility, using up-to-date information technologies to make well-grounded decisions regarding nature management in the region. Now the important tasks for teachers, ecologists, and progressive groups of the population are not only the ecological orientation of the public and providing the population with information, but also the task of promoting civic positions and stimulating social activities for democratization of ecological knowledge. The implementation of this large-scale TACIS project has resulted in:

- o Establishing the Baikal Ecological Information Network.
- o Obtaining a large number of computers.
- o Establishing contacts with ecological organizations from other countries and regions (ISAR, Social Information Agency, the American organization Sacred Earth Network, and others).
- o Participating in preparation of the state report "On the Status of Environmental Conditions of Irkutsk Oblast," which says, "In arranging ecological education of the population there must be coordinated efforts of the government organs; environmental, educational, scientific, and public organizations; and the mass media."

The importance of continuous ecological education is clear to all the participants in the Baikal Ecological Information Network. Most of them have been closely cooperating with each other and with other organizations in this important task. Another example of cooperation between local autonomous bodies and public organizations is the Russian-Canadian project on cooperation in decision-making in the field of environmental protection and, in particular, the Irkutsk component, "Water Resources Management in the Angara River Basin." During the 1998-2000 period, the project organizers combined the efforts of state authorities and public organizations of Irkutsk Oblast in arriving at a "consensus" in decision-making in the field of environmental protection. Some of the project participants are:

- State Committee on Environmental Protection
- Committee on Natural Resources
- Department of Nature Management, Irkutsk Oblast Administration
- Angara-Baikal Basin Water Department
- Irkutsk Territory Department of Hydrology, Meteorology, and Environmental Monitoring
- Irkutsk Hydro-Electric Station Administration
- Irkutskenergo Joint-Stock Company
- Baikal-Angara Department of Waterways and Navigation
- Committee on Nature Management Legislation and Ecology of the Irkutsk Oblast Legislative Assembly
- Limnological Institute, Russian Academy of Sciences (RAS)
- Institute of Geography, RAS
- Energy Systems Institute, RAS
- Institute of Geochemistry, RAS
- Institute of the Earth's Crust, RAS
- Institute of Plant Physiology and Biochemistry, RAS
- Institute of Biological Research at Irkustk State University
- Irkutsk Refrigeration Industrial Complex (state-owned enterprise)
- Irkutsk Housing Design and Construction Administration
- Science in Siberia (publication)
- Academy of Water Industry
- Children's Ecological Organization of the city of Angarsk
- Baikal Ecological Education (public organization)
- Regional Ecological Forecasting (research and production firm)
- Baikal Ecological Wave (public organization)

- o Civic Informational Initiative (public organization)
- o Irkutsk Branch of the All-Russian Nature Protection Society
- o Mayor of the Usolye Administrative Region
- o Mayor of the town of Shelekhov.

In spite of the fact that the programs and governmental decisions regarding the Baikal region were only partially realized, progress has been made:

- o The Selenga Pulp and Paperboard Plant has converted to a closed-loop water consumption system.
- o Wood drift floating along Baikal's tributaries has been stopped.
- o Collection of waste water from boats in Lake Baikal has been put into practice.
- o Pollutant emissions to the atmosphere from the Baikal Pulp and Paper Plant have been reduced.
- o Hazardous substance discharges into Lake Baikal have been reduced.
- o Lake Baikal was put on the World Nature Heritage List by UNESCO.
- o The Law of the Russian Federation "On Lake Baikal Protection" was passed.
- o The Baikal state information system has been established.
- o Norms for permissible pollutant impact on the Baikal ecological system have been worked out, and a new ecological approach is under preparation.
- o Integrated ecological monitoring of the Baikal ecosystem is being conducted.
- o A new way of obtaining drinking water from the depths of Lake Bakial has been developed and patented, and production of bottled water has been organized as an alternative type of profitable production. At the same time, experience makes it possible to identify the reasons why environmental programs being realized by local government bodies in cooperation with public

organizations and population are not completely effective.

They include:

- o Lack of a coordinated system of objectives and tasks being realized under various projects and programs.
- o Lack of an ecological basis in some programs.
- o Lack of economic, financial, and legal mechanisms due to budget constraints.
- o Methodological miscalculations, in particular, not taking into account the integrated ecological approach.
- o Unreasonable "centralization" and lack of orientation towards priorities of the concerned parties and users of the results of activities under the programs.

With regard to resource potential, this region has all the necessary qualities to be chosen as a "model" when elaborating the concept of sustainable development from the position of the Agenda for the Twenty-First Century. A rather well- preserved environment of the region, a huge resource potential, and a unique natural object-Lake Baikal with the surrounding landscapes-form a natural basis for the sustainable development process. On the other hand, the ecological fragility of the natural landscape system of the region, especially the ecosystem of Lake Baikal, will determine the high requirements for social and economic development processes, including the ethics and aesthetics of nature management oriented toward the future. Lake Baikal and the whole Baikal region should become an area for international cooperation of intellectual, financial, material, and human efforts aimed at solving the integrated problems of the survival of mankind and the preservation of the biosphere.

LIMNOLOGICAL INSTITUTE, SIBERIAN BRANCH, RUSSIAN ACADEMY OF SCIENCES

1. The Baikal International Center for Ecological Research has been created. It allows increased scientific investigations of different integrated problems.

2. Ecological passports for different enterprises and institutions functioning in the Baikal region have been developed.
3. Norms of the allowed pollutant impact on the Lake Baikal ecosystem have been developed.
4. A draft of the Law on Lake Baikal has been worked out and submitted to the State Council.
5. The technical conditions for Baikal bottled drinking water have been developed, and a patent for its production has been obtained.
6. A draft of the Federal Target Program of the Baikal Pulp and Paper Plant that solves social problems of the town of Baikalsk has been developed.
7. Microbiological and hydrobiological monitoring of the Lake Baikal ecosystem and its main tributaries is being conducted.
8. Integrated research of biodiversity in the Lake Baikal ecosystem and in the water bodies of its basin has been considerably expanded.

PUBLIC PARTICIPATION IN ENVIRONMENTALLY SOUND DECISION-MAKING: LEGAL ASPECTS CONSTITUTIONAL AND LEGAL GUARANTEES

While speaking about guaranteeing the rights of citizens to participate in environmentally sound decision-making, one normally refers to Article 32 of the Constitution of the Russian Federation as the basic document. The article states, "Citizens of the Russian Federation have the right to participate in managing state affairs both directly and through their representatives." Moreover, Article 33 of the Constitution ensures the right of citizens "to appeal in person and make individual and collective appeals to state bodies and bodies of local government." Appropriate federal legislation has not been developed. It is uncertain whether it will ever be adopted, but existing legal provisions are insufficient.

Yet, the priority of human and civil rights as well as numerous guarantees of exercising these rights has already been guaranteed in the Russian Constitution and in some laws currently in force. To be sure, we should abandon a narrow academic approach to civil rights and start protecting them in practice. The Institute of Environmental Law, hereinafter called Ecojuris, is a professional human rights organization. Ecojuris was the first in our country to start protecting environmental rights of citizens and nongovernmental organizations in practice, including the right to participate in the decision-making process. It seeks to accomplish this role on the basis of the following basic principles:

1. The Constitution of the Russian Federation shall be used directly. Part 1 of Article 15 of the Constitution states that the Constitution "shall have supreme legal force and direct effect and shall be applicable on the entire territory of the Russian Federation."
2. Gaps, contradictions, and common and controversial points in the laws shall be interpreted in favor of the citizens. The heart of this principle is Article 2 and Article 18 of the Constitution. The first one proclaims: "Man and his rights and freedom shall be the supreme value." The second one says: "Human and civil rights and freedoms shall have direct force. They shall determine the meaning, content, and implementation of laws, they shall determine the functioning of legislative and executive authority and of local government, and they shall be guaranteed by law."
3. Environmental rights (like any other human and civil rights) shall be fundamental and of high priority. State and local government bodies shall only be able to establish procedural norms for their execution and protection. This principle is based on the following articles of the Constitution:
   - Part 1 of Article 3: "The bearer of sovereignty and the sole source of power in the Russian Federation shall be its people of many nationalities."
   - Part 2 of Article 17: "Basic human rights and freedoms shall be inalienable and shall be enjoyed by everyone from birth."
   - The above cited Article 18.

4. The following principle is based on the very same articles of the Constitution: Opinions of the citizens on any activity to be carried out or on any object to be located on the territory where they live shall prevail and shall be disputed only in accordance with legal procedures.
5. The right to participate in decision-making shall be a part of the human right to a favorable environment, that, in turn, shall be an inalienable element of the right to life. This principle emerges from the following complex of articles of the Constitution and other laws:
   - Article 42: "Everyone shall have the right to a favorable environment..."
   - Part 1 of Article 20: "Everyone shall have the right to life."
   - Part 1 of Article 9: "Land and other natural resources shall be utilized and protected in the Russian Federation as the basis of life and activity of the people living on the concerned territory."
   - Article 92 of the Law "On Protection of the Natural Environment":
   - " Everyone shall have the right to life in the most favorable environmental conditions."
   - Articles 12 and 13 of the above law, guaranteeing environmental rights of the public.
6. Information necessary for the exercise of citizens' environmental rights, including the right to participate in decision-making, shall be of public interest. Classifying this information as limited access information (that is, state secrets or confidential information) shall be prohibited (Article 10 of the Federal Law "On Information and Protection of Information," based on Part 4 of Article 29 and Article 42 of the Constitution).
7. Environmental rights of citizens and nongovernmental organizations shall be ensured and protected by the whole body of laws currently in force-civil, civil-procedural, investment, information, nuclear, environmental, natural resources, and so on. We are

successfully using these principles to protect the environmental rights of citizens and nongovernment organizations as well as to protect rights in related fields, such as the right to information, to participation in managing state affairs, and to legal protection.

Ecojuris, in close cooperation with an organization it created, the Network of Russian Public Interest Environmental Lawyers, protects public interests, using the possibilities provided by the environmental legislation. These laws are rather progressive and, to some extent, pioneering in our country. Environmental lawyers- practitioners have made a substantial breakthrough in human and civil rights protection, adding environmental legislation with creative approaches to civil and civil-procedural law.

In addition to the above general principles, when protecting environmental rights we use more specific fundamental approaches and provisions of Russian legislation:

1. At the stage of obtaining preliminary agreement on location of a facility, bodies of local government shall be obliged to clarify the opinion of the population by means of local referenda and citizen meetings. Citizens, public associations, and bodies of local government shall have the right to participate in considering issues pertaining to exemptions and allotments of land plots of interest to the population (Article 28 of the Russian Federation Land Code).
2. A scheduled economic or other activity that could be environmentally dangerous in the future shall be subject to mandatory state environmental examination (Article 3 of the Federal Law "On Environmental Examination").
3. As to an activity (regardless of the territory where it is carried out) that causes harm to the health or property of citizens, their households, or the environment, citizens or organizations may turn to the courts to stop environmentally harmful activity (Article 91 of the Law "On Protection of the Natural Environment").
4. The danger of causing harm in the future may be grounds for filing a lawsuit to prohibit an activity creating such

danger (Article 1065 of the Civil Code of the Russian Federation).

5. Interests of citizens, nongovernmental organizations, and other persons may be represented in a court as well as in extra-juridical examinations of disputes by lawyers and other persons acting with a power of attorney in the traditional way (Chapter 5 of the Civil Procedural Code and Article 185 of the Russian Federation Civil Code). Besides, their interests may be represented in the above mentioned bodies on the basis of Chapter 50 of the Civil Code, "Actions without authority in the interest of another person." Conditions of actions in the interest of another person are determined by Part 1 of Article 980 of the Civil Code: "Actions without agency, other instructions, or the prior consent of the interested person for the purpose of preventing harm to his person...or in his lawful interests shall be carried out based on their benefit or usefulness..." Part 1 of Article 981 establishes an obligation to notify the interested person of action in his interest:

   "A person acting in the interest of another person is obligated at the first opportunity to inform the interested person of such action and wait for a reasonable period of time for his ratification or non-ratification of the action undertaken..."

6. Inasmuch as nature and its resources shall be the national property of the people of Russia as the natural basis of their social and economic development and well-being (Preamble of the Law "On Protection of the Natural Environment"), Article 980 of the Civil Code provides for the possibility of protecting interests not only of living people, but also of future generations. This innovative approach is being successfully used by Ecojuris. It has found support among the representatives of the Office of the Prosecutor General and has not met opposition among judges of the Supreme Court of the Russian Federation.

   The Civil Code does not establish definite forms of ratification of the actions undertaken in the interest of another person. So we have developed an application form (Table 1) for a person to implement the requirements of Article 981. This form can be used in case of representation of the interests of private citizens or groups of citizens. (Legal persons and nongovernmental organizations, in particular, fill out a similar application form, except the column on descendants.)

7. The right to participate in environmental decision-making along with other environmental rights pertains to personal non-property rights, that is to non- material values (Article 150 of the Civil Code). Therefore, in accordance with Article 208 of the above Code, legal limitations shall not be placed on the requirements of protecting these rights.
8. In 2000, a possibility of actions in the lawful interest of another person was secured in the procedural legislation, namely in new wording of Article 42 of the Civil Code.

Thus, in summary, rather vast legislation is currently in force in our country to be used in protecting public rights to participate in environmentally sound decision- making. Of course, one would like to have good special legislation concerning regulations under review. However, due to the poor quality of many new laws (issued by the "fluent pen" of the State Duma), serious anxiety exists that public rights would not be secured and extended but substantially limited.

A relatively fresh example from the environmental sphere can be presented. The new Federal Law "On Sanitary and Epidemiological Well-being" was adopted in 1999, replacing the previous one with the same title (1991). (The Code of Laws of the Russian Federation, No. 14, 1999, Art. 1650). The latter had been adopted at the height of perestroika and became the first Russian normative act to secure the citizen's right to a favorable environment as well as the right to participate in decision-making.

Part 4 of Article 5 of the law stipulated that citizens "shall have the right to participate both directly or through their representative or public associations in developing, discussing, and making decisions by state government and On Approval of Actions Undertaken by Ecojuris In accordance with the procedure established by Articles 980 and 981 of the Civil Code on protecting the lawful interest of another person (in case of appeal against the Government relating to transfer of the first group of forest lands into non- forest group lands for managing forests and using the forest fund, adopted in 1994- 1998). The public waited for the State Duma to update the wording of this provision and advance it in the spirit of the times. Instead, the provision was excluded in full from the law, and as a result the public received the toothless pre-perestroika right "to submit proposals."

It should be noted that for the last two or three years, attempts have been made by some groups of deputies and officials to submit new wording of the Federal Law "On Environmental Examination" to the State Duma for consideration, which has limited human and civil rights.

My long-standing human rights activity is evidence that our country has unfortunately remained a state not governed by laws. "Under-regulation" of some relations and incoherence of some legal norms sometimes are better from the human rights standpoint than excessive "over-regulation" undertaken by incompetent and dishonest lawmakers.

In spite of the absence of general unified mechanisms of participation in making decisions that can affect the environment and natural resources, citizens, nongovernmental organizations, and other strata of our society have "compensatory mechanisms" for such participation. This is public participation in evaluating the effect on the environment (EEE) in the environmental examination.

An EEE is a stage of environmentally sound decision-making to be carried out before the environmental examination. A new regulation on evaluation of the effect of economic and other activity on the environment was adopted in 2000 with direct participation of the author of this article (approved by the order of the State Committee on the Environment on May 16, 2000, No. 372, registered in the Ministry of Justice on July 4, 2000, No. 2302). A pioneering attempt was made in this document to regulate more carefully the procedure of public participation in decision-making. The document considers public participation to be not only the basic principle of EEE, but also an "inalienable part" of this procedure. Notification and participation of the public as well as due consideration of its opinion shall be binding at all stages of EEE, beginning with preparation of the EEE technical design (paragraphs 2.5, 4.1, and others).

In decision-making, public preferences must be revealed and taken into account. This shall be one of the results of EEE (paragraph 1.6). Part IV of the regulation is fully devoted to notification and participation of the public in the EEE procedure. It fixes the terms and order of notification, information content, and rules of collection and analysis of comments and proposals. Preliminary consultations, public discussions, and submissions of written comments shall be the main forms of citizen participation.

All these procedures are regulated in the document. For example, paragraph 4.9 stipulates that public hearings are to be arranged by local governments. All decisions related to public participation shall be documented.

The advocate of an action shall arrange public hearings on a planned activity and keep the record. The main issues of discussion as well as disputes between the public and the advocate (if any) shall be clearly fixed in the record. The record shall be signed by representatives of local government, citizens, public organizations (associations), and the advocate. The record of public hearings shall be included in the final set of documents on evaluating planned economic activity and the effect on the environment.

The new regulation, unlike the previous ones clearly stipulates the obligation to take into account information on comments and proposals of the public. A supplement of the regulation contains a list of documents to be included in the final set of EEE materials to prove the actual participation of the public in the decision- making process. All these materials shall be submitted for environmental examination (paragraphs 12.1-12.7). The following information shall be included in the materials of public hearings:

- o Means of notification of the public on the place, time, and form of the public discussion.
- o A list of public discussion participants, including names, and the names of organizations (if any), with their addresses and telephone numbers.
- o A list of issues under consideration and abstracts of presentations, and records of public hearings (if any).
- o All comments and proposals raised in the course of the public discussions, names of their authors, and materials of possible disputes between the public, local government, and advocate.
- o Conclusions of the public discussion on the environmental aspects of a planned activity.
- o A summary of public comments and proposals with the indication of those which have been or have not been taken into consideration and grounds for refusal.
- o A mailing list of appropriate information to be sent out to the public at all stages of EEE.

The principle of public participation in the environmental examination has been secured in Article 3 of the Federal Law "On the Environmental Examination" mentioned above. According to this article, any project can be a subject of state environmental examination beginning with drafts and ending with documentation justifying the license, agreement on division of production, and so on, depending on the nature and importance of a project (Articles 11 and 12 of the above law). The state environmental examination is an obligatory measure to protect the natural environment. It should prevent economic decisions which can cause harm to the natural environment. A positive conclusion of the state environmental examination is necessary to finance and implement any project and programm (Parts 1 and 2 of Article 36 of the Russian Federation Law "On Protection of the Natural Environment"). The legal consequences of a negative result of the examination shall be a prohibition on implementing the project (Part 5 of Article 18 of the Law "On the State Environment Examination").

The right of public associations to carry out a public environmental examination of the same project before or at the time of the state environment examination is provided by Chapter 4 of the above law. Public examination findings shall reflect public opinion and shall be obligatory for consideration during the State decision on realization of the project. Of great importance for public rights is Article 14 of the Law "On the Environmental Examination" providing an obligatory submission of (1) EEE results and (2) results of citizen and public organization discussions organized by local government concerning the subject of the state environmental examination. In this case, the law considers the power of local government to organize public discussions, polls, and referenda among the population on economic activity as a power in the sphere of the environmental examination (Part 2 of Article 9). Thus, the above analysis of the federal law "On the Environmental Examination" and EEE Regulations clearly demonstrates (analysis of law and regulations) that a duplication, or "overdose," of public discussions takes place in these documents. But given the great number of human rights violations in our country, this is not bad. To exercise one's constitutional right to participate in managing state affairs (Part 1 of Article 32 of the Constitution), one must participate in decision-making at all stages of the process. If it doesn't work at one stage, it may at another.

Consequently, Russian land and environmental legislation gives the public some possibilities to express views in favor of or against placing a facility or carrying out an activity on territory of their residence as follows:

- o By means of a local referendum or meeting to be held by local government at a stage of preliminary planning.
- o By means of public hearings/discussions at the EEE stage organized by joint actions of local government and an investor on a federal, regional or local level according to the importance of the project.
- o By means of a public discussion, as an integral part of the environmental examination, organized by local government. Thus, in accordance with the Constitution's provisions, public opinion shall be decisive. State decisions that are inconsistent with residents' opinions or impede expressions of such opinions are violations of

a number of constitutional rights that can be appealed to interstate bodies for the protection of human rights and freedoms, if all available internal means of legal protection have been exhausted (Article 46 of the Constitution).

EXPERIENCE IN DEFENDING THE ENVIRONMENTAL INTERESTS OF SOCIETY

Ecojuris is a nongovernmental organization seeking to execute public interest environmental law. The term "public interest environmental law" had not even existed in our country when we started our activity although some decades ago this term became popular in the United States, Canada, and other countries. Nevertheless, we succeeded in opening and introducing this direction in Russia. We began our work at the end of 1989 on the base of the Academy of Sciences' Institute of State and Law. At that time, illegal construction of the North Thermal Power Station was underway in Moscow, organized without appropriate environmental examination. Later a similar problem arose in Southern Butovo (a district of Moscow). Having realized that it was impossible to continue our work without pooling efforts of many people, we set up Ecojuris; and in 1991 it was registered as a nongovernmental organization. Since that time it has re-registered more than once because of changes in legislation and in membership.

As of now the name of our public organization is "The Institute of Environmental Law-Ecojuris." Our experts carry out consultative-judicial practice as well as research, legal drafting, education, seminars, and training not only in Moscow, but also in the regions. We hold training courses for environmental lawyers. We are currently carrying out a lawyers' training program on protecting national minorities' rights for traditional uses of natural resources. For the first few years, Ecojuris had been the only nongovernmental organization in the USSR and Russia to protect public environmental interests and civil environmental rights. But now, about ten such organizations exist in our country. Most have been created with our direct involvement. Lawyers work for environmental organizations, such as Karelia's Association of the Greens and

Kamchatka's League of Independent Experts. In 1994, it occurred to us that we should informally pool our efforts. Since that time we have been holding annual conferences of our organizations. To exchange experience and information, the informal Network of Russian Public Interest Environmental Lawyers was set up in 1997. It currently has more than forty members.

In 2000, representatives from five countries of the former Soviet Union took part in our Seventh Annual Public Interest Environmental Law Conference for the first time. In addition to the Russian network, we have established the Eurasian Public Interest Environmental Law Network to protect public environmental interests. Our colleagues from Azerbaijan, Moldova, Ukraine, Kazakhstan, Kyrgyzstan, and Uzbekistan have joined us. In each of these countries, there are one or two persons engaged in consulting, pleading cases, and other legal activities. Human rights lawyers from Belarus, Georgia, and Armenia have also expressed their wish to join the Network. Most of these countries have similar legislation and problems: the oil mafia, the fishing mafia, the timber mafia, and corruption, particularly among the highest and middle rank officials responsible for granting licenses and permissions to carry out different projects and use different kinds of resources.

Conduct of rank-and-file officials is not immaculate, yet they have a long way to go to reach the standards set by "the highest echelons." During all these years, we have been involved with law on behalf of the public. In the early 1990s, courts did not take environmental cases for examination at all. Judges did not know the environmental legislation. We brought them copies of appropriate normative acts. In such a manner, they learned about this information for the first time. To ensure that an original jurisdiction would take such a case for examination, we would sometimes have to appeal to the Supreme Court. We were the first who acquainted judges and other officials with the Constitutional right to a favorable environment and unlimited guarantee of protecting this right in court. What is more, they learned that a European Human Rights Court existed, and we could appeal to it. It was a revelation for them. Since the middle of the 1990s the judicial system has begun stirring. Judges and public prosecutors are displaying interest in our activity. They have started taking part in our seminars and delivering lectures for our trainees. Bodies dedicated to guaranteeing human rights have arisen. We won cases in Moscow and in the regions. To illustrate, in Chelyabinsk, a member of our Network in cooperation with Ecojuris has managed to gain psychological damage compensation for a child who is a third-generation radiation victim.

At present, Ecojuris has a rather complex structure. It includes a consultative center for citizens and public organizations. Muscovites and Moscow Oblast residents are able to consult the Center. People from other parts of the country can send us written inquiries. Verbal inquiries center largely around citizens' environmental rights in populated areas, including unlawful building, destruction of trees, infringement of sanitary and epidemiological norms, and neglect of environmental assessment and examination. Deforestation and unlawful construction in protected wetlands are common. It is these violations that upset people. In general, the inquiries show considerable variation, ranging from protection of domestic animals to complaints against housing quality to noise pollution.

Apart from consultative assistance, Ecojuris continues dealing with public interest environmental law. In Moscow, Moscow Oblast, and adjoining oblasts, the consultative center pleads different cases, including sanitary and epidemiological infringement, unlawful construction, and neglect of environmental impact examination on various projects. As a rule, about ten such small cases are under consideration by Ecojuris at any one time.

More complicated cases of interregional and even All-Russian interest are also being handled by Ecojuris. Considerable advances have been made on these levels. In 1998-1999, Ecojuris won two cases against the Government on the illegitimate reclassification of pristine forest lands as non-forest lands. In September 1999, we won a case against the Government on its unlawful granting of permits for the discharge of drilling wastes into the Far East seas. These cases have been won at the level of the Supreme Court. To be sure, failures also occur. We try to see that a lost case does not turn into a conspicuous failure. Each case, even a small one, is normally accompanied by a public campaign and mass media support. Letters and requests are sent to the state bodies, including the office of the Prosecutor General. Here are some concrete examples.

We actually lost the case on the St. Peterburg-Moscow high-speed railway project. The Supreme Court rejected our claim. But a large-scale mass media campaign was launched. More than three thousand supporters of our position were involved from different regions of the country. A great number of publications were issued. All TV channels broadcast reports on the matter, including on our lawsuit. We believe that this case made its contribution to stopping construction of this line. In our view, President B.N.Yeltsin reversed a substantial number of his decrees due to the threat presented by this very case. Though this case may have been lost in court, it should not be considered a failure. Ecojuris opposes President Putin's edict of May 17, 2000, on abolishment of the State Committee on Ecology and Ministry of Forest Management.

A great number of laws, from the Constitution to the environmental legislation, have been violated by this edict. The Presidential edict is a very important decision related to citizens' environmental and human rights to a favorable environment, to information, and to participation in managing State affairs. We believe the edict to be undeniably unlawful. There is not a general unified procedure for public participation in environmental decision-making in our country. Consequently, so- called "compensatory" mechanisms should have been put into operation. This would imply, that in accordance with the federal Law "On the Environmental Examination," the draft of this edict as well as the draft of the corresponding government decree adopted on the base of this edict should have undergone state examination with participation of the public. This procedure has not been observed. Therefore, we consider it to be a serious abuse of citizens' rights.

Nevertheless, the Supreme Court has ignored our claim, so we are now at the stage of appeal. We are currently developing a strategy of future actions, as we cannot let this case end without legal consequences.

HIGHLIGHTS OF PRESENTATIONS

The list of organizations represented at this workshop provides a good overview of the types of environmental NGOs that are active in Russia and the United States. There are of course hundreds of others with special interests and unique approaches-at both the national and local levels. But in general, advocacy, analytical, and educational NGOs have been well represented. At the same time, the concept of NGOs is somewhat different in the two countries. An American environmental NGO is usually perceived as an organization established specifically to contribute to environmental improvement at the national or local level, or both. Professional societies (e.g., the American Chemical Society), nongovernmental laboratories supported by the federal government (e.g., Oak Ridge National Laboratory), and departments of universities, for example, are not usually considered to be environmental NGOs, even though Russian specialists might consider them to be an important form of NGOs.

In Russia there is a long history of many types of organizations outside the formal governmental structure participating in environmental protection activities that today are considered to be environmental NGOs. They include, for example, coordinating councils established by regional governments with common environmental interests, institutes of the Russian Academy of Sciences, government- sponsored citizen organizations, museums with environmental outreach programs, and societies that promote ecology programs for students. During the past decade, hundreds of western-style environmental NGOs have been established in Russia, many with strong international ties to western NGOs. Greenpeace is probably the leading example of this trend.

Several speakers have noted, however, that some of the new Russian NGOs, with far less stature than Greenpeace, are primarily interested not in championing environmental causes, but rather in serving as a vehicle for expressing dissent with broader governmental policies and in becoming conduits for western grants. Still, many new Russian NGOs are very vigorous advocates of greater attention to environmental concerns amidst the economic collapse in the country, and they certainly have carved out a permanent niche on the Russian landscape. Some environmental NGOs in both countries are devoted to ensuring that decisions and policies taken by government, including the enforcement of environmental regulations, are in the best interests of the public.

They use direct communications with governments, the power of the mass media, and the judicial system to achieve this goal. Others have assumed responsibilities not adequately handled by government agencies, such as packaging government information and data in a form that is understandable to both specialists and the public and in developing additional data relevant to governmental decisions. Others serve as rallying points for voices of the people or provide meeting grounds for polluters, the public, and government. Others direct their energies to education and training of both professionals and the public-offering courses, preparing educational literature, and generally supplementing activities of educational institutions by sharing experiences, developing new analytical techniques, and applying new methodological approaches. Still others serve as coordinating centers for governmental authorities and specialists from different regions of the country with common interests. Then there are hybrid organizations that assume several of these tasks and additional responsibilities as well.

The workshop addressed many environmental issues, with heavy reliance on case studies; and the discussions of immediate environmental problems placed the consideration of NGOs into a meaningful perspective. In the aggregate, NGOs are interested in all aspects of environmental protection. At the same time, several differences in the agendas of NGOs in Russia and the United States seemed apparent. Of course, the differences expressed at the workshop were somewhat influenced by the individual interests of the participants.

The Russian emphasis on protection of forests and on the impacts of large-area radioactive contamination was understandable. The economic crisis has led to a deterioration of the technical and administrative capabilities to control pollution with the result that particulate and other common pollutants are of greater concern in Russia than in the United States.

Also, solid waste disposal is a serious problem in Russia, where segregation of wastes, recycling of wastes, and establishment of adequate landfills lag behind efforts in the United States. The U.S. effort, on the other hand, has increasingly focused on human health impacts of pollution. Control of toxic effluents and emissions is a high priority with risk assessment being an area of intensive development. Also, the United States is able to devote more resources to investigation and protection of biodiversity; and global environmental issues also receive increasing priority.

In both countries, scientific research plays an important role in the work of NGOs. Many Russian presentations were by specialists of the institutes and centers of the Russian Academy of Sciences, clearly an important resource for NGOs. In the United States, many NGOs now have internal scientific capabilities, which enhances their credibility in dealing with government agencies. In both countries, solid scientific data are important in convincing the government agencies, the legislative bodies, and the public to give greater priority to environmental concerns.

Turning to education and training, Russia has an impressive array of programs at both the high school and university levels. However, a recent law rescinds the long-standing requirement that an ecology component must be included in the mandatory-core high school curricula, leaving the decision on this matter up to local authorities when they prescribe the optional aspects of the curricula. Several universities have adopted "sustainable development" as a theme, and a number of NGOs work with the universities in this field. It is important that "sustainable" development not become "no" development, and the importance of economics in the work of the NGOs was recognized. One example of the tight linkage between NGOs and students is in the city of Tomsk, where students provide much of the core of the NGO movement.

The internet was repeatedly cited as an important tool for the NGOs. U.S. government agencies increasingly use the internet to disseminate important information related to their decisions; and this trend has been of considerable importance for NGOs. The role of e-mail in tightening the linkages among

NGOs with common agendas is clear; but there are many uncertainties as to the environmental data that are disseminated on the internet, given the absence of good quality control mechanisms. Nevertheless, in the years ahead, internet communications and data transfer will be central to the activities of many NGOs. Several questions were not completely answered during the workshop, and they should help provide a framework for more focused workshops on the role of environmental NGOs that could be organized in the future.

- o What additional steps can the Russian Government take to facilitate the work of NGOs? The pending legislation to update the basic environment protection law addresses the role of NGOs, but will additional amendments be necessary? As the Ministry of Natural Resources absorbs its new responsibilities for protection of the environment and protection of forests, how will it ensure that NGOs continue to have access to governmental decision-making, how will it disseminate information to NGOs, and how will it support NGO activities at the local level?
- o Given the economic crisis, should Russian NGOs emphasize cooperation or confrontation with government agencies and with the polluters? Is the judicial system sufficiently responsive to environmental concerns encapsulated in law suits to warrant greater efforts in the field of litigation- at the national and local levels? Are the councils supported by regional governments in the Urals and in Siberia useful models for replication in other areas? How can the Ministry of Defense and Ministry of Atomic Energy be encouraged to pay more attention to NGOs?
- o What are the characteristics of successful NGOs? Is support by western grants an asset or a liability? Can the Russian Academy of Sciences' new committee on cooperation with environmental NGOs facilitate cooperation among the scientific community and environmental organizations in a manner that enhances the credibility and the impact of these organizations?

CLOSING REMARKS

This workshop was characterized by active participation of the attendees and proved of importance in further improving cooperation between ecological scientists and nongovernmental organizations.

Reports of the Russian side showed that nongovernmental organizations have become real participants in dialogues during the decision-making process at local and regional levels all over the country from the Pacific Ocean to the Baltic and Barents Seas. The experience of the "Siberian Agreement" demonstrates the possibility of involving significant scientific centers for realization of large international projects.

The Kemerovo and Khabarovsk research centers of the Russian Academy of Sciences strongly contribute to establishing problem priorities, and they actively collaborate with social organizations in educational endeavors.

The workshop agenda coincides with a priority set by Agenda 21, by other UN documents concerning sustainable development, and by instruction documents of UNESCO. All speakers and discussants especially stressed the importance of scientific education and help in interpretation of complex new interdisciplinary problems.

We are very interested in the experience of the Hampshire Institute, a nongovernmental organization developing software for assessment of hazards due to different chemical pollutants in food and environment. Joint projects adapting this software for Russia can meet with support in our regions. Without doubt the experience of our American colleagues in database technologies would be very useful for us in making information available to everyone.

Reports devoted to interaction with the mass media, social organizations, and decision-makers were of significant mutual interest. Undoubtedly, the reports by Professors Kraft and Kokhanova and by Ms. O'Connell gave food for thought. These themes can serve also as research areas for joint projects. All the participants came out in favor of continuation of such workshops. I expect the Cooperation Section of the Russian Academy of Sciences Scientific Council on Ecological Problems and Emergency Events will take into account these wishes in their planning for 2001.

In conclusion, I would like to turn to comments by Dr. Gibbons. He expressed his thought that the scientist's duty is to explain to the society outward phenomena, being based on the most advanced scientific concepts. It is a challenging task to help people make proper decisions in a condition of global indeterminacy and continuously changing environments. The coming millennium will be characterized by the increasing importance of quality of life, human health, and education. Natural resources are finite, but knowledge and development of human intelligence are infinite. Let me wish all colleagues every success in this important field.

SCIENTIFIC COUNCIL ON ECOLOGICAL PROBLEMS AND EMERGENCY EVENTS

The Scientific Council on Ecological Problems and Emergency Events (hereinafter called the Council) was established for general coordination and further development of basic and applied research activities of the Russian Academy of Sciences in ecology, environmental protection, and emergency events (natural and man-made catastrophic processes). The Council is a coordination and consultative unit working on a voluntary basis and attached to the Presidium of the Russian Academy of Sciences.

The Council works in cooperation with the government and with other institutions of Russia, foreign countries, and international organizations dealing with scientific research in ecology, environmental protection, and emergency events. The main purposes of the Council are the following:

1. The general coordination of research carried out by the Russian Academy of Sciences on ecology, environmental protection, and emergency events.
2. Development of an electronic library based on research materials of the institutes of the Russian Academy of Sciences on ecology, environmental protection, and emergency events. The library should be of interest to users of Russian information networks and for connection to the Internet.

3. Analysis and synthesis of research results obtained by institutions of the Russian Academy of Sciences on environmental protection and natural and man-made catastrophic events.
4. Preparation of proposals and recommendations for the Presidium of the Russian Academy of Sciences concerning problems of ecology, environmental protection, and emergency events.
5. Preparation of materials concerning problems of ecology, environmental protection, and emergency events according to the needs of state agencies addressed to the Russian Academy of Sciences.
6. Promotion of ecological research including interdisciplinary research in the institutions of the Russian Academy of Sciences.
7. Promotion of ecological examination of projects and facilities of the state involving scientific institutions of the Russian Academy of Sciences.
8. Promotion of links of the scientific institutions of the Russian Academy of Sciences with governmental bodies, Russian ecological organizations, including public ones, and foreign organizations dealing with problems of ecology, environmental protection, and emergency events.
9. Promotion of links of the scientific institutions of the Russian Academy of Sciences, dealing with problems of ecology, environmental protection, and emergency events with the Russian and foreign mass media.
10. Participation in the organization of scientific meetings on the problems of ecology, environmental protection, and emergency events.
11. Cooperation with international scientific organizations, foreign scientific institutions, and individual foreign scientists on problems of the Council.
12. Promotion of joint activity of scientists from different departments by establishing interdepartmental and international research groups in ecology, environmental protection, and emergency events.

STAFF AND STRUCTURE OF THE COUNCIL

The main structural units of the Council are:

- o The Bureau of the Council.
- o Regional divisions of the Council on the problems of ecology, environmental protection, and emergency events in the Far East, Siberia, the Urals, and the European part of Russia.
- o Sections on the following problems: catastrophic processes, ecological problems of the atmosphere, ecology and wildlife conservation, ecology of continental waters of Russia, ecology of the world ocean, ecology of the lithosphere and underground waters, information support for ecological research, ecological problems of education, interaction with nongovernmental and international ecological organizations, social and economic problems of ecology, and methods and technologies of ecological research.

4

NGOs and the World Bank

The NGO community is concerned about the impact of World Bank funding and "partnerships" with NGOs, especially those in Third World countries. Some charge that the Bank, with its enormous wealth, is able to "buy" small grassroots NGOs in the South, to gain legitimacy for its projects. Those sympathetic to the Bank's programs argue that this process of "dialogue" or "partnership" makes the Bank sensitive to the needs of people at the local level.

According to Bank documents, the Bank "has made a special effort to engage local NGOs in its operations, given their on-ground presence and firsthand knowledge of the needs and interests of the poor." The Bank's engagements in these projects has increased rapidly, so that by 1994, 115 (about half) of the Bank's lending projects had provisions for NGO involvement. In 1991 and 1993, the rate was about 30%. In the period 1973-1988, the rate was just 6%.

The Bank has developed a number of programs to promote "closer Bank-NGO collaboration." These include "social funds" to finance community-based projects, direct contracts with NGOs to carry out segments of loan projects, special grant programs and "new initiatives" including funding of NGO participation in international conferences. To further its work in this area, the Bank has set up a new NGO Unit, which maintains extensive computer-based files on NGOs. The Bank's Economic Development Institute also runs special training programs for NGO representatives. Millions of dollars are now flowing from the Bank into the hands of NGOs. The Bank likes NGOs because they are part of the "private sector" and their activities are often a substitute for the state. They symbolize "self-help" approaches to social problems as opposed to collectivist ones. But the Bank prefers certain kinds of NGOs over others. Judging from the NGOs it chooses to have a "dialogue" with, it prefers environmental NGOs to trade unions, docile outfits to truly grassroots groups, libertarian NGOs to socialist or communitarian ones.

The Bank has now incorporated many NGOs into consultative or dialogue bodies, but the process got under way some time ago. By the mid-1970's the Bank started organizing "specialist workshops" to which it invited NGO experts on such topics as forestry, water and energy. In 1981, the Bank took another step by setting up the World Bank-NGO Committee and soon the Bank participated in co-financing a few local projects with its NGO partners. The major intermediaries on the NGO side were the Geneva-based International Council of Voluntary Agencies and the Brussels-based Cooperation internationale pour la developpement et la solidarite. Other NGOs criticised these new arrangements as secretive and unrepresentative and they denounced those who participated in the Committee.

The Bank co-optation process moved into high-gear as the Bank helped set up a group of its critics (and provided them with funding!) in a body called the NGO Working Group on the World Bank, established in 1984. But other NGOs kept their distance and in 1988 organized a counter-meeting for the first time at the Bank-IMF annual meeting in Berlin. These counter-meetings have put forward very harsh views of the Bank and held tribunals to judge the social impact of the Bank. The counter-meetings have been held every year.

Another vehicle for the Bank's policy dialogue is the Council of the Global Environmental Facility, which has a small number of NGO members. The Bank has also hired NGO staff, like John Clark of Oxfam, and it is increasing a program by which it brings NGO staff into the Bank on an "exchange" basis. There is even a proposal now for an "NGO funding window" at the Bank.

The Bank stepped up its efforts on the NGO front in 1995 by sponsoring the Brussels Conference on Hunger and Poverty in November, along with the International Fund for Agricultural Development. The conference drew over 1000 representatives of aid groups, NGOs and others. It drew up a five-point "action plan" which included setting up "popular coalitions" among international agencies, governments and grassroots organizations.

The conference decided that the main weakness in current international and national actions to fight hunger and poverty is "insufficient participation by the poor in decisions affecting their daily lives." Critics of this and other Bank initiatives point out that the Bank itself, with its harsh "conditionalities" and interventionist structural adjustment progams in nearly a hundred countries is itself one of the world's most important barriers to democracy. Thus a "popular coalition" involving the Bank is a contradiction in terms. It would only perpetuate the problem, rather than solving it.

The Bank has also sponsored regional meetings with NGOs. On 24 April 1996, the largest such meeting ever held in Asia brought together 70 NGOs in Manilla at the University of the Philippines. A considerably smaller meeting had been held the year before in Delhi. The Bank also organized regional meetings in Africa and in Latin America and the Caribbean. In all cases it tried to enlist NGO partners in what it calls a "policy dialogue."

In 1996, the Bank incorporated one of its most forceful critics -- the Washington-based Development Group for Alternative Policies (D-GAP) -- into a Bank-funded program which involves substantial numbers of (mostly Southern) NGOs in a "review" of Bank structural adjustment policies in 10 to 12 developing countries. This initiative, known as SAPRI (Structural Adjustment Participatory Review Initiative), was finally launched on 14 July 1997 (Bastille Day) at a public ceremony. NGOs have been organized into a "Civil Society Network" which included some 500 organizations at the time of the launch. These steps give the Bank and appearance of openness and accountability, but in the final analysis they do not change the essence of power at the Bank or in the affected countries. NGOs will have to work by pursuasion; they will not have any direct voice in the Bank's decision-making process nor in its fundamental mission.

By the summer of 1997, the participating NGOs had already grown sceptical and frustrated with their role. As D-GAP Communications Director Tony Avirgan wrote in the June issue of Bank Check:

> The civil-society organizations involved in SAPRI are not naive, however, about the possibilities of the exercise resulting in a fundamental change in the World Bank's economic policies. In fact, it is not lost on anyone that, while the Bank uses SAPRI to demonstrte that it is doing something on the adjustment issue with its critics and civil society generally, it is considering tightening the adjustment noose around the necks of borrower governments.

The new Bank President, James Wolfensohn, has proved to be a brilliant public relations figure and a skilled tactician. From his first weeks in office, he has projected himself as a dedicated reformer intent on changing the Bank into a different kind of institution, truly working in the interests of the poor and the downtrodden. He has spent considerable effort to talk to NGO leaders and assure them of his good intentions. But Wolfensohn like most other Bank presidents has a background as a profit-driven businessman. Before coming to the Bank, he worked as head of his own Wall Street investment banking firm. Bank critics point out that previous Bank presidents also began their term with talk of eliminating poverty, innovative approaches to development, empowerment of people and other such jargon.

Wolfensohn himself noted at his first annual meeting of the Bank in the fall of 1995 that the number of those in absolute poverty in the world has increased from 1 billion to 1.3 billion in the past five years, confessing that the Bank's strategies have failed to improve income distribution. Wolfensohn's predecessor Lewis Preston also admitted that the Bank had failed to act effectively to stem environmental degradation. Such statements from the Bank's highest officials, seem to confirm NGOs worst fears. So did the notorious Wappenhans Report (1992). Written by a high Bank official and originally intended for internal use only, the report concluded that a very high proportion of the projects for which the Bank had made its loans had unsatisfactory outcomes.

In spite of these failures and the deep opposition to the Bank's "policy-based lending," the Bank's power and money seem to have a substantial and growing influence on NGOs. The Bank has proved that it can cause splits among NGO coalitions between those who accept Bank funds and those who don't. To the extent that the Bank uses NGOs to assess the effects of Structural Adjustment and the extent of poverty and hunger, some NGOs may feel pressured into seeing the world from the Bank's perspective, rather than the perspective of their own members or constituents. Or at the very least they may be pursuaded to soften their criticism, because they come to see the latest Bank leadership as acting in good faith.

As a counterweight to NGOs that are "incorporated" by the Bank, a strong and increasingly well-organized international network of critical NGOs has emerged, linking those that do not hesitate to point out frankly the devastating effects of the Bank, the Fund and other International Financial Institutions (IFIs).

The "Fifty Years is Enough" network is the leading international network with hundreds of members world wide. At a regional level and national level, NGOs have also formed coalitions and networks. In March 1995, 35 groups came together to form the Brazil Network on Multilateral Financial Institutions. NGOs have also formed the Latin American and Caribbean Network on Multilateral Banks, with focal points in Montevideo (Intituto del Tercer Mundo, a part of Third World Network) and in Washington (Bank Information Center).

But even the most committed of the IFI critics face a serious problem: how to bring real accountability to these enormous, secretive and very powerful institutions. Some would like to demolish them, a perspective implied in the "Fifty Years is Enough" campaign slogan. This view has strong support on both the libertarian left and on the libertarian right, among those who believe in minimum government and maximum "free market." The reformists, who hope to make the IFIs more accountable, mostly focus on three strategies: (1)forcing greater disclosure, (2)engaging in "dialogue" and public campaigns, and (3)using the leverage of powerful member governments, especially through work with the US Congress.

IFI activists of all persuasions have often stressed the enormous, undemocratic power of the Bank. Christian Aid (UK) had a 1995 Bank campaign entitled "Who Runs the World." No one thinks that the Bank's new Public Information Center (opened January 1994) will make it adequately "transparent" or accountable. But, surprisingly enough, few IFI activists have looked to the UN as a possible means of accountability and control. But there are signs that this perspective may be emerging. If so, the coalition for the democratization of the UN may gain a very important potential partner.

TRANSPARENCY BEGINS AT HOME

Civil society organisations gathered on this island, ahead of the annual meeting of the World Bank (WB) and the International Monetary Fund (IMF) in neighbouring Singapore, have launched a 'global charter' demanding transparency from the finance institutions.

This initiative, which argues that the public's right to information has greater weight than the WB-IMF's willingness to be transparent, marks a new direction that non governmental organisations (NGOs) are taking from their usual mission -- targeting governments that deny the right to freedom of opinion and information to their citizens.

"Taking on the Bank and other international financial institutions is our new rallying cry. We have expanded our mission," Toby Mandel, law programme director at 'Article 19', the international media rights watchdog, told IPS in an interview shortly after the launch on Sunday. "The charter aims to pry open the highly secretive practices of the WB-IMF. These public bodies must be as open as the governments they are calling upon to be transparent." Countries such as India, Mexico and South Africa have a better structure of openness and have national laws concerning the right to information that make it easier for citizens to secure documents than at the Bank, he added. "We should get information not when they (WB-IMF) want to release it, but when we, the people, want it."

"The right to access information held by public bodies is a fundamental human right," states the 'Transparency Charter for International Financial Institutions: Claiming our Right to

Know' in its preamble. "A two-way flow of information provides a foundation for healthy policy development, decision-making and project delivery."

The charter has set out nine principles to compel the financial powerhouses to fall in line with the United Nations Universal Declaration of Human Rights, which guarantees the right to "seek, receive and impart information and ideas". Among them are the public's right to access information held by the IFIs, "regardless of who produced the document and whether the information relates to a public or private actor".

The second principle stresses that IFIs should automatically disclose "a wide range of information about their structures, finances, policies and procedures". The third principle calls on the IFIs to be completely transparent and offer "access to decision-making", which even means public access to draft documents. And to strengthen the public stake in this issue, the sixth principle calls for the creation of an "independent and authoritative body" to review requests for information that the IFIs deny. "Anyone who believes that an international financial institution has failed to respect its access to information policy, including through a refusal to provide information in response to a request, has the right to have the matter reviewed."

The charter is the work of the Global Transparency Initiative, a coalition of eight freedom-of-information (FoI) groups, including Article 19, the Washington D.C-based Bank Information Centre (BIC), the Manila-based Access to Information Network, the London-based Brettons Woods Project and the Cape Town-based Institute for Democracy in South Africa. It comes two years after the FoI groups rallied under this new banner to bring the financial institutions under their critical gaze. The launch of this charter also marks a vote of no confidence in the Bank's existing "disclosure policy", which was initiated in 1994 to make some of its records accessible to people. "Compared to 15 years ago, the Bank is disclosing more information now. But there is no right for the people to demand the Bank to disclose the information they need," said Jennifer Kalafut, of BIC, at the launch of the charter.

"Do they disclose reports and performance audits? No," she revealed. "Are the board of directors open about the decisions that are made? No." "The World Bank should change to accept transparency as a right," she added. "The problem is that they are stuck with a paradigm that they are the ones to choose what information must be released." Activists and researchers meeting here for the three-day International People's Forum (IPF) are throwing their weight behind the charter. Those that IPS spoke with welcomed this initiative as part of an on-going global drive to force WB-IMF to be more open and transparent at a time when these institutions are demanding that national government address corruption and ensure transparent functioning.

"This (charter) will help us audit any World Bank and ADB (Asian Development Bank) projects in Bangladesh," said Reza Chowdhury, secretary of Campaign for Good Governance, a network of 700 grass roots groups, based in Dhaka. "This also exposes the Bank, which is currently pushing a new programme to fight corruption. If it does not recognise the public's right to information of its records, it will be difficult for the Bank to lecture to governments."

According to Stephen Mandel, senior researcher at the New Economics Foundation, a London-based think tank, "the Bank refuses to reveal how decisions are made and the voting records of the board of directors, which is useful in holding the executive directors in each country accountable".

UK 'THREAT' TO WORLD BANK BRINGS A LITTLE CHEER

The British government statement that it is withholding some funds from the World Bank has drawn conditional praise from aid agencies.

Britain's international development secretary Hilary Benn has announced that the government will hold back 50 million pounds (95 million dollars) from the World Bank unless the institution eases lending conditions to developing countries ?- in effect stops forcing poor countries to privatise their public services and open up markets to foreign competition.

The money in question is not enough, says the Charity War on Want. "The sum mentioned by Benn is a tiny fraction of the 1.3 billion pounds (2.4 billion dollars) pledged to the Bank by his department over the next three years, and the threat therefore lacks the necessary bite," the charity said. John Hilary, Director of Campaigns and Policy at War on Want, said: "Hilary Benn has got the right idea but the wrong numbers. We commend the decision to withhold funding, but the threat should be made a real one." Hilary said that "the free market policies of the World Bank have condemned many developing countries to greater poverty, and the UK government should have nothing to do with such policies. Benn should withhold all funding from the World Bank and IMF until they drop these harmful conditions on poor countries."

But other groups say that the move is nevertheless a significant one. "We want the UK government to put pressure on the World Bank and the IMF," Anna Thomas from Christian Aid told IPS. "By making this move, the government is putting pressure, and we are very pleased to see that. And if they do not respond, then we would like to see the government route more money for development through other channels."

Much development aid from the World Bank and the International Monetary Fund (IMF) has long been tied to demands for opening up of market sectors in countries receiving the aid. Britain and Norway are among few countries that do not tie development aid to demands for liberalising economic policy.

The small but significant move could well have strong impact, Thomas said. "The evidence for a need in World Bank policy is coming from its own research," Thomas said. "The World Bank is currently reviewing the conditionalities attached to grants and lending, so we hope it will respond to the UK move." Christian Aid has been in the forefront of demands since July this year for the British government to put pressure on the World Bank to change its policy.

Britain's World Development Movement welcomed the move as a "partial victory" for campaigners. "If the purpose and effect of this initiative is to stop the Washington-based institution from forcing developing countries to 'liberalise' their economies and privatise services then the British government is, at last, accepting WDM's argument that aid should not be tied to such conditions," said WDM director Benedict Southworth.

"Mr Benn is responding to the calls of campaigners by signalling a welcome first step and establishing a benchmark against which the future actions of government will be measured." Southworth added: "The minister has established the principle that Britain's contribution to the international financial institutions is to be made dependent on these bodies accepting that developing countries ought to be able to make their own economic decisions. If this approach is pursued it would transform the prospects of developing countries."

Any change of policy by the World Bank would come as an important signal for all development aid through governments or multilateral lending agencies. Aid agencies within Britain are now planning to pile on the pressure for the government to do more. "We now urge Britain to go the extra mile and withhold all its monies," Christian Aid's head of policy Charles Abugre said in a statement. "Until these organisations fundamentally reform and allow poor countries space to develop they will remain a busted flush which we must not underwrite."

NGOS BOYCOTT WORLD BANK MEETINGS

More than 80 non-governmental organisations announced they were boycotting the International Monetary Fund and World Bank annual meetings that began today in Singapore, in protest at the host government banning at least 27 accredited activists and many others from entering the country. The NGOs were to make a formal statement on Friday but organisers told the Guardian this afternoon that 80 groups had already agreed to the boycott and more were expected.

"We estimate this means at least half of the 500 NGO activists due to attend the meetings will not do so," said Donartus Marut, of the International NGO Forum on Indonesian Development. Oxfam, Greenpeace and the World Development Movement (WDM) are among the more prominent organisations now avoiding the official meetings, although some still intend to go to Singapore in an unofficial capacity or hold events away from the official venue. "We're joining the boycott to show solidarity with our partners and allies who were denied access to exercise their fundamental rights, through freedom of expression and association, to attend the meeting," said Taylor

Thompson of Oxfam. Among the 27 activists is a Briton, Martin Powell, of WDM.

Murray Benham, WDM's head of campaigns, said he could not understand why the organisation was banned. "We've clearly got a long history of criticising the bank and the fund and recently issued a report calling for the bank and fund's abolition and replacement with other mechanisms," he told the Guardian. "But you wouldn't have thought a fairly academic report would put us beyond the bounds of acceptance."

Singaporean police have said the banned activists pose a threat to security, law and order. They have banned all outdoor demonstrations in connection with the meetings and have designated an area the size of a volleyball court for indoor protests. In the past week the World Bank and IMF have repeatedly issued strong statements condemning Singapore's decision.

The World Bank's president, Paul Wolfowitz, today told about 50 activists that the ban meant Singapore was reneging on a three-year deal. "The most unfortunate thing is what appears to be a going-back on an explicit agreement," he said. "So far we've had no satisfactory explanation why." Mr Wolfowitz is scheduled to meet senior Singaporean ministers later today and is expected to protest against the ban. Shortly before the meeting the government softened its position slightly, saying it might allow the activists in if they travelled to Singapore. "We will assess at the point of entry whether they pose a security or safety risk," the Singapore organising committee for the event said in a statement. "If we judge the risk to be acceptable for that particular activist, we are prepared to allow him or her in. However, we cannot guarantee that all 27 activists will be admitted to Singapore."

Singapore has also banned the holding of a civil society forum that traditionally is held in parallel to the official meetings. Some 800 NGO activists are instead gathering on the neighbouring Indonesian island of Batam from tomorrow until Sunday. Following alleged pressure by the Singaporean authorities the Indonesian police have ordered all outdoor events at the forum to be cancelled.

IMF-WB Exposed by Ban on NGOs at Singapore Meet

Attempts to stop an International People's Forum (IPF) on the Indonesian island of Batam, planned to coincide with next week's annual meeting of the World Bank (WB) and the International Monetary Fund (IMF) in Singapore, reflect badly on the finance institutions and expose their 'anti-people' policies, say forum organizers.

"In the first place we wanted to have it (the Sep. 15-18 forum) in Singapore but, because the government there would not allow it, we went to Batam which is close to Singapore," said Kusfiardi (one name), coordinator for the Indonesian chapter of the international non-governmental organization (NGO) 'Anti-debt Coalition', a forum member.

"Some of us will also be attending the IMF-WB meeting since we have registered and got accreditation. Batam is the most logical place to hold the parallel meeting because it is a 45-minute ferry ride away," explained Nadia Hadad, spokeswoman for the Jakarta-based organizer of the IPF, the International NGO forum on Indonesian Development (INFID).

But, earlier this week, the provincial police chief of Batam sent a letter to the INFID organizers informing them that the parallel event has been banned on the grounds that it could harm relations between Indonesia and Singapore. Reports in the Indonesian media on Saturday said Indonesia had deployed its anti-terror squad 'Detachment 88' at sea ports in Batam to scrutinise passengers arriving on the island, which INFID claims was clear indication of collusion between Singapore and Jakarta. A few years ago Singapore had signed an agreement with Indonesia to develop Batam as an offshore economic zone that could take advantage of capital from Singapore business interests and cheap labour in Indonesia.

The Batam police chief also cited security reasons for banning the IPF from the island, which INFID thought ridiculous. "Our intention is to respond to the IMF-WB meetings where we (IPF) will be discussing issues that are also discussed at the official events. We have no intention of attacking the Singapore government. We are talking of issues that are very critical to Third World countries like Indonesia, the Philippines and others," Hadad told IPS. "Batam police's decision goes against the spirit of openness in Indonesia (since the fall of Suharto)," said Kusfiardi. "But the decision doesn't come from Batam police-- it comes from pressure from the Singapore government and the IMF-WB. There are a lot of Singapore investors in Batam and they say that it (the forum) will discourage investment". Kusfiardi said the severe restrictions on civil society groups in Singapore and Indonesia show that "they (IMF-WB) are not committed to what they preach (to developing country governments)," he added. The reference was to the agenda of WB president Paul Wolfowitz to bring up the issue of good governance and corruption at the annual meeting.

Hadad told IPS that, under Indonesian law, INFID does not need a permit to hold the forum. They just need to inform the police three days in advance of an event so that necessary security can be arranged. "While we don't actually need a permit we submitted, with good intention, on Aug. 1, a letter to the police regarding our events --but we did not get any response". Apparently, the police move was in response to statements issued by local NGOs in Batam, claiming to be part of INFID, saying that there were plans to send people to Singapore for protest march. "But that was not us and we were not planning to take our protest march to Singapore. We don't know even who these NGOs are," Hadad said. 'Jakarta Post' reported on Friday that the police decision has the support of 18 local NGOs in Batam that expressed fears that the IPF will undermine investments on their island, which attracts thousands of workers from across Indonesia to work in factories set up by foreign investors. However, the influential daily also said that there is speculation that local NGOs are being paid off by business interests.

The letter from Batam police, which has been obtained by Jakarta Post, said that fears have been expressed by employers in Batamindo industrial estate, that the gathering would "have an influence on their workers". Batamindo is a major investment by Singapore companies with the estate's operational headquarters in Singapore. The estate employs thousands of workers, mainly young women, who come from villages in Java and Sumatra islands and live in dormitories inside the complex. "It is our right to express our opinions. We are not involved in destruction," notes Kusfiardi . "It is the IMF-WB policies which are destructive to lives of people in the developing countries. We're expressing our views on these policies". Kusfiardi argues that the Singapore government wants the IPF in Batam banned because "they want to have a meeting with relatively no problems, so that they can position themselves as a major venue to hold such large conferences and, in turn, make a lot of money".

IMF-WB issued a joint statement from Washington on Thursday, calling upon the Singapore government not to block "properly accredited civil society representatives" from attending their meeting. "We have consistently opposed any restrictions on full participation and peaceful expression of views. Open dialogue with civil society is also important for the effective operation of our institutions," they said in the statement.

Kusfiardi, however, is sceptical of IMF-WB claims to being supportive of civil society participation at the Singapore meeting. "The IMF and WB are using Singapore to protect themselves from protests and demonstrations against their policies (which are destroying lives in developing countries)," he argues. "These institutions want to be seen as development experts, but in most cases their policies are not working and they don't want to be open to criticism (by civil society groups)."

While IMF-WB said they have given accreditation to some 500 NGO representatives from more than 45 countries, it is becoming increasingly clear that the Singapore government will not allow many of them to enter the city-state or participate in the annual meeting.

Essentially that would mean that authorities in Singapore would not honour a memorandum of understanding requiring the government "to assure expeditious entry procedures, including the issuance of visas when required and warranted for any observers and other persons included in the categories of participants specified in the annual meetings requirements manual, who are accredited to or invited by the organizations to be present for the meetings."

Civil society activists have been accusing the financial institutions of not being serious about enforcing that commitment by the Singapore government. Hadad said INFID received a letter from IMF-WB on Friday informing them that Singapore has banned its members. But, she said, the WB director in Indonesia has told them that he was negotiating with the Singapore government to get the ban reversed. INFID, she said, is listed to speak at a number of official fora between civil society and IMF-WB at Singapore.

INFID's executive director Donatus Marut also said he had been informed by IMF-WB that, although accredited, Singapore would not allow him to attend the meetings. While the letter assigned no reason, he believes it may have to do with his lead role in organizing the planned forum at Batam. "This situation puts IMF-WB into a difficult situation," Hadad argued. "It harms the image that they have been building so far of being open to dialogue about the impact of its policies with civil society groups."

CAN WE REFORM THE INTERNATIONAL FINANCE INSTITUTIONS?

Over 2006, the Global Call to Action against Poverty agreed to launch a month of mobilization on the 16th September (to coincide with the IFI Annual Meetings) building up to a climax on a global white band day on the 17th October. The month will be launched with highly visible public awareness-raising street actions, stunts and media events. These actions will culminate in a global white band day of mobilization around the International Day on Eradication of Poverty, on October 17th.

Civil society organisations that attended the "Strategy Session on the International Monetary Fund" at the Institute for Policy Studies in Washington, DC, on the occasion of the IMF-World Bank 2006 Spring meeting drafted a Consensus Declaration and Strategy Paper titled "The IMF: Shrink It or Sink It", which has been circulated globally for endorsement in advance of the critical Fall meeting of the Bretton Woods institutions that will be held in Singapore on 13-20 September 2006. The paper clearly states: Like old nuclear reactors, the

IMF is dangerous and, many argue, must be retired. The optimum solution to the problems posed by such Jurassic institutions is to decommission them. But if this is not yet possible at this point in the case of the Fund, then its power to do harm and its reach must be drastically curtailed.

Another important contribution to the debate comes from the Global Unions Group and the World Confederation of Labour with their joint statement to the 2006 Annual Meetings of the IMF/WB titled: "Reform of the IFIs to Create Effective Instruments Against Global Inequity and Financial Instability". The international trade union movement proposes a more consultative approach by rethinking the roles that they currently play.

According to the statement, the international financial institutions (IFIs) could play a positive role in favour of a more equitable globalization, but this would require developing totally different approaches on issues such as trade liberalization, privatization and labour market deregulation, which have been imposed on developing countries through the IFIs' loan conditions or coercive policy advice. Even though much more needs to be done, the progress made over the past year in debt cancellation for poor countries shows that, when the IFIs choose to work in cooperation with the global trade union movement and other civil society organizations, important advances can be made towards achieving the Millennium Development Goals.

I want to reflect here on the opportunities that the upcoming Annual Meetings of the IMF/WB offer us. Following new mandates given to the IMF at last April's spring meetings, the annual meetings are scheduled to discuss implementation of decisions aimed at enhancing the IMF's role concerning international financial stability in a global economy characterized by unsustainable trade imbalances, commodity price pressures, currency fluctuations and sharp inequalities of income. The new mandates include multilateral consultations of "systemically important members", increased surveillance over exchange rates, and the design of a new crisis-prevention loan facility. The annual meetings will also discuss proposals for changing the distribution of votes and representation in the governing structures of the IMF.

These Annual meetings have always been important occasions for social movements, people's organizations, NGOs and other formations to hold international activities and actions at the site of the meetings, that articulates critique, express protest and assert alternatives to the role, policies and operations of these institutions.

While the analyses, positions and calls of these movements and groups are not homogenous, there is no debate that the IMF and the WB cannot be allowed to operate the way they have been doing in the past. Profound changes have to take place, and these changes will not happen without active public intervention and pressure not only on the IMF and WB but also on the governments that are in control of these institutions. Moreover, what is agreed by all is that the International Monetary Fund is perhaps at its most vulnerable state in years. It is suffering a triple crisis--a crisis of legitimacy, a budget crisis, and a role crisis--that is unparalleled in its 62 years of existence.

A Legitimacy Crisis: The Fund's reversal of fortune stems mainly from the Asian financial crisis, which brought down the famed tiger economies in the summer and fall of 1997. The Asian crisis was the "Stalingrad" of the IMF, and it never really recovered from it. The Asian financial debacle gave impetus to an ongoing review of the structural adjustment programs that the Fund, along with the World Bank, had imposed on over 90 developing and transition economies since 1980. Few of these had succeeded in bringing about the growth, reduction in inequality, and decrease in poverty that the countries undertaking these programs had been promised. Indeed, IMF "shock therapy" programs in Russia and Eastern Europe added millions of people to the poverty rolls in the 1990s.

In 2002, with the Fund still reeling from the Asian financial crisis, Argentina collapsed, defaulting on $100 billion of its $140 billion foreign debt. Perhaps more than any other country in the world, Argentina had followed to a "T" the neoliberal prescriptions of the IMF, including radical deregulation, radical tariff liberalization, and financial liberalization. When this mix of policies unraveled in 2001 and 2002, so did the IMF's credibility since it had thrown in billions of dollars in stabilization loans in support of them. A Budget Crisis: The crisis of legitimacy has had financial consequences. In 2003, the Thai government declared it had paid off most of its debt to the IMF and said it would soon be financially independent of the organization. Indonesia ended its loan agreement with the Fund in 2003 and recently announced its intention to repay its multibillion dollar debt in two years. A number of other big borrowers in Asia, including the Philippines, India, and China, mindful of the devastating consequences of IMF-imposed policies, have refrained from new borrowings from the Fund. Now, this trend has been reinforced by the recent moves of Brazil and Argentina, which, in paying off all their debts and declaring financial sovereignty, have implicitly asserted that they do not want to borrow again. What is, in effect, a boycott on the part of its biggest borrowers is translating into a budget crisis since over the last two decades the IMF's operations have been increasingly funded from loan repayments by its developing country clients rather than from the contributions of wealthy Northern governments, which deliberately shifted the burden of sustaining the institution to the borrowers. The upshot of these developments is that payments of charges and interests, according to Fund projections, will be cut by more than half, from $3.19 billion in 2005 to $1.39 billion, in 2006 and again by half, to $635 million in 2009.

A Role Crisis: The erosion of the Fund's role as a disciplinarian of debt-ridden countries and an enforcer of structural adjustment has been accompanied by a search to find a new role. An attempt by the Group of Seven to make the Fund a central piece of a new "global financial architecture" by putting it in charge of a "contingency credit line" to which countries about to enter a financial crisis would have access if they fulfilled IMF-approved macroeconomic conditions fizzled out as it was pointed out that the spectacle of a government seeking access to the credit line could itself trigger the financial panic that the government sought to avert.

The IMF attempts to present itself as a "lender of last resort" for developing countries. But, for many Asian countries, a regional institution, which understands the complexities of a region better than the Fund and which would thus be less indiscriminate in imposing conditionalities, is the answer. There is also movement in Latin America towards a regional institution where one of its functions would be to serve as a source of capital and as a lender of last resort: the Bolivarian Alternative for the Americas (ALBA), pushed by Venezuela, Bolivia, and Cuba.

But, one objection goes: East Asia and Latin America have significant capital resources to serve as a pool for a regional lender of last resort. But what about capital-poor Africa? This is the concern that has made many African governments reluctant to distance themselves from the Fund. One could oppose that, instead of relying on the IMF, African governments could possibly draw on the cooperation of relatively capital-rich developing countries such as China, Venezuela, India, and South Africa to set up a regional institution that would serve as a lender of last resort.

CAMPAIGN DEMANDS

Responsibility in the broader context of the MDGs The IFIs would achieve greater legitimacy if they ensured that their policies were fully consistent with broadly accepted goals such as poverty eradication and the Millennium Development Goals (MDGs). Instead, the IMF's managing director issued a statement in June announcing that the IMF would seek to define "limits of Fund accountability and responsibility in the PRS [poverty reduction strategy] process and in the broader context of the MDGs".

By turning its back on the MDGs, the IMF will make itself more irrelevant to the needs of the global community. Whether it be in designing a new emergency credit facility to assist countries in financial crisis or in redesigning the distribution of votes and representation in the IMF's governing structures, the IMF must assure that its financial instruments protect the interests of the most vulnerable members of society. The Fund should thus refrain from adopting an emergency credit facility which would require the borrowing country to adopt macroeconomic policies that increase job losses or to reduce social expenditures.

RAPID IMPLEMENTATION OF DEBT CANCELLATION COMMITMENTS

One year after the decisions of the World Bank and IMF, taken at the 2005 annual meetings, to cancel the debts of several poor indebted countries, we welcome the fact that the debt cancellation initiative has allowed the recipient countries to devote more of their resources to fighting poverty and improve the welfare of their citizens. We also urge the World Bank and IMF to build upon the momentum of last year's decision by providing debt cancellation to more countries. Noting that the African Development Bank (AfDB) already agreed to debt cancellation of eligible African countries, the international trade union movement calls on the Inter-American Development Bank (IDB) to follow the example of the AfDB and implement its own programme this year.

Debt cancellation must be implemented quickly and efficiently, without subjecting countries to burdensome economic policy conditionality. Countries like Haiti, which will see its debt relief delayed at least three years because of conditions attached to the debt relief programme, should not have to continue paying service on odious debts while its citizens are forced to forgo basic education, health and social services. The economic policy conditionality attached to debt relief, such as privatization, trade liberalization, or the requirement that countries adhere to IMF prescriptions of spending limitations, is often at odds with the MDGs, which put health, educational, and social needs at the centre of the development agenda. We call on the World Bank and IMF to honour their endorsement of the MDGs as well as their commitments to promote country ownership of development strategies by ceasing to attach economic policy conditionality to debt relief.

STOP REDUCING THE COSTS OF PUBLIC SERVICES

Two of the Global Union Federations, Public Services International (PSI) and Education International (EI), have frequently informed the World Bank that certain efforts to reduce the costs of public services can undermine the quality of services and eventually hinder achievement of the MDGs. For example, EI has objected to the Bank's requirement that some African countries hire "volunteer teachers" as a condition for receiving financial assistance for education. The policy exists purportedly to achieve the attainment of MDG 2 of universal primary education at lowest cost possible, but EI has pointed out that the hiring of unqualified teachers leads to schooling of dubious quality.

EI's position was recently supported by a report on Evaluation of World Bank Support for Primary Education issued in July 2006 by the Bank's own Independent Evaluation Group, which warned that the World Bank and client countries "will need to resist the persistent temptation to increase access first and improve learning outcomes later, since experience has shown that it is difficult to retrofit quality onto a system that is operating at a low level of performance". The practice of requiring some African countries to hire under-qualified teachers has continued.

STOP USING THE DOING BUSINESS INDICATORS

The report of the World Commission on the Social Dimension of Globalization, published in 2004, called for increased coherence between the IMF, World Bank, WTO, International Labour Organization (ILO) and other relevant UN bodies. A central recommendation was that the creation of full and productive employment and decent work were key instruments for poverty eradication and equitable development. Unfortunately, both the IMF and World Bank have limited their participation in the follow-up to joint discussions that analyse some labour and development issues, rather than engaging in policy coherence initiatives as the World Commission report recommended. In addition, the main instrument used by the IMF and World Bank in promoting labour market reforms has been the blueprint set out in the annual Doing Business report prepared by the Bank's Private Sector Development department, in which workers' rights and decent work objectives are clearly made subservient to investors' rights. The basic approach of Doing Business is that any labour law or regulation that is perceived to be an obstacle to the unfettered rights of private investors should be removed. The World Bank's Doing Business web site hails Palau - a Pacific island country of 21,000 inhabitants that is not an ILO member and has no labour code - as the world's overall "Best Performer" in terms of labour regulation. According the World Bank's Doing Business data base, Palau merits the Best Performer designation because, among other exemplary features, it allows workers to be required to work up to 24 hours per day and up to 7 days per week. For an employee having 20 years of seniority, employers are required to provide zero days of annual leave.

The World Bank should remove labour market regulation from the mandate of its private sector development department and stop using the Doing Business indicators as a basis for its labour market reform proposals. Any IMF or World Bank involvement in labour reforms should require that the reforms be based on tripartite dialogue involving unions, employers and government, and are consistent with the core labour standards and with other ILO conventions ratified by the country.

FIGHTING ALL KIND OF CORRUPTION

We welcome the World Bank's recent focus on improving transparency and governance in its client countries in an effort to eliminate corruption. However, this effort must be complemented by increased attention to the activities of private corporations, usually based in industrialized countries that are frequently implicated in corruption as much as the host government. The Bank's demand for greater openness on the part of the governments to which it lends will have far more credibility if the Bank were to improve the far-from-perfect transparency of its own operations. Additionally, the Bank's anti-corruption campaign will only be as effective as its seriousness in defending and supporting the "whistleblowers" - be they trade unions, other civil society organizations, the media, or the Bank's own staff - that expose corruption. Free and independent civil society organizations act to counter the "undue influence by powerful corporations", which the Bank's report identifies as an "underlying source" of grand corruption in some countries. Unions and other civil society groups are in a position to organize and mobilize the public to demand accountability from government. While the World Bank will naturally work with governments to address corruption, an effort to support and strengthen civil society organizations must be at the heart of its approach.

Democratizing those Institutions

A redistribution of representation in the IMF and the World Bank must not be limited to increasing the vote of a few emerging economies but should also ensure an enhanced presence of the countries where the IFIs' policies have the biggest impact, notably low-income countries, many of which are African. The current situation at the IFIs' boards, where only two executive directors represent 47 sub-Saharan African countries while thirteen directors represent 30 OECD countries is just unacceptable.

We reiterate that the IMF must recognize the importance of civil society consultations to the success of its work, and must continue to pursue active engagement with trade unions. The consultations should be expanded to discussion of lending operations as well. Although they are currently negotiated in secret between the IMF and the government, loan agreements should be determined through more transparent and open discussions, including the trade unions and other civil society organizations. Join the International Peoples Forum vs the IMF and the World Bank.

With Asian movements taking the lead, an international group of networks, movements, campaigns and NGOs are convening an International Peoples Forum vs the IMF and the World Bank on September 15 to 17, in Batam-Indonesia, a few days before the official meeting of the IMF and WB. The Global Call for Action against Poverty will be co-convening the Forum, and will launch its Month of Mobilization. Mobilization in Batam will be echoed by activities in capitals worldwide.

Through the International People's Forum, we aim to:

- o Encourage international citizens intervention and action during the occasion of the Sept 2006 IMF-WB Meeting (beyond Asia); Project the international character of citizens initiatives and movements vs these institutions
- o Provide space for citizens groups and movements to give expression of their critiques, demands and alternatives vs the IMF and WB, and address specific

issues relevant to the context and agenda of the Sept 2006 IMF and WB Annual Meeting

- o Promote linkages and solidarity among various groups involved in educational, campaigning and advocacy work on the IMF and WB, and facilitate venues for exchanges, joint study and strategizing, collective action
- o Exercise and uphold the right of citizens to freedom of expression and assembly.

A major conference on alternatives to the IMF on the issue of "lender of last resort" should also be organized in 2007, with comprehensive research work undertaken this year in preparation for this event.

The IFIs' 2006 annual meetings are called upon to help define an appropriate role for the IMF in dealing with major global challenges to economic stability, to develop a coherent and effective World Bank strategy for combating corruption, and to make both of the IFIs more relevant to achieving development goals. Civil society organizations have shown their capacity to work in cooperation with the IFIs in order to make progress on debt cancellation for highly indebted countries and to ensuring that the IFIs' operations respect the internationally agreed labour standards. Consultation and cooperation with civil society organizations will be key to achieving successful reforms of the IFIs so as to make them into effective instruments against global inequity.

World Bank Delays NGO Consultations

The World Bank says it has postponed a consultation with civil society groups in Berlin on its proposed social and environmental guidelines for lending after the NGOs boycotted the event and threatened to launch protests instead.

A World Bank spokesperson told IPS that Wednesday's meeting was postponed until an undisclosed date in December; civil society groups say it was cancelled. The schedule change follows a meeting in London on Nov. 1 that was attended by only one group. Other gatherings have already been held in Tokyo and Washington; many groups also boycotted those consultations and staged protests. The NGOs (non-governmental organisations) are angry because they say the meetings are merely a "public relations exercise" and that the Washington-based bank is not serious about giving a greater say to indigenous and local people affected by bank-financed projects carried out by international companies.

The bank has scheduled other consultations with NGOs in Bangkok, Johannesburg, Moscow, Washington and Tunis before the end of 2004. The bank's private sector arm, the International Finance Corporation (IFC), said in August it was opening its doors for talks on its rules and guidelines for lending, and that it would launch public consultations as it updates its environmental and social safeguard policies. The IFC is also reviewing another policy on information disclosure. The IFC has loaned 16.8 billion dollars worldwide since 2003. From its founding in 1956 through 2003, it has lent around 59 billion dollars to 2,990 companies that worked in 140 developing countries. The World Bank is the world's largest public-sector lender to developing nations, while the IFC lends to companies whose projects are supposed to contribute to development in those countries.

The bank, an institution dominated by the group of eight most industrialised countries (the G8) is often accused of working on behalf of the interests of western-based corporations and local elites at the expense of the poor, the environment and social norms in developing nations. Bank officials have long denied the allegations, arguing their mandate is to help reduce poverty and that bank loans have lifted millions of people worldwide out of poverty.

The groups that boycotted the Berlin meeting include War on Want, World Development Movement, Bretton Woods Project, Friends of the Earth and the World Wildlife Fund (WWF). Only anti-corruption NGO Transparency International (TI) attended the meeting in London.

The review of the IFC's standards and guidelines is particularly critical because several public and private institutions, including other banks, take their cues on social and environmental standards from the agency. "This whole consultation process is a sham," said Friends of the Earth (Germany) spokesperson Markus Steigenberger, in Berlin. "There is too little time and too little information available. The meetings are effectively no more than a World Bank public relations exercise. They provide no venue for meaningful consultation, especially for those most affected by IFC operations," he added.

According to Hannah Ellis of Friends of the Earth England, "although we are aware that the potential consequences of these environmental and social safeguards review are huge, not just for IFC financing but for the potential impact on the whole international financing sector, we feel that this kind of consultation is unconstructive." NGOs say they want the IFC to stop financing companies with poor environmental and social records until they change their practices, and to ensure that its investments are environmentally and socially sound. The IFC guidelines recommend how to deal with such issues as natural habitat, indigenous peoples, involuntary resettlement, dam safety and cultural sites.

The review is also important because the agency has promised to incorporate into it some recommendations from the Extractive Industries Review, an independent assessment of the World Bank's involvement in funding oil, gas and mining projects. Earlier this year the EIR final report suggested the bank bail out of mining and gas projects and re-channel the money into developing renewable energy sources. The bank has said it will accept some EIR recommendations, but that it opposes ending investment in oil and gas projects because that would do more harm than good to the developing nations that rely on cash from those projects.

Among other things, the review is supposed to determine whether indigenous communities have the right to say "no" to an IFC project, whether some environmentally vulnerable areas should be protected from any kind of development and how international pollution standards should be modified. The groups say the World Bank is snubbing their proposals to the review, including that standards should be strong, clear and binding, that local people should be able to have a decisive say in projects and that the IFC should be subject to international law. "The IFC is sacrificing its social and environmental norms to meet industry demands," said Steigenberger. "But they are supposed to protect people and the environment. How can the

World Bank Group justify weakening rather than improving its social and environmental standards?"

Critics add that without their participation, the review will be meaningless. "The World Bank, to maintain or to gain any legitimacy, must be accountable to its shareholders and to the communities who are investing, and in order to do that it must have constant constructive dialogue with representatives of civil society," Ellis said.

The bank denies it has turned down requests from the NGOs to further open the meetings and give more power to local and indigenous groups. "We are getting a lot of substantial NGO input from those who attended the regional workshops à we had over 30 NGOs represented in Manila for instance," David Cowan of the IFC's communications department told IPS on Friday. "So we do want them and we do want to hear from them and we want to hear from them on the substance, and if they feel something is weak point out where it is," he added. "There is no sense in which the draft policy is a done deal. We are looking for input from all stakeholders. It means governments. It means clients and of course it means civil society groups and academics."

Groups See Hope for Debt Cancellation for Poorest Countries in Upcoming Meeting

Non-governmental organizations (NGOs) that have been campaigning for years for writing off tens of billions of dollars in debt owed by poor countries to international financial institutions (IFIs) say their dream may soon be realized, perhaps as soon as just nine days from now.

That's when the finance ministers of the Group of Seven (G-7), the world's wealthiest governments, will meet to decide whether to back a joint British-U.S. proposal to cancel all of the debt owed by 33 of the world's poorest nations to the World Bank, the International Monetary Fund (IMF), and regional multilateral development banks. "We are counting down to freedom from debt," said Marie Clarke, national coordinator of Jubilee USA Network, at a rally across the street from the U.S. Treasury Tuesday. "We are encouraged by Treasury's apparent support for full multilateral debt cancellation, but time is running out. We need action, not more words, on October 1 when the G-7 meets."

The NGOs, which include Africa Action, Oxfam, Physicians for Human Rights (PHR), among many others, have been heartened by recent reports that the Bush administration, which is eager to get Iraq's creditors to cancel over 100 billion dollars of debt, has line up solidly behind a debt-cancellation initiative that was first put forward by British Prime Minister Tony Blair at the June Group of Eight (G-8) Summit in Georgia. The administration, which clearly believes that support for the British proposal would give it more leverage in arguing for debt relief for Iraq, is also eager to highlight Bush's "compassionate conservatism" just five weeks before the November elections and sees debt relief - particular if it does incur direct costs to the U.S. taxpayer - as a well-timed vehicle for such a demonstration.

The plan is designed to replace the eight-year-old Heavily Indebted Poor Countries (HIPC) initiative, which was designed to reduce the debt of some 41 eligible countries to more manageable levels in exchange for their implementation of far-reaching economic reform programs designed to make their economies more attractive to foreign investment. So far, 27 countries that together owed the IFIs a total of about US$100 billion have seen their debt reduced by about $30 billion. That reduction translates into roughly a halving of their annual debt service payments. While that represents a substantial savings, most of HIPC's beneficiaries continue to pay more in debt service each year than they spend on health and education, a situation that debt campaigners argue is morally indefensible, particularly because much of the original debt was incurred by western-backed dictators who misspent or, in some cases, embezzled the money.

Even some IFI officials now concede that the debt relief provided by HIPC has been inadequate, particularly in light of the HIV/AIDS crisis in sub-Saharan Africa, which has not only overwhelmed local health systems, but has dragged down economic growth which in turn makes it much harder for countries to repay the debt the owe. "These debts are fundamentally illegitimate," according to Salih Booker, executive director of Africa Action, a grassroots group that led the anti-apartheid campaign in the U.S. during the 1970s and 1980s. "They undermine African efforts to address HIV/AIDS and other challenges, and they should have been canceled a long time ago." "There is an explicit and intimate linkage between debt and death (in poor countries)," noted Holly Burkhalter, PHR's Washington director, who released a letter from 150 doctors around the world calling for total debt cancellation. She said the debt was wreaking havoc in already-overstretched health systems.

Despite the Bush administration's backing for the proposal, it is not yet a done deal, according to the NGOs and administration officials. A number of other G-7 members, which, besides the U.S. and Britain, include Canada, Germany, France, Italy, and Japan, have voiced objections. They have argued that total debt cancellation could make it more difficult or even impossible for countries to reestablish their creditworthiness and that the administration's proposal for paying the costs associated with cancellation - through the Bank's own resources and sales of gold held by the IMF - could inflict long-term damage on the lending ability of both institutions.

At the same time, however, Bush's backing for the initiative should give it new momentum. His past insistence that other western governments forgive a higher percentage of Iraq's debt than HIPC offered to much-poor countries had irritated other western governments. French President Jacques Chirac, in particular, had explicitly objected to giving Iraq greater debt relief than far more needy countries. Some activists said they feared that the cancellation initiative may still get caught up in trans-Atlantic tensions resulting from the Iraq invasion. "We have a saying in Africa," said Njoki Njoroge Njehu of the '50 Years is Enough' campaign, a coalition of groups that oppose the IFIs' structural adjustment programs (SAPs). "When elephants fight, it's the grass that gets hurt."

For that reason, the NGOs are backing the Anglo-U.S. proposal, although many would go much further than what will be put on the table at the October 1 meeting. Jubilee's Clarke said her group opposes any SAP-like conditions imposed on beneficiary countries in exchange for debt cancellation. Many development NGOs criticize SAPs because the burden of structural adjustment has often fallen disproportionately on the poor and most vulnerable sectors of the population. "We are looking for 100 percent debt cancellation without conditions," she said. She added that debts should be cancelled for more countries than the 33 that are targeted by the current proposal. Many other poor countries who do not meet the technical requirements of HIPC are nonetheless paying far too much in debt service, she noted.

The G-7 meeting is to take place on the eve of the annual meeting of the boards of governors of both the World Bank and the IMF at their headquarters in Washington. The G-7 and other western countries have sufficient voting power on the boards of the two agencies that, once they agree on an initiative, its adoption is virtually assured.

ECOSOC/BWI Meeting: Joint NGO Statement

Joint NGO Statement delivered by Martin Khor, Director of the Third World Network, on behalf of the civil society community, at the concluding plenary session of the Special High Level ECOSOC Meeting with the Bretton Woods institutions and the WTO, at the ECOSOC Chamber, United Nations, New York.

Two years ago, when the Monterrey FFD Conference was held, there was considerable momentum generated in which governments pledged to work within a coherent policy framework led by the UN to address critical finance and development issues. The CSOs too had hopes that the FFD process would help to tackle the problems.

Two years later, we find that this political momentum has dissipated. And that the problems of finance and development have remained or worsened. The debt crisis continues for many countries, and more countries are on the brink of financial crisis, aid is still inadequate, capital flows remain unregulated, there are large currency fluctuations and other forms of financial stability, an impasse in multilateral trade relations, the continuing crisis in commodities, and a huge net transfer of resources from South to North.

The need to strengthen the FFD process

The theme of this year's session meeting is coherence, coordination and cooperation. But in the title there is a fourth C, which is context, the context of the Monterrey Consensus and of finance and development. This fourth C is the most vital, because context is key. Coherence, coordination and cooperation are only the means. We must cohere, cooperate and coordinate in line with certain principles and policies, which form the context. If we cohere and coordinate according to the wrong lines and context, it would be worse than not having coherence at all.

There is also a fifth C, and that is capacity. The capacity of the FFD follow up process and mechanism to meet the challenge. We know the seriousness of the problems. But in comparison the follow up capacity is extremely light and weak. We only have, annually, this one-day event. It is even only called a meeting. No doubt the name of the meeting has been embellished with the terms "special" and "high level", but that does not hide the fact that this is only a one-day event, lacking a firm institutional framework. There is also the biannual FFD dialogue, which is an expanded version of this meeting. And besides these few days of discussion, there is hardly any other official events, except for a few hearings. In contrast, the UN has a Commission on Sustainable Development for environment and development issues, and a Commission on Social Development for social issues. Surely the set of issues contained in finance and development deserve at least a Commission within which the discussions can take place and actions can be followed up.

Similarly, the secretariat servicing the FFD, however high the quality of its work, is too weak and has inadequate resources, given the enormity of the problems. The present mandate is grossly insufficient and thus cannot effectively affect the outcomes that are needed. This weak framework must be supplemented or expanded:

1. This spring one-day meeting should be expanded to two or three days to enable more serious dialogue and the dialogue should include the planning of actions.

2. Task forces (that include NGO representatives) should be established to discuss and propose actions on various issues, such as debt, financial flows, trade and finance. They can meet in between the annual meetings and biannual dialogues.
3. The intergovernmental process should be strengthened. A Commission on Financing for Development should be established. There should be a bureau of government representatives to coordinate affairs in between the annual meetings.
4. The UN secretariat or parts of the secretariat handling FFD matters should be strengthened. It should regularly produce more detailed and high-quality papers and reports on the range of FFD issues that can inform on the latest situation and provide suggestions and guidance. It should organize forums, task forces and meetings on the various key issues.
5. The role of NGOs should be strengthened in the process and in the expanded mechanisms.

The FFD is still an orphan child in search of parents. It needs the father of an effective intergovernmental process and the mother of a strong secretariat that can nurture it, and the NGOs can be the brothers and sisters that help develop the child. The problems are so serious, we need not only to keep them alive, but to keep them burning bright in order to make any progress. The NGOs feel that the governments and the UN system must redouble and retriple the efforts to reach an outcome of development, empowering people, reducing inequality, bringing about sustainable development that delivers health, food, jobs and a clean environment.

Development requires that there be enough financial resources, financial stability, and the channeling of financial resources to productive investments in appropriate economic and social activities with clean environment processes, and that that fulfill human needs in the context of sustainable growth and development. Where do we stand today on financing for development? The situation is very disappointing. The following is a summary of a few of the key issues.

Comprehensive Treatment of External Debt

On the issue of external debt, there has been very little progress. The situation is still unresolved for most developing countries that have a debt problem. A comprehensive and systematic solution should now be found for all groups of countries. As the representative from the IMF reported just now from the discussions in one of the roundtables, having a debt overhang is very detrimental to a country's growth and ability to meet the Millennium Development Goals, as excessive debt prevents the use of resources for useful activities (such as education, health and basic infrastructure) and impedes investment.

Thus a comprehensive approach is now required. For low income countries, the HIPC initiative has not succeeded, and it is time that there be debt cancellation for all low-income countries, including those that are not now categorized as HIPC For middle income countries facing a debt servicing problem, the problem must also be resolved, otherwise it is possible some of them will slip into the category of low-income. For these countries, there should be debt relief or partial debt cancellation.

For countries facing the danger or possibility of debt default, they should have resourse to a systematic and fair debt workout mechanism in an international framework agreed to by all. In the absence of this framework, countries may have to initiate their own debt workout solutions, and they should not be blamed when they seek such unilateral solutions. The concept of debt sustainability has to be revised, keeping in mind that a country has to ensure there is sufficient finances to meet the needs of its citizens.

Reconsider Loan Conditionality

The unpopular and largely discredited structural adjustment policies underwent a metamorphosis into the PRSP process, with the popular terms poverty reduction, participation and country ownership added on. However the core economic content has remained the same. Thus the same problems as were in the structural adjustment programme remain in the PRSP. At the least, there should be a reconsideration of the macroeconomic, trade and financial liberalization aspects of these loan conditionalities.

- o The macroeconomic core policies have been pro-cyclical and contractionary, contributing to stagnation or recession. They should be reconsidered and in their place there should be counter-cyclical pro-growth recovery policies.
- o The conditions for financial liberalization (free inward and outward movement of capital flows) should be reconsidered in view of the recent evidence of harm that capital mobility can cause and has caused to many countries.
- o The conditions for rapid trade liberalization, especially import liberalization, have to be changed, in view of the damage to the domestic industrial and farm sectors casued by imports of cheap products resulting from excessively rapid tariff reduction.

Reform of the International Financial System

The framework for international finance is in disarray with the rise of instability and volatility in capital flows, in currency rates, and with financial crises afflicting more countries. But the international community has been dragging its feet in re-building a system that leads to financial stability.

The following are urgently needed:

- o An international system of regulation of capital flows, at least to prevent speculative activities that generate volatility and financial crises.
- o An international framework that enables individual developing countries to regulate inflows and outflows of various types of funds (including credit, portfolio investment and foreign direct investment).
- o A system that stabilizes exchange rates among the currencies that are used for interanational transactions, as well as the currencies of the developing countries.
- o A reform of the roles and governance systems of the Bretton Woods institutions.

Trade and Finance

As we know, trade flows have a major effect on financial resources. The current impasse at the WTO is an opportunity to re-balance the multilateral trade system and re-orient it to the needs of developing countries. The following are some of the measures required:

- o Revise the WTO's agriculture rules so as to prevent the dumping of subsidized products at artificially cheap prices. This "dumping" practice is contributing to import surges in many developing countries, with effect on rural livelihoods and also on the trade balance. Northern agricultural subsidies should be eliminated and phased out as soon as possible. Developing countries should be permitted to protect their small farmers on grounds of food security and rural ovelihoods. The worst scenario, which quite possibly mat materialse, would be for Northern protection to continue, while developing countries have vto reduce their tariffs further under WTO rules or loan conditionality.
- o On industrial products, developing countries must be allowed the flexibility to choose the pace and rate of their liberalization. In previous Rounds, developing countries by and large had such flexibility. However, many developing countrues have suffered deindustrialisation, with closure of local industries, due mainly to loan conditionality of the Bretton Woods institutions. In the WTO, there are several proposals for a non-linear formula which if accepted would drastically reduce the industrial tariffs of developing countries and threaten the viability of their local industries. Another result is increased imports and wider trade deficits, affecting financial resources.
- o The so-called Singapore issues of investment, competition, transparency in government procurement and trade facilitation, should be dropped from the WTO agenda. Most developing countries are against having WTO agreements on these issues as they would severely constrain their development policy space. These issues are so controversial that they have impeded progress in

other areas. Since there was an offer by the main proponent of these issues to drop three of these issues in the Cancun Ministerial meeting, and they are no longer demandeurs of these issues, it would now be timely to drop these issues altogether and thus pave the way for more goodwill for negotiating the other WTO issues such as agriculture.

- o On patenting of drugs, the developing countries should now establish national policies and laws to enable measures such as compulsory licensing so that morfe affordable medicines can be supplied to patients.
- o The commodities crisis continues to afflict a large number of developing countries. A comprehensive international approach should be taken, including the revival of cooperation among producer and consumer countries to facilitate realigning of supply to demand, and stabilization of prices at levels that can meet the needs of developing countries.

Participatory Governance

The imbalances in global governance in trade and finance have contributed to the lack of benefits and the problems facing developing countries in the area of financing for development. A democratization of the Bretton Woods institutions and the WTO is required, for develop0ing countries to participate more equitably in decisions that affect them. The current method of selecting the IMF managing director, the position of which is seen as the prerogative of European countries, is only a topical example of the inequities of the global systems of economic decision-making. The finance situation in the world and in developing countries has not improved since Monterrey and in some areas it has deteriorated. The FFD process must be revitalized, on the basis of fundamental rethinking. Coherence and cooperation in policy should be based on this rethinking. We need to switch from the one size fits all policy conditionality of the Bretton Woods institutions, and tailor policies to fit the needs of each country.

We need to move away from the "level playing field" assumptions of the WTO, and instead build the development dimension into the heart of the rules and operating principles of the system.

We need to switch from the concept of "mainstreaming trade and financial liberalization in development" to the more appropriate concept of "mainstreaming development needs into trade and finance policies and systems." We need to move from a piecemeal and unsatisfactory approach to debt, and have a comprehensive treatment of the problem, and to build a new international financial architecture that regulates capital flows and end the series of financial crises.

We need to reverse the net outflow of financial resources from the developing countries, and to tackle the factors that lead to this drain so that resources flow to the developing countries instead.

And finally we need to bridge the democratic deficit in the global institutions. The quotas in the Bretton Woods institutions are long outdated, lack fairness and legitimacy. The WTO decision-making system should be modernized, and make the transition to a truly multilateral and democratic organization where developing countries are allowed to fully participate. More space must be given to civil society so that its voices can be heard.

The NGOs have in recent years played an increasingly important role in FFD related issues. For example, the Jubilee campaign succeeded in increasing public awareness and mobilizing public opinion on the need for settling the debt problem. The NGOs are committed to continuing and increasing our work in the FFD issues and arena. We hope the governments and the UN system will be up to the challenge too.

PRSPS: 'POLITICAL SPACE' AT WHOSE EXPENSE?

The four years of experience with Poverty Reduction Strategy Papers (PRSPs) have resulted in countless reports and seminars discussing the merits of this new development vehicle. Some questioned from the start the capacity and willingness of donors to devolve control over economic and social policies of 'developing' countries. There is a belief that while PRSPs have only departed from previous programmes in their increased emphasis on social spending, they are nonetheless a worthwhile exercise because of the unprecedented 'political space' they have opened for local NGOs to participate in designing public policies.

But increasingly commentators argue that not only do PRSPs not widen the range of policy options from which governments can choose, they have the potential to hamper or undermine existing democratic structures, and consolidate the hegemony of creditors' interests in the development policy arena. This is well argued in two recent papers, Poverty Reduction Strategy Papers: a New Convergence by Craig and Porter and Merging in the Circle, the Politics of Tanzania's Poverty Reduction Strategy by Gould and Ojanen.

'Development without Enemies': PRSPs as a Technocratic, Depoliticised mode of Governance

As noted by Craig and Porter, an academic and an official at the Asian Development Bank, PRSPs tend to ignore power issues and the political economy of poverty and inequality. They are the result of a broad consensus at the international and national level that combines economic integration, good governance and investment in human capital, a "Third-Way remorphing of neo-liberal approaches". A sign of this growing consensus is perhaps that when new governments come into power, they do not feel the need to revise their PRSP. Interestingly the supposed universal applicability of the PRSP approach to all countries contradicts pronouncements by the World Bank and the IMF that one-size-fits-all approaches do not work.

Craig and Porter argue that PRSPs are best seen as "'inclusive' liberal approaches held together and legitimated by [...] apparently apolitical catchwords like participation, partnership, and community". In effect they consider the emerging convergence in policies for poverty reduction as "an attempt to generate a level of global to local integration, discipline and technical management of marginal economies, governance and populations unprecedented since colonial times".

Gould and Ojanen, in their paper for the University of Helsinki, agree that PRSPs reflect a "depoliticised mode of technocratic governance", in accordance with a tradition in the development industry of "effecting far-reaching political solutions via technocratic measures". Their case study of Tanzania found that the PRSP resulted from a partnership between a core group of players (an 'iron triangle' of donors, state and non-state actors forming a "transnational policy elite") who share a narrow social and ideological background. This includes lifestyle and vocabulary, but also a commitment to "'managerialism' (a faith in the expertise of the professionalized 'new public manager' to achieve optimal policy outcomes) and 'budgetism' (a faith that the optimal allocation of public resources through official budgetary mechanisms constitutes the government's main tool for addressing social issues)." Aid industry efforts to build capacity of public institutions in Tanzania create "a corps of depoliticised budgetists" who "have made a survival strategy of adapting themselves to the roller-coaster ride of donor whims". In this context the PRSP has "deteriorated into an exercise of 'budgetism', rather than a genuine consideration of the various policy alternatives available to Tanzania".

The 'Consultative Imperative': Opening Space for Whom?

Many NGOs argue that while PRSPs are not perfect and the core macroeconomic framework remains untouched, at least the new framework has created political space for local civil society actors, often pushing them to get better organized to influence political processes in their country. The assumption therefore seems to be that PRSPs can reinforce democracy and offer opportunities for the poor to get their voice heard (if not translated into core policy priorities), with NGOs playing the role of facilitators.

However a number of critics have questioned how the space opened has been filled, at what cost, and at whose expense. David Brown, of the UK's Overseas Development Institute, argues that the discretionary element inherent in this model of participation can create a "quiescent form of representation, for there are no entitlements. On the one hand, those who continue to be excluded under the discretionary arrangements have no legal right to demand representation. On the other, those who are included will be put under pressure to accept whatever they are offered, on the grounds that, as supplicants, they could have received much less". This can be at the expense of democratic structures that are bypassed, often because they are considered corrupt or inefficient, as opposed to capable technocrats of the 'iron triangle' described in the case of Tanzania.

Despite pronouncements by the Bank and the IMF that legislators should be more involved in PRSPs, Gould and Ojanen argue that in the new consultative mode of development policy formulation, "the dominance of the public policy arena by a narrow corps of transnational development professionals occludes the possibility of deepening democratic oversight". Representative democratic structures (imperfect as they might be) are bypassed, but structures of clientelism are left intact. In what becomes in effect a 'fast-track democracy', "legitimacy of post-SAP policies is being sought through the establishment of direct channels of communications" with NGOs used as brokers to bring 'the poor' directly into the policy arena.

The actors who capitalize the most on the political space opened by the 'consultative imperative' opened by PRSPs are not necessarily domestic actors but rather international NGOs, whose "well-resourced, highly professional exponents of 'global civil society' have managed, by entering into an opportunistic albeit tense alliance with public bi- and multilateral aid agencies, to co-opt the narrow political space precariously occupied by those few domestic actors". However the authors also argue that "far from conspiring to capture political space for its own sake, transnational private aid agencies would prefer to see domestic actors taking the lead".

The incredible amount of ink and paper used to discuss the merits of PRSPs shows the unease of NGOs and academics with the recycling of the concept of participation by the World Bank and the IMF. This in turn has led to the emergence of the concept of participation as the "new tyranny". At the very least these studies show that participation is no panacea and may be a distraction or worse in the context of the steep hierarchies that operate within developing countries and the aid industry.

The Myths and Dangers of PRSPs

Poverty Reduction Strategy Papers (PRSPs), required by the IMF and the World Bank for access to debt relief and concessional assistance, are loaded with a number of myths that should be debunked.

The Myth of 'National Ownership'

According to these two institutions, PRSPs are country-driven and reflect the priorities of each country in its fight against poverty. They insist that PRSPs are drafted through a large participatory process involving the government, civil society organizations (CSOs) and the private sector. But 'national ownership' is more theoretical than real. In many cases, CSOs have been frustrated by the process and have found they had been used more as an alibi, or guinea pigs, than considered as genuine partners. Democratically-elected parliaments have been bypassed. And the fact is that African governments put in PRSPs what the Bretton Woods Institutions (BWI) would like to see, rather than what the poor really want. The reason: PRSPs have to be consistent with the BWIs' preferred policies in order to get their endorsement.

The Myth of 'Pro-poor' Policies

There is a big gap between policies that are in the interest of the poor and those that the BWIs consider as sound. The privatisation of public and essential services, like water, health and education, is at the core of the BWIs' policies and has contributed to spreading poverty. A case in point is Senegal where, because of water privatisation, poor groups in urban areas pay 3 to 4 times more than rich groups. The liberalisation of the country's groundnut sector, imposed by the BWIs, cost more than 400 jobs following the dissolution of transport company SONAGRAINES, and led millions of peasants and their families to the brink of famine. The Government had to draw up an Emergency Relief Plan to avoid a national catastrophe. Price deregulation and the elimination of subsidies have squeezed the purchasing power of average citizens, leading more than 64% of people surveyed in the Senegalese PRSP to say that their situation has deteriorated over the last five years, a period of supposedly high growth rates.

The Myth of 'Poverty Reduction'

How, under these circumstances, can the IMF and the World Bank claim that PRSPs aim at reducing poverty? The forced liberalisation of the groundnut sector in Senegal led to a sharp fall in agricultural production in 2002. This, in turn, resulted in the decline of economic growth from 5.6 % in 2001 to an estimated 2.4 % in 2002. This translated into an income loss of roughly $200 million for a country where two out of three citizens live under the poverty line. In many other countries, local industries have been destroyed by cheap imports in the name of free trade imposed by the BWIs. No wonder in Sub-Saharan Africa about 500 million people live on less than $2 a day. This number is projected to rise to more than 600 million in 2015, despite all the fuss about the Millennium Development Goals. So long as PRSPs, like the now discredited Structural Adjustment Programmes (SAP), are within the framework of the neoliberal model, they will generate more poverty than they reduce.

After spreading poverty at an unprecedented scale in Africa, the IMF and the World Bank are trying to mislead world public opinion, especially in the North, into believing that they are really committed to poverty reduction. Their real mission is to promote the interests of global capitalism by opening Africa's economies to multinational corporations and financial speculators and by transforming them into markets for Northern countries' products.

This should be clear to everyone, especially NGOs familiar with these institutions' philosophy and policies. Yet some Northern NGOs which have been among the leading critics of SAPs and at the forefront of the struggle for debt cancellation, have bought the BWIs' propaganda. They have found some merits to PRSPs and think that with an emphasis on more spending for social sectors, PRSPs could help alleviate poverty, despite the fact that they leave intact the neoliberal macroeconomic framework. The same NGOs think that the PRSPs provide an opportunity for their partners in the South to influence national policies toward more pro-poor policies. This explains why some big Northern NGOs have literally forced their Southern partners to participate in the PRSP process. This paternalistic attitude has been condemned by numerous Southern NGOs, especially African NGOs, during the last African Social Forum, in Addis Ababa, in January 2003. A sincere partnership should be based on mutual respect and trust. African and other Southern NGOs are mature enough to know what is best for their people and what course of action to follow. Northern NGOs should respect that choice and support it rather than dictate what they think is best.

In conclusion, what the BWIs are trying to achieve with the PRSPs is to:

" create the illusion of poverty reduction while continuing the same failed policies;

" promote a superficial national consensus on short-term poverty reduction programmes at the expense of a serious reflection on long-term development policies;

" drive a wedge between so-called 'reasonable' and 'radical' civil society organizations; and shift the blame to HIPC governments and citizens for the inevitable failure of the PRSPs.

We should not walk into this trap!

US Blocks Stronger African Voice at World Bank - NGO

The Bush administration is blocking proposed reforms to the World Bank's governance structure that would modestly increase the representation of African countries on the Bank's governing board, according to a non-governmental organization (NGO) that monitors the institution. The reforms are supposed to be discussed at an informal meeting of the Bank's executive board Monday, according to the British-based Bretton Woods Project, but the U.S. executive director to the Bank, Carol Brookins, has called for halting the discussion due to what she claims is an absence of consensus on the subject. Brookins' office declined to comment for this story.

"The U.S. government attempt to kill off discussion of proposals on reforms to rebalance Bank and (International Monetary) Fund (IMF) governance gives more ammunition to critics who say these institutions are just tools of the richer nations," said Alex Wilks, the Project's co-ordinator. NGOs and developing countries have long demanded reform of the Bank's governing board that would give poor countries a stronger voice. Now, the executive directors of the world's industrialized countries control about 60 percent of the vote, and the U.S. government, with close to 20 percent of the vote, can effectively veto changes in the Bank's charter that require a super-majority of 85 percent of voting shares.

On the other hand, the 46 sub-Saharan African member-countries together control just a few percent of the board's total voting power and, between them, have only two directors on the executive board of both the Bank and the IMF. The executive boards decide on what loans and credits are approved. The Bank is the world's largest single source of development finance: it provides about 20 billion U.S. dollars a year in loans, credits and guarantees.

For more than a decade, governments and NGOs have called on Bank members to reform the board's voting structure in order to give a proportionately greater voice to poor countries on the grounds of both fairness and of promoting a greater sense of responsibility and "ownership" of the institution and its operations to developing countries. In March 2002, the report of the Financing for Development summit in Monterrey, Mexico -- in which Bush himself participated -- stressed "the need to broaden and strengthen the participation of developing countries in international economic decision-making and norm-setting". It called in particular for the Bank and the IMF to enhance participation of developing countries in "their decisions-making".

The Bank's executive board has been discussing what steps it could take in this regard for some time, according to a 15-page discussion paper prepared for a Jun. 23 board meeting by Bank management that was obtained by the Project. The paper sets out various options for structural reforms that would not require amendments to the articles of agreement, therefore "can be blocked by the U.S. government". Citing statements by governments and the Bank's policy-making Development Committee during its April meeting, the memo notes that "political will does exist" for reforms. "There is a willingness to give serious consideration to these more demanding options at this time in order to 'strengthen the international dialogue and the effectiveness of these institutions' (i.e., the Bank and the Fund)", the memo states. The paper goes on to propose a number of changes, the most important of which include raising the combined voting shares of developing countries from the current 39 percent to 44.3 percent and increasing the number of executive directors who represent sub-Saharan African countries from two to three.

But Brookins has reportedly circulated a memo that opposes further discussion on such structural reforms and instead proposes creating a fund to provide extra research capacity for the executive directors from developing countries. That is "more than ironic", considering the proposals would not have far-reaching implications on how the Bank operates, says Pam Foster, Coordinator of the Halifax Initiative Coalition. The United States would retain its veto, for instance, she said in an interview. But she fears the U.S. move will have a "chilling" effect on reformers on the Development Committee, led by South Africa. "It puts a significant damper on any enthusiasm that was bubbling around reform efforts," adds Foster, whose Ottawa-based group is made up of Canadian civil society organizations working to transform the international financial system.

The U.S. memo could also effectively remove governance reform from the agenda of the Bank-IMF annual meetings in September, she speculates. According to Wilks, "this example of a large country throwing its weight about in global institutions shows precisely why reforms are needed". "If the U.S. gets its way, then international summit commitments will again prove to be worth less than the paper they're written on."

More Bad News for Small Farmers

A Ministerial Declaration on Policy Coherence, issued simultaneously with the creation of the World Trade Organization (WTO) in 1995, stressed the need to achieve greater coherence in policy-making among financial and trade institutions. Building upon the declaration, the WTO signed cooperation agreements with both the World Bank and the International Monetary Fund (IMF). In the following years, the

WTO, World Bank and IMF have intensified efforts to achieve "policy coherence."

The influence of the international financial institutions (IFIs) in the trade policies of their borrowing countries is not something new. Already in the 1980s they had begun to make stabilization and structural adjustment loans, which usually intended to restructure the whole economy of the borrowing country along the premises of an export-led growth strategy. Slashing tariff and non-tariff restrictions and reducing subsidies were, therefore, among key prescriptions in those loans. There are, however, other more subtle but equally powerful mechanisms by which IFIs have influenced trade policy in borrowing countries. For example, the role that they play as providers of research and training to policy-makers in developing countries, their assessments of country policy and institutional environments and their trade-related technical assistance programs are also important in shaping trade policy in developing countries and excluding the search for valid alternatives. A look at the influence that IFIs have had in the past in prying open agricultural markets in developing countries provides many reasons to worry about what greater cooperation among them and the WTO actually means for food security and farmer's livelihoods.

For example, before the creation of the WTO, many developing countries reduced tariff protections and subsidies to farmers in order to abide by conditionalities attached to loans they desperately needed in order to repay growing external debt. At the same time, industrial countries, in no need to borrow from the IFIs, were able to maintain large agricultural subsidies and tariff barriers. Thus, small farmers in the South were forced to compete with Northern-based transnational food companies that benefited from protection by their governments. The WTO Agreement on Agriculture, to a great extent, locked-in the degree of liberalization existent in both the South and the North, without addressing such imbalances. Moreover, low tariff and subsidy levels that previously were the matter of policies in Southern countries became the matter of trade rules enforceable through trade sanctions. Thus, liberalization that had been open to the possibility of reversal became irreversible in practice. But the "coherence" among the institutions does not stop there. Indeed, after the creation of the WTO, the IFIs have continued to promote reduction of tariff and subsidy protections to farmers oftentimes below the levels allowed by the WTO.

IFI programs promoting the privatization of publicly provided services have led to states withdrawing from their role in the provision of irrigation, seed distribution and extension services that allowed poor farmers to receive them at a subsidized rate. This was regardless of whether subsidized provision of these services was considered legal under the WTO. The privatization of services has tended to drive rates up. Small farmers have been the most hard hit by rate hikes as the prices to pay for fertilizers, seeds, or water is often a key factor in the viability of their business. The IFIs have also promoted domestic and international financial liberalization. This has often led to the removal of sources of subsidized credits on which small farmers with scarce assets and uncertain incomes due to the price volatility of their products, need to rely in order to pay for the increasing costs of their inputs. Food state-marketing boards have also been targeted under IFIs programs in several countries, which means depriving small farmers of government marketing and distribution oversight. As a result, small farmers, facing increasing costs, reduced access to finance and unfair competition, end up losing their lands, which is leading to increased land concentration. Again, as industrial countries are not the borrowers in the IFIs institutions, these extra pressures are only exerted on farmers in developing countries, thereby working largely to the advantage of industrial countries and their corporations. The imbalances in the voting structure of the IFIs, where industrial countries hold more than 60 % of the votes, cannot be underestimated when analyzing the interests that their policies systematically benefit in the area of agricultural trade.

In the face of policy coherence efforts pursued by financial and trade institutions, it is important that NGOs, networks and movements working on food security issues improve their understanding of the ways in which the policies of financial institutions intersect with rules of the multilateral trading system. The advocacy efforts aimed at benefiting poor farmers in the South will no doubt be more effective if they deal with trade and financial areas not as separate, but in an integrated fashion. For example, developing countries' debt problems are greatly exacerbated by the decline of commodity prices on which they are dependent for exports. Thus, the establishment of a commodity policy or agreement that improves the prices of such commodities is a goal that would benefit both groups working on farmers and on debt issues.

At the same time, an integrated approach to trade and finance creates the potential for new civil society alliances that capitalize on synergies among civil society groups. Both civil society groups seeking reforms to the trade system and those seeking reforms to the IFIs should be proactive in proposing an alternative agenda on coherence. Civil society groups should challenge the official policy coherence agenda by putting forward a vision of what genuine policy coherence built around the protection of food security and the rights of small farmers should look like.

Furthermore, such an integrated approach would allow the extension of alliances beyond groups focusing purely on food security issues. Policy coherence as a trend is having a negative impact on the right of access to essential services, like education and health, as well as the ability of states to regulate foreign investors and support domestic entrepreneurs. Thus, an improved understanding of the common ground shared with other constituencies affected provides a fertile ground for joining forces in research, campaign and advocacy efforts.

Civil Society Lags as Economic Gurus March on Mideast

As international financial institutions (IFIs) race to carry economic initiatives to the Middle East, groups that monitor the spread of corporate globalisation are at risk of falling behind, raising concerns that the region could end up an unmonitored corporate playfield. Although the newfound interest in the Middle East was kick-started by Washington's plan to transform Iraq into a free-market model for the rest of the region after its Mar. 20 invasion, several organisations were quick to follow suit. The United States now says it has managed to convince the G8 group of the most industrialised nations, whose ministers met this weekend in France to donate funds for the reconstruction of the country.

The donors also say they plan to meet to discuss the economic future of the U.S.-occupied country, which could be held in Tokyo in mid-June.

The Geneva-based World Economic Forum (WEF), known for its high-profile annual meetings in the alpine resort of Davos that attract the world's corporate and political luminaries, said last month it would convene an extraordinary meeting in Amman, Jordan under the theme "visions for a shared future", Jun. 21-23.

The move to the Middle East continued unabated last week when President George W. Bush launched a proposal for a so-called "free trade" agreement with countries of the Middle East that is likely to be modelled after controversial agreements like the North America Free Trade Agreement (NAFTA).

Among other things, that deal gives private firms the right to sue governments if their labour, health or environmental laws are seen to be barring the way to private-sector investment. The U.S.-Mideast agreement is expected to be finalised by 2013.

In Iraq, administration officials, many hailing from the private sector, are fast replacing the Saddam Hussein dictatorship, opening the oil-rich country further to corporate executives, U.S. bankers and goods.

Also, two of the most controversial institutions in the world economy, the World Bank and the International Monetary Fund (IMF) - often accused of force-feeding strict austerity programmes and export-oriented policies on poor nations, further dragging them into poverty - say they are readier than ever to work in the region.

The organisations are working now on assessing Iraq's debt for Middle Eastern creditors, and will follow that by considering the financial needs for the reconstruction of the country.

Their Middle East presence is bound to continue, as the IMF and the Bank are slated to hold their annual meeting this September in Dubai's Gulf City.

In another telling sign, the IMF devoted the entire issue of its quarterly 'Finance and Development' magazine to the Middle East, with articles brimming with advice on how the region's countries should dismantle their social protection systems and reduce their public sectors.

The organisations' officials, including Sena Eken, assistant director in the IMF's Middle East Department, said the volatile region should focus on "promotion policies", "payment methods", "management remuneration" and the like, "rather than 'hardware' such as clinics, schools, roads and wells".

That's not all. On Jun. 21-22, an informal "mini-ministerial" meeting of the World Trade Organization (WTO) will take place in the Egyptian Red Sea resort city of Sharm el-Sheikh to discuss opening markets to a range of international goods and services, as well as resolving differences over access to medicines for poorer countries.

The meeting, one of several in the run-up to the WTO ministerial conference Sep. 10-14 in Cancun, Mexico, will include trade gurus like U.S. Trade Representative Robert B. Zoellick and European Trade Commissioner Pascal Lamy.

"Obviously, the Middle East and the Muslim world are now the new tourist destinations for international financial institutions and their corporate culture," said Anuradha Mittal, co-director of the U.S.-based Institute for Food and Development Policy (Food First). "It's like an economic invasion after the military invasion," she added in an interview.

But despite corporate globalisation's evident new interest in the Middle East, think tanks and civil society groups that monitor the IFIs and other major players appear to be dragging their feet.

The U.S.-based Centre for Global Development, which calls itself one of the few independent think tanks devoted to following globalisation trends, features no expert on Middle East economics.

And while other reputable think tanks like the Brookings Institution and the Institute of International Economics (IIE) abound with experts and formal officials well grounded in security or the Arab-Israeli conflict, almost none specialise on the business side of the region or its involvement in corporate globalisation.

Civil society groups, which influence the work of the World Bank, the WTO and IMF, along with U.S and E.U. foreign trade policies in areas like Latin America, Africa and East Asia, have, by comparison, been far less outspoken on the Middle East. They too lack programme officers or watchdog activities on the work of oil corporations, corporate executives or the IFIs in the region. Prominent groups, like the Bank Information Center, and energetic activist organisers, like the 50 Years Is Enough network, also lack Middle East expertise and coverage.

This despite the fact the area was not far from the operations of those international economic players, even before the invasion of Iraq and the burst of interest in the area.

USAID has its biggest international offices and staff in Egypt, a country of 72 million people who have been suffering under the staggering neo-liberal economic reforms of the authoritarian regime of Hosni Mubarak. And Israel receives more foreign aid from Washington than any other nation - more than 3.5 billion dollars annually. Both think tanks and civil society groups cite funding and the fragility of civil society groups in the region for their failure to monitor attempts by the United States and other Western economic powers to drag the Middle East further into their orbit. "I think there is a weakness there of course," said Njoki Njehu of Washington-based 50 Years Is Enough. "It will still be a definite challenge in the future because of the limitations of civil society groups in the region and the nature of the (brutal) regimes there and how they are so unaccountable to civil society."

One new local group is The Anti-Globalisation Egyptian Group (AGEG), whose Arabic acronym means "burning fire". In April, Wael Khalil, an activist with the group, told IPS the WEF initiative would "play into our hands and not into their (WEF's) hands. They are creating yet another new point of mobilisation and resistance. Their efforts won't come to pass."

But with the IFIs already in the area, think tanks and civil society groups might want to consider their absence if they want to remain what they claim to be - global.

IMF, World Bank Join Forces with WTO

Attempts by global financial institutions to synchronize their policies on developing nations threaten to further entrench a one-sided approach to development, fuel instability, and widen the gap between the world's rich and poor, watchdogs of the institutions warned Monday.

The alarm comes only a day before two of the world's major wardens of the global economy, the Washington-based World Bank and International Monetary Fund (IMF) were to meet in Switzerland with the Geneva-based World Trade Organization (WTO) to develop a common approach to world economic policies called the "coherence agenda."

The meetings will be attended by senior officials of the increasingly controversial bodies, including IMF Managing Director Horst Koehler, WTO Director General Supachai Panitchpakdi, and World Bank President James Wolfensohn.

Prospects of the meeting, under the umbrella of the WTO General Council--the organization's highest level decisionmaking body in Geneva--sends shivers down the spine of critics of the international financial institutions (IFIs), who see their policies as counterproductive and in the service of a few rich nations and their sprawling corporations.

"This will limit the room for choices and policy space," said Aldo Caliari from the Washington-based Center of Concern, one of 40 groups that signed a petition opposing the meetings and warning of the possible consequences. "It's like being forced to shop from one shop--same policies and same goods."

The IFIs say their meeting will help strengthen the global multilateral trading system, which they consider an anchor of strength and stability in the world economy. Developing nations will benefit by getting increased market access for their products in rich developed countries, they add.

But analysts here say the record and the structure of the organizations, especially the two Bretton Woods Institutions, the IMF and the World Bank (named for the place in the U.S. state of New Hampshire where they were launched in 1944) bodes ill for developing nations. "When you understand how much power the industrial countries hold in the governance of the Bretton Woods institutions, you realise why the trade agenda supported by these institutions tends to be aligned with the negotiating interests of those same countries within the WTO," said Caliari. The voting structures of the IMF and World Bank are heavily biased towards rich countries. Their leaders, for instance, are chosen through processes open only to U.S. and European citizens.

The IMF and the Bank have for years been peddling trade liberalization, deregulation, privatization and budget austerity to developing countries, and the results, critics say, are disappointing. Feverish privatization urged by the Bank and the Fund, especially of public services like water and utilities, has smoothed the way for foreign corporations to supply these services and introduce commercial pricing systems, which have often led to higher rates for poor citizens, jeopardizing their access and pushing them further into poverty.

"Economies of developing countries have been characterized by slow and erratic growth, increased instability and rising income gaps," said the groups in their Monday statement. "With the WTO, such misguided and failed policy reforms are being progressively locked in through trade law backed by the threat of economic sanctions through its dispute settlement mechanism. Under the new distributions of roles to be discussed Tuesday, the IMF and the Bank would help ease the way for full liberalization of trade by offering "technical and financial support." The Washington-based organisations would "assist" developing nations to manage lower revenues because of reduced tariffs, withstand a period in which their trade preferences in industrialized nations are eliminated, secure funds to support increased trade and, finally, help create export- oriented economies.

The IMF and the Bank would also raise the profile of trade in borrowing countries' Poverty Reduction Strategy Papers (PRSP) and Country Assistance Strategies (CAS), documents developed with the support of the two lenders that function as borrowers' economic roadmaps.

In return, the IMF and World Bank will receive observer status in the trade negotiations committee, which handles individual negotiating issues at the WTO and its subsidiary bodies, coupled with a role at the WTO secretariat, a body often accused of bias on disputes between rich and poor countries.

Critics say these plans should cause even more concern. They say so-called "technical assistance" is really one way to force-feed the same policies on developing nations rather than give them the tools to develop independent views and, possibly, development options. "Technical assistance is being used as a political tool to win support for a 'development agenda' that is heavily disputed in the WTO," said Shefali Sharma from the Geneva office of the Institute for Agriculture and Trade Policy in a statement. "No amount of technical assistance in implementing policies that, in effect, handicap and shackle developing countries in the WTO, can improve gains towards development."

Cooperation between the three bodies is not new. The WTO director general often attends meetings of the IMFC--the assembly of the IMF and Bank governors--and of the development committee, the senior decisionmaking body of the institutions. Most recently, he attended the IMFC meeting in April 2003 and briefed finance ministers on the Doha trade negotiations and work program, according to WTO documents.

The IMF and the World Bank have also been paying greater attention to trade issues in the past few years, both in the course of their regular country work and research papers. Documents have been flooding out of the two organizations in support of "free" trade.

In 2002, they issued a joint staff paper on "Market Access for Developing Countries' Exports," which examined patterns and costs of restrictions and distortions on developing countries' exports.

Rich Nations Continue to Wield Power in Global Bodies

Officials of global organisations and rich nations rarely admit it but civil society groups and developing countries say the sad fact has not changed: multilateral bodies meant to help create a global community are in fact undemocratic.

From the World Trade Organization (WTO), the International Monetary Fund (IMF), the World Bank and the

United Nations, to Interpol and the World Health Organization (WHO), dozens of international agencies now work to regulate world trade, telecommunications, transportation, labour, business, health and the environment, among other issues.

In almost all of those bodies, poor and powerless nations, like Somalia and Afghanistan, are under-represented while the rich and powerful, like Britain and the United States, operate with almost unchecked authority and overwhelming power.

Some non-governmental organisations (NGOs) are impatient to see real change. "We talk about democratic and accountable organisations so we could live in a truly global community, where a country like the United States, instead of boasting of being a superpower, becomes a true part of the global community," says Anuradha Mittal, co-director of California-based Food First, a group that has called for the rule of law in global bodies. "We are talking about that multilateral system of checks and balances, when countries like Sudan and India, or countries like the United States, all adhere to the same principles."

That is unlikely under the current structures of those institutions. At the United Nations, the mother of all agencies and one of the most respected worldwide, the 15-member Security Council, the only international body with powers to declare war and peace, is a stark example of global inequality. The council is heavily weighted in favour of the five big powers - the United States, Britain, France, China and Russia - which all exercise veto power over its decisions.

Although the 191-member New York-based U.N. General Assembly works on the principle of one-country, one-vote, the Security Council is almost at the mercy of the five veto-wielding powers, except in those instances when they themselves disagree, as in the recent debate over using force in Iraq.

The democratic discrepancy also infests economic institutions. At the Washington-based International Monetary Fund (IMF) and World Bank, seats and votes are still allocated according to member countries' economic bulk, leaving poor nations defenceless before heavyweight nations like the United States and Japan. The Bank and the Fund each have 184 members, including developed and developing countries, and

24 board members representing countries or groups of nations. But while the 46 sub-Saharan African countries, for example, are represented by only two executive directors on the boards of the Bank and Fund, eight rich nations, including Germany, France, Britain and the United States, are represented by their own executive directors.

Directors from rich countries now control more than 60 per cent of the votes at the World Bank and IMF, while the U.S. administration has veto power over any extraordinary vote requiring a super-majority.

Even in institutions like the Geneva-based WTO, which theoretically operates under consensus and technically gives each member country veto power, practice is different. Some 28 of the WTO's 146 member nations do not even attend most of the organisation's meetings for the simple reason that they lack the resources to set up diplomatic missions in the expensive Swiss city of Geneva. But those countries still figure as part of the consensus when decisions are made.

And while the WTO system is set up so that all members participate in preliminary discussions and decision-making meetings, in practice negotiations are limited to select groups of countries, known as "green rooms", often hand picked to include the European Union, the United States, and Japan.

In several cases, the system "has operated against the interests of the developing countries", says Bhagirath Lal Das, India's former chief negotiator under the General Agreement on Tariffs and Trade (GATT).

The list of "unbalanced" institutions that are supposed to represent all parts of the world equally is lengthy, as noted by the anti-globalisation movement, which has vigorously raised the issues of transparency, democracy and accountability using colourful marches, street protests and public events.

Civil society groups have noted that attempts aimed at redressing such balances have been largely futile and often meet with strong resistance from the beneficiaries of the status quo. Over the last 10 years, a U.N. working group has been discussing proposals to restructure the Security Council with the aim of providing equitable representation to the world's developing nations, who comprise over two-thirds of the membership of the world body.

The proposals include veto power status to developing nations from Asia, Africa and Latin America. The veto contenders include India and Indonesia from Asia; Mexico, Argentina and Brazil from Latin America; and South Africa, Nigeria and Egypt from Africa.

But the working group has remained deadlocked and unable to devise a compromise formula to make the Council more representative of the United Nations. The deadlock has been caused both by opposition from Western powers to an enlarged Security Council and to the abolition of veto powers, and by divisions among developing nations as to which of them should sit on the restructured body. In April, a renewed drive to give developing countries more say in running the IMF and the World Bank, two agencies accused of drowning poor nations in poverty and debt, netted only lip service from rich nations and promises to keep the issue alive for future consideration.

At the WTO, despite pressure from civil society groups, Washington in December brushed aside criticism and exercised its power when it blocked a decision that could have backed developing countries' right to access low-cost medications. "This is exactly what we want to see go," said Mittal. "That this 'who has the gold, has the law' is a mentality that has to go. That mentality of the superpower has to go. Nobody should be above the law."

World Bank Supports Community-Driven Development in Bangladesh

The World Bank today approved a US$18.2 million credit for a project to help poor and vulnerable groups in Bangladesh increase their inclusion in and ownership of local development initiatives. The project will support the efforts of the Government of Bangladesh and non-governmental organizations, who are working to amplify the voice and support the ideas of those who are typically excluded from development decisions, in particular the poorest of the poor and women.

The credit will finance a Social Investment Program Project to be implemented by Bangladesh's Social Development

Foundation (SDF), a not-for-profit company, established by the Government in 2001, and comprising representatives from both civil society and the Government. The project work will be concentrated in two districts: Jamalpur and Gaibandha, which rank among the highest in poverty incidence in Bangladesh, in terms of both income and human development.

Over an initial four-year period, the project will help strengthen the SDF's capacity to deliver key messages and information about the project at the national level and to assist with community mobilization and local level planning. It will also assist the SDF in its efforts to analyze results from project implementation in order to subsequently scale up and institutionalize successful approaches to community-driven development. The project will also support institutional development at the local level to help create awareness and motivate poor people in rural areas to develop village organizations. It will support them in developing Community Action Plans (CAPs) which will help prioritize communities' needs for small-scale infrastructure and social assistance based on informed choices. The communities will be expected to show ownership by contributing at least 15 percent of the expenditures of approved infrastructure initiatives while the project will finance the remaining balance.

"The concept for this project originated in a remote area in Bangladesh where poor people talked about the non-income dimensions of poverty," said Wahida Huq, a World Bank Senior Operations Officer and Task Team Leader of the project. "They spoke about powerlessness, gender inequalities, poor local governance, and their exclusion from basic services, such as health and education, and from participation in development processes. The pilot project will encourage innovative approaches to address these aspects of poverty and particularly to reach out to nearly half a million poor and vulnerable people."

She added that the pilot project will also help strengthen local governance by empowering community organizations, promoting participatory planning processes, and creating functional spaces for participatory local governance.

The social assistance program will focus on typically excluded people and will support inclusion of disabled people in development processes, increasing awareness about health and nutrition issues, development of livelihood skills, programs to assist pregnant women, legal assistance for the poorest and most vulnerable groups, implementation of tribal development plans, and financial support for emergency relief to the victims of natural disasters. The project will also support private financing, on a pilot basis, of community utilities. It will test new approaches which will leverage participation and financing from various service providers of basic utilities, such as piped water supply and off-grid electricity, anywhere in the country where opportunities exist.

Overall, the project is aimed at helping the country develop an inclusive process which will identify demand and address social development needs in a manner which will contribute to improved local institutional development. It is designed to help demonstrate cost-effective and participatory means for implementing small-scale rural infrastructure and social assistance projects. It is also intended to help Bangladesh, at the national level, to identify emerging successful procedures and to replicate good practice throughout the country.

The no-interest credit from the International Development Association (IDA), the World Bank's concessional lending arm, is to be repaid with a 0.75 percent service charge over a period of 40 years after a 10 year grace period.

A Civil Discourse

Noting that globalization, civil society, and governance were prime topics at the World Economic Forum in Davos and the World Social Forum in Porto Alegre, Dr. Kumi Naidoo brought his views on three of the "biggest issues presently facing humanity" to Washington yesterday as part of the World Bank's Presidential Fellows Lecture series. Past lecturers have included United Nations Secretary General Koffi Annan, Nobel laureate Amartya Sen, novelist Chinewa Achebe, and former President of the European Commission Jacques Delors. Naidoo is Secretary General and CEO of CIVICUS, an international alliance of more than 600 networks and organizations in 110 countries working to strengthen civil society and participatory democracy worldwide. A social activist, Naidoo was a member of the anti-Apartheid movement and founded the South African NGO Coalition. Bank President Jim Wolfensohn said in his introductory remarks that "our institution has benefited over the years tremendously from interaction with civil society-not always comfortably and certainly very critically, but I think the criticism has helped us to modulate the way we do things."

In his lecture, Naidoo stressed the contradictions inherent in globalization-the benefits versus the costs, the emergence of transnational crises such as HIV/AIDS, and the trend towards strengthening multinational corporations and supranational institutions at the expense of local control.

"Important decisions affecting people's lives and well-being are made in non-transparent ways in supranational institutions that are not accountable to citizens and not accessible to citizen engagement," said Naidoo to illustrate the perception by many activists that democratic decision-making is on the decline. Citing recent surveys examining trust in political institutions, Naidoo explained that traditional notions of governance-including representative democracy-have broken down in the context of globalization and produced a "democracy deficit." Yet this decline in trust does not necessarily suggest a rise in apathy, as witnessed by the resurgence of civil society involvement in policy discussions such as those around debt relief.

"Given the shift of power from national to global levels, it has become a critical priority for civil society to be engaging at a global level, yet it is here that the democratic deficit is felt most strongly," remarked Naidoo in noting that this especially holds true for institutions such as the Bank and U.N.

Likewise, Naidoo views legitimacy as the primary challenge for civil society itself. In response to critics who argue that civil society groups only represent themselves, Naidoo notes that civil society organizations operate on the "perform or perish" principle, given that contributions are not guaranteed through taxation or membership contributions and that their performance will largely dictate future funding levels. Furthermore, codes of ethics and standards of excellence are being adopted by civil society at the national level in many countries.

Regarding openness to engagement with civil society, Naidoo said that the Bank has come far, but still has a long way to go. Asked what would be two things the Bank could do to improve its interaction with civil society, he said the Bank should incorporate gender equity at the meso-, macro-, and micro levels of its work, and adopt a rights-based approach to development that puts economic and social justice as the guiding principle in its operations.

Fellow activist in the anti-Apartheid movement and presently Managing Director of the World Bank, Mamphela Ramphele, closed the lecture by saying, "Your being willing to come and engage with us in such a thoughtfull way--on some of the real difficult questions that we all face--is an indicator that the direction the Bank has taken on engaging civil society is being reciprocated by the decision of civil society to engage the Bank."

Open Statement on Steps to Democratize the World Bank and IMF

NGOs circulated this statement discussing the structural inadequacies of the IMF/World Bank and ideas for reform. The final statement complete with signatories will be available on April 10, 2003 at www.brettonwoodsproject.org/topic/reform

Following the Monterrey conference on Financing for Development a number of official discussions are underway about changing the governance regime of international institutions. Civil society organisations and others have long pointed out that the World Bank and IMF wield enormous power over developing country governments, yet have severe shortcomings in their legitimacy and effectiveness. The undersigned organisations and individuals hereby put on record a statement of some of the key problems with World Bank and IMF governance and their demands for minimum steps to improve it.

1) Rebalancing Board Composition and Voting Power

The Executive Boards of the World Bank and IMF do not give all countries an equal opportunity to represent themselves. Seats and votes are allocated to countries according to their economic size or historical significance. The 46 Sub-Saharan African countries have just 2 Executive Directors on the Bank and Fund Boards to represent them all, while 8 countries have a single Executive Director each. Rich country Executive Directors currently control over 60 per cent of the votes at the World Bank and IMF. The US government has a veto on decisions requiring a super-majority. The dominance of the richer countries remains the case despite the increasing levels of income to the Bank and Fund from borrowing country loan repayments. We demand that:

a. There be a reallocation of Board seats and votes to ensure that all member countries are fairly able to represent themselves and that creditor and borrower countries have an equal allocation of votes;
b. There be no more than 10 countries per constituency, and rotation of Board members among different countries in the constituency;
c. No one country should have a veto on any decisions.

2) Making Governing Bodies Transparent

The World Bank and IMF have made progress in recent years in the transparency of some of their documentation. This has not, however, extended to the Boards of the institutions. We believe that, as these institutions make decisions which affect the welfare of people across the world, citizens have a right to know what positions their representatives are taking within their governing structures.

We demand that:

a. The agenda, transcripts, summaries and minutes of World Bank and IMF Board meetings be published so that parliamentarians, civil society groups, academics and others can see who is taking what positions at these important institutions. Exceptions to this principle should be narrowly drawn and based on a clear indication of harm that would result from disclosure of specific information.
b. Board members should express their position with formal votes rather than informal indications of position.

3) Opening Leadership Selection

The leaders of the World Bank and IMF play an important role in defining the directions of their institutions, chairing their boards and representing them publicly. They are currently selected in a non-transparent process which limits applications on the grounds of nationality. The European countries nominate the IMF Managing Director while the USA nominates the World Bank President and the IMF Deputy Director. This is unacceptable. The minor steps agreed recently to improve the selection processes have not gone nearly far enough.

We demand:

a. the introduction of a transparent process for selecting the heads of both organizations. This should involve all member countries and significant stakeholder groupings and assess candidates on merit, regardless of their nationality. In fact geographical diversity in top positions should be actively encouraged.

4) Reversing Mission Creep

The World Bank and the IMF have taken on so many roles that they have branched out to cover areas and issues way beyond their mandate and competence. By encroaching on the mandates of other multilateral institutions. By doing so they have increasingly deprived UN specialized agencies and bodies with expertise in particular fields of the freedom to propose effective policies. Indirectly this has also undermined the participation of developing countries in global policy-making and agenda-setting.

Choosing a Better World

These past two years have not been easy ones for the world. Too soon after we toasted a new millennium full of hope, we have seen terrorism, economic recession and disrespect for human rights put fear and uncertainty in the hearts of people in rich and poor countries alike. Continuing conflicts, droughts and floods, collapsing markets and deepening poverty have taken a heavy human toll, particularly in Asia, Africa and Latin America. How to make a better world possible for all is what civil society representatives from around the globe will be debating this week at the third World Social Forum (WSF) in Porto Alegre, Brazil. And these are the same challenges that we are grappling with - and yes, debating - at the World Bank.

Whether in Porto Alegre, Bamako or Washington DC, such debates are important. Certainly no one in civil society nor in the World Bank can claim to have all the answers to these enormous challenges.

Yet what I believe is promising is the evidence of a growing consensus among those of us working in international agencies, and leaders in government, business and civil society, that we can begin to solve these problems only if we forge a new development path linking economic growth to social and environmental responsibility. Without social equity, economic growth cannot be sustainable. Without enlarging the real opportunities available to all citizens, the markets will work only for the elites. This means providing everyone with access to education, health care, decent work and - as the new Brazilian president Lula has pointed out - with at least three meals a day. The events of September 11, 2001, helped drive home the message to people everywhere that there are not two worlds - rich and poor. There is only one. We are linked by finance, trade, migration, communications, environment, communicable diseases, crime, drugs and certainly by terror.

Today, more and more people agree that poverty anywhere is poverty everywhere. Our collective demand is for a global system based on equity, human rights and social justice. Our collective quest for a more equal world is also the quest for long-term peace and security.

This growing consensus is playing out in the emergence of a global partnership for poverty reduction. At the recent United Nations conferences in Monterrey and Johannesburg, and at the launch of the Doha round of World Trade Organization (WTO) negotiations, developed countries pledged to help developing countries by strengthening capacity, increasing overseas development assistance, opening markets to trade and reducing agricultural subsidies.

In turn, developing countries pledged to institute sound economic management policies and promote good governance.

Rich and poor countries alike have reaffirmed their commitments to achieving the Millennium Development Goals. At the World Bank, we have now reoriented our strategy to help developing countries meet the Goals - including halving poverty, ensuring basic education and health for all, promoting gender equality and protecting the environment - and pressing the richest countries to meet their obligations under the Goals to help the poor.

Over the next 50 years, we will likely see world population grow from 6 billion to 9 billion, with almost 95 percent of that increase going to the developing world. Food needs will double, annual output of carbon dioxide will triple, and for the first time more people will live in cities than in rural areas, placing an enormous strain on the social fabric, on infrastructure and on the environment. If we are to meet our common goal of reducing poverty, we estimate that we will need an average annual growth rate of the world economy around 3.5 percent - giving us, perhaps, a US$140 trillion world economy by 2050. But it must be responsible growth - growth that takes full account of social and environmental concerns.

Responsible growth means greater transparency so that publics can track government policy. People rightly demand to know what their governments are doing, to be consulted and to have a say in their own destinies. This is where civil society, at the local, regional, and global levels, can play a critical role. Civil society groups are helping give voice to the voiceless, delivering essential services and building local capacity, especially in regions where government presence may be weak or because they come from poor communities themselves.

For too many years, the World Bank, like many others, ignored civil society. Over the last decade we have been actively engaging civil society organizations throughout the world in policy dialogue and in the projects we finance. There is no doubt in my mind that we have civil society advocacy to thank for progress on debt relief and on the environment, and for the better implementation of Bank projects. And the role of civil society groups at the local level and on the world stage will continue to grow. My colleagues and I have followed the debates which have occurred during the WSF during the past two years, and we will discuss with interest ideas and proposals which emerge this year. But while debate remains needed, it is not enough. We must also act. We must harness all available resources - from the public and private sectors, international agencies and local communities - in implementing innovative solutions that will reduce poverty.

The future is in our hands, we are not hapless bystanders. We can influence whether we have a planet of peace, social justice, equity, and growth or a planet of unbridgeable differences between peoples, a planet of wasted physical resources, of corruption and terror. We can create a renaissance of values and social justice, freedom from want and fear. We will not agree on every issue, but we can agree that a better, and more humane, world is possible - and we can work much more closely together to make it a reality.

The World Bank Defends Its Record on Human Rights

Senior officials from the World Bank and NGO representatives use the Human Rights Forum to discuss the outlines of a "rights based approach" to poverty lending by the World Bank.

Two senior officials from the World Bank used a November 24 meeting of the Georgetown Human Rights Forum to defend the Bank's human rights record against NGO criticism, and asked for practical advice on what is meant by a "rights-based approach to development."

In a wide-ranging two-hour debate, which drew an audience of 300, Ian Johnson, Senior Vice President for the Environmentally and Socially Sustainable Development Network at the World Bank, insisted that the Bank has made a series of major changes which have enabled the Bank to become a central player in promoting the rights of the poor.

Mr. Johnson also said that the Bank's operations evaluation unit might consider undertaking human rights assessments of Bank projects, and that the Bank could provide support for the new UN Convention on the rights of migrant workers as part of its work on "human movement."

But Mr. Johnson also explained that promoters of human rights with the Bank have difficulty "selling" rights to their colleagues in operational departments, and to the Bank's 24-member Executive Board. He himself had looked at the policies of agencies like the UNDP and UNICEF, which have adopted a "rights-based approach," and found little practical difference in their operational programs from one day to the next.

Mr. Johnson heads an internal World Bank task force on human rights which is due to report to the Bank president, James Wolfensohn, so his views were listened to with considerable attention. Also appearing on the panel was, Judith Edstrom, Sector Manager for Social Development at the Bank and another member of the task force.

The NGO community was represented by Irungu Houghton, US Program Coordinator for ActionAid USA; and Mike Jendrzejczyk, Washington Director of the Asia Division for Human Rights Watch. Both gave practical examples of how the Bank could integrate human rights into its programs - not least by intervening on behalf of NGOs who work on key Bank programs, such as HIV/AIDS and the internet.

They also argued that an integrated policy on human rights would allow the Bank to play a "unique role" at the nexus of poverty and development, and that it had a responsibility not to lend to governments which violate their obligations under international human rights treaties.

The World Bank lends about $20 billion annually, and has immense power to shape the economies of smaller countries. Human rights NGOs have long complained that many Bank's projects and programs (particularly structural adjustment and large infrastructural loans) harm human rights, and urged the Bank to integrate human rights more into its lending. The Bank's standard response has been that formally embracing human rights would violate its articles of agreement, which forbid political interference in the domestic affairs of member governments.

At the same time they maintain that many Bank loans, on education and health, make it possible to realize social and economic rights. Mr. Johnson told the audience that the Bank's articles must be respected, as with any institution, but that they were being less "rigidly" interpreted than in previous years. He also noted a series of major changes at the Bank, which have allowed it to become an important partner in the fight against human rights:

- o Defining poverty: The Bank's definition of poverty has evolved from per capita income to social exclusion and disenfranchisement, and even more broadly to "the extent to which people are fragile or vulnerable within the society." This makes it easier to define poverty in terms of human rights violations.
- o Safeguard policies: The Bank has drawn up several policies aimed at cushioning those who are affected by Bank programs (i.e. indigenous peoples). These, said Mr. Johnson, are more stringent than any other comparable institution including credit export banks.
- o The Bank has established a 3-person independent inspection panel (one of whom is a Georgetown professor) which hears complaints by individuals who have been adversely affected by Bank projects. The panel has heard 27 cases and occasionally forced the Bank to change direction.
- o Mr. Johnson said he favored economic growth, but also conceded that economic inequality is growing. This, he said, was outside the Bank's control. He cited contributing factors like the "scandalous" OECD agricultural subsidies, which currently amount to about a billion dollars a day - equal to the combined GDP of Sub-Saharan Africa.
- o Social and economic rights: The constraint on the Bank's ability to fund social programs, and so realize social rights such as the right to health, is not money or staff. In fact, the number of Bank officials working on health has grown quickly to 150. The real constraint is "demand" for such programs in the borrowing countries. This needs more promotion by the Bank.
- o The Bank has decentralized its operations and appointed an NGO liaison officer in all of its country offices. This brings it more into contact with community needs and allows it to work directly with civil society.

- The Bank is increasingly supportive of rule of law programs - to the point where the Bank's Legal Department even provides technical assistance in areas like domestic abuse.
- The Bank has intervened discreetly on behalf of NGO leaders, and human rights defenders, who have been attacked or jailed by governments - where it feels this will likely succeed.

While commending the Bank for publicly engaging in the human rights debate - something that would have been unthinkable ten years ago - both NGO speakers said the Bank could do much more. Mr. Houghton said that the Bank had forced his own government, Kenya, to put the repayment of its debts before the rights of Kenyan citizens - and that this was even enshrined in the constitution. By promoting the downsizing of government and structural adjustment, he said, the Bank undercuts the rights of the poor and creates greater vulnerability.

According to one study by ActionAid, this had led to the lifting of price controls and the ending of food subsidies during a famine in Mali. The result was that hoarders held back food and "made a killing" on the market, while Malians actually died from starvation.

Mr. Jendrzejczyk, from Human Rights Watch, gave several practical examples of a "rights-based" approach. He commended the Bank for supporting rule of law programs, but urged it go further. In one example, he said, China was establishing legal aid centers in impoverished rural areas. The Bank should provide these centers with legal expertise, and make them better able to work on abuses such as the trafficking of women, which plague this "huge country in transition."

Mr. Jendrzejczyk also complained that the Bank's commitment to civil society was often "pro forma," and urged the Bank to intervene more actively on behalf of human rights defenders and NGOs which support for key Bank programs. For example, the Bank was investing heavily in the internet and committed to bridging the "digital divide." Yet it had failed to intervene when China arrested a computer programmer named Houng Qi who set up the first human rights website in China.

The Bank had also declined to press the Indian government to provide protection for victims of HIV/AIDS discrimination in India - even though ending discrimination could be key to the success of a massive Bank program to combat HIV/AIDS.

Both Mr. Houghton and Mr. Jendrzejczyk argued that the Bank could do itself a favor by integrating human rights more into its lending. Mr. Houghton said this would provide the Bank with a new "paradigm" for its lending, and also position the agency to play a unique role at the nexus between both branches of rights (civil/political and social/economic) and development. It would also ensure that the Bank does not get "left behind" by other agencies in the international system.

Once again, the real problem for Mr. Johnson was practical - how to get colleagues, borrowing governments and the Bank's Board to buy into such an approach. Unlike other UN agencies of bilateral aid agencies, he said, the Bank does not have a diplomatic arm which allows it to challenge governments, and that governments would not accept any challenge to their sovereignty. "It won't wash."

If the Bank wants to advance such arguments, said Mr. Johnson, it will need to use other allies in the international system with a more formal mandate for human rights. Even consultations with civil society had been difficult, he said. The Bank had organized 32 consultations with 1,000 indigenous representatives during the redrafting of a new Bank policy on indigenous peoples. Still, the indigenous felt dissatisfied and under-represented. This, he said, pointed to the need for new institutions better able to handle such consultations, or a radically new approach to consultations.

Mr. Johnson did, however, suggest that the Bank' Operations Evaluation Department might be an appropriate forum for conducting human rights assessments of Bank programs and projects. This has long been a demand of human rights organizations. One questioner, from Friends of the Earth (USA), said assessments would allow for much better engagement by civil society in the borrowing countries and also a more public appreciation of the trade-offs involved when the Bank makes a loan. Mr. Johnson did not rule this out, although he said it would have to be acceptable to the Bank's Executive Board. "Would it (the Board) be interested? I don't know. I just don't know."

Giving the Public a Voice in the Protection of the Global Environment: Avenues for Participation by NGOs in Dispute Resolution at the European Court of Justice and World Trade Organization

Traditionally, sovereign states have been the sole legitimate actors in the field of international relations. States alone have negotiated multilateral agreements, accepted binding international commitments, and enforced international obligations. However, in an increasingly globalized society, the traditional concept of international law as the "law of nations" no longer reflects the realities of international society. Modern international society includes a range of non-state actors that are increasingly demanding a voice in international organizations and [*48] processes.

Non-governmental organizations (NGOs) are among the most dynamic and influential groups of non-state actors in the international legal field. In its broadest sense, the term "NGO" covers a wide variety of groups and entities, such as members of the scientific community, non-profit groups and associations, business entities, legal organizations, members of the academic community, and individuals. This paper uses the term "NGO" to mean non-profit environmental groups and associations that derive their legitimacy in the international arena, at least in principle, from their close link with general public constituencies. Even within this subdivision of NGOs, there is a wide range of groups - grassroots community organizations, national environmental groups, and international associations like Greenpeace - with a diversity of funding, expertise, organizational capacity, and representation.

In the context of the global environment, where issues often transcend national boundaries, NGOs are arguably more effective guardians of the public interest in environmental protection than States preoccupied by national self-interest. In recognition of NGOs' contribution to environmental protection and the importance of public participation in resolving environmental issues, states have been increasingly willing to allow NGO participation in multilateral negotiations on environmental issues and in the formulation of international environmental policy. Nevertheless, the international community has been reluctant to grant NGOs the power to intervenc in suits to enforce states' international environmental obligations. However, recent developments in two international fora - the European Court of Justice (ECJ) and the dispute resolution process of the World Trade Organization (WTO) - suggest new avenues for NGO participation in environmental dispute settlement. These developments may serve as precedent for greater public involvement in other international tribunals deciding environmental cases.

Critics have suggested that the lack of public participation in the ECJ and WTO decision-making processes has undermined the effectiveness of their respective environmental programs. In the case of the ECJ, the inability of concerned individuals and organizations to compel the European Community (interchangeably referred to as Community or EC) institutions to comply with Community environmental law is alleged to contribute to a "democratic deficit" within the European Union (EU). Similarly, the closed and exclusive dispute resolution process of the WTO is said to undermine its legitimacy to rule on the legality of environmental policies with trade effects.

Part II of this article examines the existing opportunities for NGOs to compel Community institutions to comply with Community environmental law. It then assesses possibilities for enhanced NGO involvement under the new European Convention on Access to Information, Public Participation in Decision-Making and Access to Justice in Environmental Matters. Part III examines the WTO dispute settlement process and discusses potential new avenues for NGO participation available under a recent ruling of the WTO's Appellate Body. Finally, Part IV of the article discusses whether NGO participation in the decision-making processes of the ECJ, the WTO, and other international tribunals affords the public an effective voice in international environmental decision-making.

NGO Participation in Disputes Before the European Court of Justice

A. Opportunities for NGO Participation in the ECJ Under the Present Legal Regime: Interpretation of Article 173 in the Greenpeace Case

In contrast to many tribunals in the supranational legal system, the ECJ already allows significant NGO participation. NGOs may notify the European Commission when Member States allegedly breach Community environmental laws and lobby the Commission or a Member State to bring the matter before the ECJ. Alternatively, NGOs may, where permitted by national rules of standing, bring legal proceedings in Member States' domestic courts based upon causes of action created by Community environmental law. NGOs have also used the "preliminary reference procedure" to obtain ECJ rulings on questions of Community environmental law raised in national courts. However, the ability of NGOs to initiate proceedings in the ECJ to contest the legality of the actions of Community institutions under Community law is strictly limited by article 173 of the Treaty Establishing the European Community, which provides that "any natural or legal person," which would include an NGO, may only institute proceedings directly against a Community institution if the "person" is the addressee of the institution's decision or the decision is of "direct and individual concern" to the person. Thus, in order for an environmental NGO to take direct action against a Community institution's decision, it must be able to demonstrate that it is directly and individually affected by the act in question.

In a series of cases involving economic issues, the ECJ held that persons were "individually" concerned by a decision if it "affects them by reason of certain attributes which are peculiar to them or by reason of circumstances in which they are differentiated from all other persons and by virtue of these factors distinguishes them individually just as in the case of the person addressed." ECJ jurisprudence thus requires the identification of a "closed class" of affected individuals in order to invoke the criterion of "direct and individual concern."

In Greenpeace International & Ors v. Commission of the European Communities, a number of environmental NGOs and other concerned individuals challenged a European Commission decision to disburse approximately 12 million European Currency Units to Spain for the construction of two power stations in the Canary Islands. The applicants contended that the disbursement violated the Commission's obligation to protect the environment because it had failed to ensure that a prior environmental impact assessment was conducted in accordance with Council Directive 85/337/EEC. The Commission contended that the applicants had failed to establish standing to challenge the decision. The Court of First Instance upheld the Commission's decision, relying on the settled case law establishing the criteria of "direct and individual concern." The applicants appealed the decision to the ECJ.

The appellants argued that the nature and character of the environmental interests affected by the Commission's decision required a different approach to article 173 standing than that relied upon in previous cases dealing with economic interests and rights. The appellants contended that transposition .. "closed class" requirement to the environmental context would create "a legal vacuum in ensuring compliance with Community environmental legislation, since in this area the interests are, by their very nature, common and shared, and the rights relating to those interests are liable to be held by a potentially large number of individuals so that there could never be a closed class of applicants...." In the appellants' view, this void could not be filled by the possibility of bringing proceedings before national courts, because such proceedings challenge only a Member State's failure to comply with Community law and not the lawfulness of Community action under Community law. The appellants relied on the broader standing requirements in some Member States, the case law of the ECJ, the declarations of Community institutions and Member States on environmental matters, and a range of international environmental instruments to support a broader reading of article 173's standing requirements in environmental cases. In particular, the appellants argued that environmental associations may establish standing where "their primary objective is environmental protection and they can demonstrate a specific interest in the question at issue."

The ECJ rejected the appellants' argument, holding that the Court of First Instance's interpretation of article 173 was consistent with the ECJ's case law. The Court also found that national court proceedings commenced by a number of the appellants - although concerning different subject matter than the proceedings in the Court of First Instance - were based on the same rights afforded to individuals by Directive 85/337. The Court believed that the appellants' rights would be adequately protected by the national courts, because the national courts could refer questions of EC law to the ECJ for interpretive rulings if required.

The Greenpeace case highlights the difficulties environmental NGOs face in attempting to mount a direct challenge to Community action allegedly taken in contravention of Community environmental law. The "closed class" criterion is difficult, if not impossible, to satisfy in the context of environmental rights, which are inherently shared by the community at large. Moreover, environmental associations are not recognized as having any special competence to bring enforcement proceedings, despite their particular interest in environmental protection. By denying the general public a right to proceed directly against Community institutions allegedly violating Community law, the ECJ has arguably undermined the ability of EC environmental laws to achieve their articulated goals.

Impact of the Aarhus Convention on NGO Standing in the European Community

The Convention on Access to Information, Public Participation in Decision-Making and Access to Justice in Environmental Matters (Aarhus Convention) was concluded under the auspices of the United Nations Economic Commission for Europe (UNECE) at its fourth "Environment for Europe" Convention in Aarhus, Denmark in June 1998. All the members of the European Union, as well as the European Community itself are signatories to the Convention. The Convention will come into force nineteen days after receipt of the sixteenth ratification. The Convention is one of the first binding international instruments to recognize "the right of every person of present and future generations to live in an environment adequate to his or health and well-being." The right is guaranteed by three types of procedural rights that each Party undertakes to provide:

(1) access to information;

(2) public participation in decision-making; and

(3) access to justice in environmental matters.

The Convention clearly imposes obligations on both States and regional economic integration organizations, like the European Community, that ratify it. Given the inclusion of Community institutions within the scope of the Convention, the question arises whether the right of access to justice, which the European Community will be obligated to guarantee if it proceeds with ratification, will overcome the standing limitations imposed upon NGOs by the Greenpeace case.

Article 9 of the Aarhus Convention provides for access to justice in environmental matters. The article requires Parties to ensure access to justice in three circumstances:

(1) Parties must ensure access to a review procedure before a court or another independent and impartial body established by law for any person who considers that his or her information request has been ignored, wrongfully refused, inadequately answered, or otherwise not dealt with in accordance with the Convention's access to information provision under article 4;

(2) Parties must ensure access to a review procedure before a court or another independent and impartial body established by law for "members of the public concerned" to challenge "the substantive and procedural legality of any decision, act or omission subject to the provisions of article 6" (dealing with public participation in decision-making), and "where [review is] so provided for under national law ... of other relevant provisions of this Convention"; and

(3) Parties must ensure access to administrative or judicial procedures for "members of the public ... to [*56] challenge acts and omissions by private persons and public authorities which contravene provisions of its national law relating to the environment."

Although article 9 specifically refers to rights of access to justice within the framework of "national legislation" or to challenge acts allegedly in contravention of "national law," these rights may also provide a remedy against improper actions of the European Community. The obligations of the Aarhus Convention fall on each Party without distinction. Moreover, the definition of "public authorities" is expressly extended to the institutions of regional economic integration organizations who become Parties to the Convention. As discussed above, the European Community will become a party to the Convention upon ratification. Thus, there is a strong argument that the references to "national law" must be construed as extending to Community laws where the "Party" or "public authority" at issue is the European Community or one of its institutions. The provisions of paragraphs (2) and (3) of article 9 offer the greatest potential for NGOs seeking to bring enforcement actions against Community institutions.

Public Participation Remedy Under Article 9(2)

Article 9(2) of the Aarhus Convention obligates the Parties to provide access to justice to members of the public having either a "sufficient interest" in a matter or "maintaining impairment of a right." Parties must determine whether an applicant has sufficient interest or maintains an impairment of a right in accordance with the requirements of national law and consistent "with the objective of giving the public concerned wide access to justice within the scope of the Convention." Many environmental NGOs will meet the definition of "the public concerned" in article 2(5) of the Convention. Moreover, NGOs may also have rights capable of being impaired for the purposes of invoking article 9(2).

Whether the language of article 9(2) creates an obligation to provide a remedy to NGOs in matters involving activities subject to article 6 remains in question. The confusion arises because article 9(2) obligates the Parties to allow citizens to "challenge the substantive and procedural legality of any decision, act or omission subject to the provisions of article 6." Article 6 applies to "decisions on whether to permit proposed activities listed in annex I," as well as other decisions, not listed, which have a significant effect on the environment, where a Party determines that such activity is subject to the provisions of the article. Article 6 goes on to specify a number of procedural requirements to ensure that members of the public are able to participate in decisions within its ambit. If article 9(2) only creates an obligation to provide a remedy where a Party fails to make provision for public participation in accordance with article 6, the reference to challenging the "substantive ... legality of any decision" would be superfluous, since the requirements of article 6 are procedural in nature and do not necessitate the making of a decision by a public authority, but only the taking of some action. Instead, the reference to challenging the substantive legality of decisions "subject to the provisions of article 6" suggests that the remedy allows challenges to the decisions of public authorities that permit annex I activities or other included activities with a significant effect on the environment. Activities encompassed by annex I include power stations and other major installations and projects which might have harmful environmental effects. However, the decisions encompassed by article 6 (and hence potentially challengeable under article 9(2)) are only those decisions on whether to permit the proposed activity. Generally, permitting decisions will be within the jurisdiction of the member States rather than Community institutions. Therefore, a decision concerning funding to support the construction of power stations, such as that in the Greenpeace case, would most likely not be considered to be a decision "on whether to permit" the activity.

Challenges to Contravention of Environmental Laws under Article 9(3)

Potentially the most far-reaching of the Aarhus Convention's access to justice provisions is that contained in article 9(3). Access to justice for members of the public to enforce environmental laws was a hotly debated issue in the negotiations leading up to the Aarhus Conference. The result of this debate is reflected in the terms of article 9(3), which provides:

In addition and without prejudice to the review procedures referred to in [articles 9(1) and (2)] above, each Party shall ensure that, where they meet the criteria, if any, laid down in its national law, members of the public have access to administrative or judicial procedures to challenge acts and omissions by private persons and public authorities which contravene provisions of its national law relating to the environment.

As members of the "public," NGOs are entitled to challenge the actions of public authorities that contravene environmental laws. Prospective challengers, however, must "meet the criteria, if any, laid down in [a Party's] national law." In the EU context, where NGOs seek to challenge the actions of Community institutions that allegedly contravene provisions of Community environmental laws, these criteria would seem to include the article 173 requirements of "direct and individual concern." Rather than preserving the status quo, however, the Aarhus Convention, if ratified by the European Community, may provide a basis for the ECJ to reconsider its application of the "direct and individual concern" criterion in environmental cases.

The European Commission actively participated in the negotiations leading to the conclusion of the Convention in Aarhus. In its declaration upon signature of the Convention, the European Community expressed its full support for the Convention's objectives: "considering that the European Community itself is being actively involved in the protection of the environment through a comprehensive and evolving set of legislation" it is important "not only to sign up to the Convention at Community level but also to cover its own institutions, alongside national public authorities." The Community declared that "the Community institutions will apply the Convention within the framework of their existing and future rules on access to documents and other relevant rules of Community law in the field of the environment." At the first Meeting of the Parties, held in Chisinau, Moldova in April 1999, the European Commission informed the participants of the Community's intent to ratify the Convention.

If the European Community proceeds to ratify the Aarhus Convention, it will formally recognize the right of every person in the Community, including both present and future generations, to live in an environment adequate to ensure his or her health and well-being. The preamble to the Convention links this right to access to justice in environmental matters, stressing that "effective judicial mechanisms should be accessible to the public, including organizations, so that its legitimate interests are protected and the law is enforced." The preambular language is buttressed by reference to international environmental instruments recognizing both the right to live in an environment permitting dignity and well-being, and the importance of public participation in environmental issues.

Thus, the Convention expressly recognizes that the right to live in an environment adequate to health and well-being depends upon access to procedures to vindicate that right. If citizens are to take advantage of this right, at a minimum, they should have the ability to enforce environmental laws promulgated by all levels of government. Since the right is conferred on "any person," including one of a future generation, imposition of a "closed class" requirement would prevent individuals and public organizations from challenging European Community actions that infringe upon the shared right through failure to comply with the provisions of Community environmental law. The Community's acceptance of the Convention's broad right to environmental health, together with its recognition that access to judicial procedures is necessary to exercise that environmental right, makes a strong case for the ECJ to reconsider its use of the "direct and individual concern" standing criteria in environmental matters. If the ECJ fails to broaden the standing requirements of article 167, then NGOs could vindicate the environmental right declared by the Aarhus Convention when that right is threatened by the actions of Member States, but not when it is threatened by the failure of a Community institution to comply with Community law. Such an incongruous result is inconsistent with the obligations placed upon all Parties to the Aarhus Convention.

Opportunities for NGO Participation in the World Trade Organization

The WTO Dispute Settlement Process

Until recently, the dispute settlement process of the WTO's General Agreement on Tariffs and Trade (GATT) was relatively impenetrable for NGOs. Under the dispute settlement provisions of the 1994 General Agreement on Tariffs and Trade, Government Members have the sole right to initiate complaints and intervene in proceedings. Panels and the Appellate Body are obliged to consider only the submissions of governmental parties or interveners, and there is no obligation for governments to release their full submissions to the public. Hearings are conducted out of public view, and only parties to a suit and governmental interveners have the right to make oral submissions to a panel.

This restrained, exclusive process serves the GATT well when dealing with technical issues concerning tariffs because it allows panels to render timely and diplomatic solutions. However, with the successful reduction or elimination of most explicit tariffs on international trade, GATT institutions are increasingly focused on the Member Governments domestic policies, including environmental laws, that allegedly create barriers to free trade. Recent high profile trade and environment disputes, such as Tuna/Dolphin, Shrimp/Turtle, and Beef Hormones, as well as the looming EU-U.S. dispute regarding trade in genetically modified organisms, expose the lack of transparency and the perceived democratic deficit in the GATT/WTO dispute resolution process.

Corresponding with the increase in the number of trade and environment disputes coming before the GATT/WTO, the recent Uruguay Round amendments to the GATT give greater weight to panel and AB decisions. For example, GATT rules formerly required that panel decisions be adopted by a consensus of the GATT Council in order to bind the parties. The new rules of the Dispute Settlement Understanding (DSU) make panel and AB decisions binding unless the Dispute Settlement Body (DSB) decides by consensus (including the vote of the successful party) not to adopt the report. As a practical matter, the rule change makes panel and AB rulings dispositive in every case. The new rule empowers panel "judges of international trade" to rule that governments must amend or repeal trade-restrictive domestic laws or risk the imposition of trade sanctions.

Environmental NGOs have long argued for better access to the WTO dispute settlement process to enable them to voice their concerns regarding conflicts between environmental policy and trade liberalization norms. Two main arguments are advanced to support greater NGO participation in the WTO dispute settlement process. First, allowing NGOs with environmental expertise to provide factual material and legal arguments to panels is likely to lead to better-informed decisions from panels dealing with trade and environment questions. Second, NGO participation will enhance the legitimacy of the WTO by allowing the public to have a voice in the consideration of environmental policies with trade impacts. The international community's growing use of the WTO as a forum for deciding environmental disputes, coupled with the WTO's influence on domestic environmental policy, have resulted in intensified NGO appeals for participation in the WTO dispute settlement process. The AB's recent ruling in the Shrimp/Turtle dispute suggests that a new avenue for participation by NGOs may indeed be on the horizon.

New Avenues for NGO Participation in the WTO

The Appellate Body Ruling in the Shrimp/Turtle Dispute

In Shrimp/Turtle, a number of developing countries challenged a US regulation that prohibited shrimp imports from countries that failed to require turtle excluder devices (TEDs) on shrimp harvesting nets. Following the wake of the furor over the Tuna/Dolphin disputes, the environmental NGO community was intensely interested in the dispute because of its significance to the ongoing development of international environmental law. Accordingly, two groups of environmental NGOs submitted briefs directly to both the appointed Panel and the parties to the dispute. The World Wide Fund for Nature submitted one brief, while the Center for Marine Conservation and the Center for International Environmental Law jointly submitted another.

The U.S. urged the Panel to avail itself of any relevant information in the two documents. In contrast, the complainant states requested that the Panel not consider the briefs in its deliberation of the dispute. The Panel noted that article 13 of the DSU granted it the power to seek and select the sources of information to be used in making its decisions. The Panel held that it could not accept the NGO briefs because accepting non-solicited information would be incompatible with article 13 of the DSU. Nevertheless, the Panel permitted the parties to incorporate the NGO briefs, or parts of the documents, in their own submissions. The U.S. took advantage of this opportunity by designating Section III of the Center for Marine Conservation and the Center for International Environmental Law brief as an annex to its second submission to the Panel.

On appeal to the AB, the U.S. challenged the Panel's interpretation of article 13, arguing that nothing in the DSU prevented the Panel from considering unsolicited briefs. The AB first examined the question in terms of the legal rights of NGOs to have their submissions considered by a panel. The AB stressed that the WTO dispute settlement process is limited to the Members of the WTO. Thus, only parties to a dispute or governmental interveners have a legal right to have their submissions considered by a panel. Accordingly, a panel is legally obligated to consider only the submissions made by the parties and governmental interveners. However, the absence of a legal obligation to consider the NGO submissions did not dispose of the matter.

The AB next examined the scope of a panel's authority to review the NGO briefs under the DSU. The AB noted the comprehensive nature of a panel's authority under article 13 of the DSU to seek information and technical advice from "any individual or body" considered appropriate, or from "any relevant source." Because of the panel's comprehensive authority, the AB held that panels have broad discretion to:

- Accept or reject, or make some other appropriate disposition of information or advice sought and received;
- Determine the need for the information and advice in a specific case;
- Ascertain the acceptability and relevancy of information or advice received; and
- Decide the weight, if any, to be ascribed to the information or advice.

The AB further noted that article 12.1 of the DSU authorized panels "in effect to develop their own Working

Procedures, after consultation with the parties to the dispute." The AB emphasized that panel procedures should allow sufficient flexibility so as to ensure high-quality panel reports while not unduly delaying the panel process. According to the AB, articles 12 and 13 of the DSU, taken together, afford a panel "ample and extensive authority to undertake and control the process by which it informs itself of both the relevant facts of the dispute and of the legal norms and principles applicable to such facts." This broad authority remains subject to a panel's duty, pursuant to article 11 of the DSU, to decide cases based on an objective assessment of relevant facts and applicable law.

Based on the panels' broad authority under the DSU, and the panels' mandate under article 11 in particular, the AB held that the Shrimp/Turtle Panel read the word "seek" too literally. The AB overruled the Panel, holding that the Panel could accept unsolicited submissions:

> In the present context, the authority to seek information is not properly equated with a prohibition on accepting information which has been submitted without having been requested by a panel. A panel has the discretionary authority either to accept and consider or to reject information and advice submitted to it, whether requested by a panel or not. The fact that a panel may motu proprio have initiated the request for information does not, by itself, bind the panel to accept and consider the information which is actually submitted. The amplitude of the authority vested in panels to shape the processes of fact-finding and legal interpretation makes clear that a panel will not be deluged, as it were, with non-requested material, unless the panel allows itself to be so deluged.

Although overruling the Panel's interpretation of article 13 of the DSU, the AB upheld the Panel's decision to accept the NGO submissions as part of the US brief.

In deciding the US appeal, the AB itself had to decide whether to accept and consider three new NGO amicus briefs attached to the US submission, as well as a revised brief submitted directly to the AB by the Center for International Environmental Law. In a preliminary ruling, the AB accepted all the amicus briefs. However, the AB asked the U.S. to indicate the extent it agreed with, or adopted, the legal arguments in the NGO briefs attached to its submission. The U.S. balked at fully adopting the NGO briefs, stating that it agreed with the legal arguments of the NGOs "to the extent those arguments concur with the U.S. arguments set out in our main submission." Given the tentative and qualified manner in which the U.S. accepted the NGO briefs, the AB, while admitting the briefs, limited its analysis to those legal arguments advanced in the main US submission.

Impact of the Appellate Body's Shrimp/Turtle Ruling on Future NGO Involvement with Disputes in the WTO

The AB's ruling in the Shrimp/Turtle dispute is significant for two reasons. First, it creates new legal avenues for NGO to influence WTO panels and the AB. Second, the increased external participation resulting from the ruling has the potential to reshape the WTO dispute settlement process.

New Legal Avenues for NGO Participation

The AB's decision creates two avenues by which an NGO brief can now come before a panel. First, the AB decision makes it clear that WTO Members may attach NGO briefs to their own submissions to a panel or to the AB. Mere attachment of a brief to a party's submission does not seem sufficient, however, to guarantee its consideration by a panel or the AB. Instead, the AB's ruling suggests that a panel or the AB is obligated to consider material presented in an attached brief only when the submitting party expressly adopts that material. Second, the AB's decision allows NGOs to submit briefs directly to a panel or the AB. When a brief is directly submitted to a panel, the panel retains the discretion to accept or reject the brief. While it is clear that panels will exercise extensive discretionary authority in the process of preliminary selection and consideration of NGO briefs, this discretion is not completely unconstrained. A panel that acted arbitrarily in determining whether to consider or reject information in an NGO brief would likely breach the requirement of article 11 of the DSU that it make an objective assessment of the matter. A finding of irrelevancy in relation to material submitted by an NGO could be construed as finding of law, and therefore be subject to review by the AB.

Thus, panels receiving NGO briefs may no longer be able to dismiss them without consideration. At the very least, they are probably required to read NGO submissions in order to determine their relevance to the dispute. This process of review alone may have the beneficial effect of exposing panels to different factual information and legal arguments beyond those advanced by the parties. Another possibility is that the briefs may make a panel aware of deficiencies in the evidence presented by the parties, prompting the panel to seek additional expert advice.

Consequences of the Shrimp/Turtle Ruling for Dispute Resolution Practice and Reform

The ability of disputants to attach an NGO brief to its submissions, coupled with the likelihood that a panel or the AB will rely more heavily upon briefs endorsed by a party, will likely lead NGOs to lobby disputants to attach NGO amicus briefs to their submissions. NGOs may be expected to pressure parties to adopt expressly the factual information or legal arguments presented in their briefs in order to ensure that a panel or the AB will consider them. James Cameron and Stephen Orava suggest that NGOs may also lobby a non-party Member Government to intervene in a dispute and to adopt the NGO's positions as part of its submission.

Even more significant reforms to the dispute settlement process are likely to be generated by the AB's authorization of NGO submissions directly to panels. A number of commentators (135) have argued that by allowing direct submission of briefs to panels, the system could be overwhelmed by an influx of unsolicited material. As a practical matter, however, panels are more likely to be favorably disposed towards briefs that consolidate the views of a number of NGOs, are concise, and raise novel arguments not advanced by the parties to the dispute. While observance of these practical matters may reduce the number and volume of briefs, the likelihood that panels in high profile disputes will receive numerous documents from a variety of non-State actors raises the question of whether the procedural route for such information should be formalized. The AB's ruling indicates that panels have broad authority to develop their Working Procedures in consultation with the parties to the dispute. Panels, therefore, might develop Working Procedures to govern the receipt of NGO submissions, the preliminary assessment process for amicus briefs, and procedures for confirming formal acceptance and distribution of submissions to all parties involved in the dispute.

However, broader reforms of the DSU may be necessary to address issues raised by the AB's ruling. The AB's ruling in favor of direct submission of briefs by non-governmental actors is not expressly limited to submissions by NGOs. Many NGOs fear that wealthy business entities will use the new procedural rules regarding access to the WTO dispute settlement process more extensively than public interest groups. NGOs have also been the target of criticism. Some critics suggest that many non-profit environmental groups fail to represent the views of the international public at large and that NGO involvement in disputes before the WTO will likely exacerbate the existing bias towards the environmental views and values of developed countries.

These concerns suggest the need for multilaterally agreed-upon amendments to the DSU to determine which non-state actors are given access to panels and to establish a screening process for organizations that claim public interest status. Additional reforms may be necessary to facilitate effective participation by NGOs, and possibly others, in the dispute settlement process. Suggested reforms include requiring parties to make their submissions public prior to the hearing, permitting submitters to be present at panel hearings, and allowing submitters to present brief oral arguments amplifying the positions set forth in their briefs or in answer to questions raised by panels. Such reforms are feasible because two powerful WTO Members - the EU and the U.S. - support changes to the DSU to enhance the transparency of the dispute resolution process and to mandate panel review of amicus briefs.

Do NGOs Give the Public a Stronger Voice in the Protection of the Global Environment?

The Benefits of NGO Involvement in International Fora

The principal rationale for allowing greater NGO access to international tribunals engaged in environmental dispute resolution is to increase public participation in decision-making that affects the global environment. Central to this rationale is the claim that NGOs better represent the public interest in global environmental protection than do states. NGOs may protect the environment better than states for four principal reasons.

First, NGOs are able to conceptualize problems and solutions without borders. Unlike states, which are primarily concerned with protecting their sovereign interests, NGOs are more likely to take a global approach to environmental problems, a crucial step when those problems have transboundary dimensions. Not only are states restrained by territorial concerns, they may also be more reluctant to take action to enforce international environmental obligations because they lack the necessary resources, their own environmental record is not perfect, or they fear jeopardizing other strategic or economic relationships.

Second, states rarely have the luxury of being able to focus on a single concern like environmentally-focused public interests groups can. Many disputes raise a variety of other economic and social concerns that may lead states to overlook or downplay arguments concerning the environmental effects of a particular measure. Moreover, in disputes before WTO panels, state representatives are frequently drawn from a country's trade department and may have little knowledge of, or interest in, the environmental aspects of the dispute. In these situations, environmental NGOs can often help bring a tribunal's attention to environmental issues that states have neglected to address, either deliberately or out of ignorance.

Third, NGOs, which commonly maintain relationships with individual citizens, are arguably more representative of public opinion on environmental issues than states balancing a variety of competing concerns. Environmental NGOs with membership encompassing citizens in non-democratic countries, or countries which are not members of international organizations such as the WTO, may also be able to act as a voice for the voiceless. Some interests that states tend to neglect in the domestic context, such as those of future generations, may find an effective voice through the efforts of NGOs.

Fourth, NGOs are increasingly sophisticated international actors with access to a wide range of resources and expertise. NGOs may possess better information than governments on environmental issues. In addition, NGOs often exercise strong political power in domestic matters and have the ability to undertake activities that governments cannot.

The Drawbacks of NGO Involvement in International Fora

While environmental NGOs have the potential to make tremendous contributions to environmental decision making at the international level, legitimate concerns still exist about allowing NGOs unrestricted access to international environmental dispute resolution processes. Environmentally focused NGOs may not accurately balance the public interest in environmental protection against other concerns such as economic development. Moreover, allowing greater NGO access to environmental decision-making will privilege the ideas and interests of the Western constituencies NGOs generally represent at the expense of the interests of developing or newly industrialized countries. In the WTO context, developing countries often bear the brunt of NGO-endorsed domestic environmental measures that create barriers to trade in goods produced by developing countries. In the EU context, Eastern European countries pressing for membership in the Union have criticized NGOs for favoring the interests of Western European citizens. Tensions have developed between grassroots NGOs and "professional" NGOs, with public distrust of the latter.

Allowing greater NGO involvement in international dispute settlement may unfairly privilege environmental NGOs over other groups, such as business entities, that also have legitimate interests in the outcome of the disputes, particularly trade disputes. Many environmental NGOs, especially in Western countries, already have significant influence on environmental law and policy-making at both the national and international level. Arguably, NGOs do not need additional rights to enforce environmental laws, because their views are already adequately reflected in the law and policy-making process. If environmental

NGOs are afforded greater rights of participation, perhaps the same rights should be afforded to all non-state actors, including corporate interests and business entities, in order to ensure that all have an equal voice in international law and policy-making. Full-scale participation in international environmental decision-making by myriad non-state actors would almost certainly overwhelm the institutional structures of bodies like the WTO and the ECJ, and is unlikely to lead to more effective representation of the public interest. On the other hand, if participatory rights are to be limited to "public interest" non-governmental actors, a practical issue arises as to how to identify which groups are "suitable" to participate in decision-making processes.

Suggestions for Sensible Regulations on NGO Involvement in International Fora

While concerns over the drawbacks of NGO involvement are legitimate, they do not pose insurmountable obstacles to greater participation of NGOs in international environmental dispute resolution. NGOs have much to offer, particularly through the provision of environmental expertise and by giving a voice to public concerns about environmental protection, if granted direct rights of participation in the ECJ, WTO, and other international tribunals. Experience with NGO participation in dispute resolution in other jurisdictions, for example in the United States Supreme Court, indicates that tribunals are well able to regulate NGO involvement and to utilize and weigh NGO input properly when resolving disputes. Greater institutional constraints in the international setting may mean that tribunals do not have the resources to devote to screening individual applications and submissions by NGOs. However, such considerations do not dictate the exclusion of NGOs from the international environmental dispute resolution processes altogether. Rather, they suggest the need for development of a process of accrediting NGOs in the international environmental arena to ensure an empirical basis for determining their claimed representativeness and expertise.

The criteria established by the United Nations Economic and Social Council for determining which NGOs may hold consultative status with the organization provide a precedent for screening processes that could be used in other international fora. The criteria include assessments of the NGO's structure, its public accountability, and its sources of funding. In addition, the rules limit NGO involvement to those groups with expertise relevant to the work of the organization. These kinds of broad criteria are sufficient to allow a wide range of groups access to international tribunals, while at the same time providing a measure of quality control. Even with an accreditation process for NGOs seeking direct participatory rights in international tribunals, concerns may still exist that only the wealthiest groups - large national or international Western-based NGOs - will have the resources to take advantage of these rights. Accordingly, international organizations and tribunals may find it necessary to provide resources and funding to some less-established NGOs in order to ensure fair representation of all eligible groups.

CONCLUSION

The ECJ and the WTO dispute settlement processes illustrate two fora at the international level where new avenues for greater NGO participation in environmental decision-making are evolving. The developments in these two major international tribunals may stimulate similar reforms in other bodies dealing with the resolution of international environmental disputes. Indeed, the Aarhus Convention requires parties to "promote the application of the principles of [the] Convention in international environmental decision-making processes and within the framework of international organizations in matters relating to the environment."

In the ECJ, the perceived "democratic deficit" created by its ruling in the Greenpeace case may be remedied by implementing the Aarhus Convention's access to justice provisions. The Convention may give NGOs standing to bring their own suits in the ECJ to challenge acts of Community institutions that allegedly violate Community environmental law. If the European Community proceeds to ratify the Convention, the ECJ may need to reconsider its interpretation of the "direct and individual concern" criteria of article 173 to allow the public and NGOs to vindicate the environmental right expressed in the Convention.

In the WTO, NGOs have been granted the ability to voice their concerns, but they have not been guaranteed that their voice will be heard. Nevertheless, the AB ruling in the Shrimp/ Turtle dispute allows for submission and consideration of NGO amicus briefs to panels and the AB in some cases. At the very least, this innovation should lead to better-informed panel decisions in the areas where trade and environment overlap. The ruling may also spur more far-reaching reforms of the WTO dispute settlement process that increase its transparency and accessibility for non-state actors.

Legitimate concerns remain over allowing NGOs unrestricted access to international environmental dispute resolution processes. These concerns can be addressed by instituting procedural screens that limit NGO involvement in international disputes to those NGOs that have particular expertise in relevant areas and adequately represent the public. Ultimately, enhanced NGO participation in international tribunals should ensure that, in the environmental area, where States are often inadequate representatives of the public interest in environmental protection, international law develops in a way that will protect and preserve the environment for the benefit of current and future generations.

5

NGOs and the Transnational Finance

This essay, which explores the capacity of NGOs to run transnational campaigns targeting financial markets, is divided into two sections. The first section clarifies the definition of NGOs and evaluates their potential, providing examples of successful campaigns run by NGO coalitions. The particular power of the environmental movement is also explored here. The second part examines the increasing involvement and effectiveness of NGOs in global financial markets, with particular emphasis on the importance of institutional investors.

NGOs and Transnational Action

Global capital is not the only important political force organised transnationally; indeed, many of the groups known as non-governmental organisations (NGOs) also seem to have the capacity for global reach. Certainly, this transnationalism is feted in much of the literature, where it is often suggested that NGOs form a nascent 'international civil society' (see, for example, Clark, 1995: 514). NGOs may also be increasingly supplanting parties and trade unions as favoured forms of political involvement. Some scholars claim that "the plurality of interests and forms of resistance associated with NGOs signals the demise of the vanguardist role of the proletariat or any other privileged group in producing social transformations and reflects the popular disenchantment with political parties and unions as forums for expressing social dissent" (Fernando and Heston, 1997: 9). The Western European trend seems to be in this direction, as since 1945, the public's interest in politics has increased, but participation in political activity outside party lines has increasingly been supplanting active party membership (Wainwright, 1994: 193).

Though their potential is much celebrated, and indeed they are paid a great deal of attention generally, NGOs are quite difficult to clearly describe. This is because they are such a diverse set of organisations; by definition, all those that are 'non-governmental'. There are more than 25 000 international NGOs, with widely varied goals, operations and levels of funding (Economist, 1999c: 22). Even when the definition is restricted to those NGOs involved in political campaigning, the heterogeneity of their agendas remains immense. For example, in the recent WTO conference in Seattle, a seminal event for so-called 'anti-globalization' NGOs, 20% of the 776 NGOs registered for the conference lobbied for more open markets (Bayne, 2000: 136).

Notwithstanding their diversity, some generalisations about the nature of campaigning NGOs are possible. They are largely single-issue social movements, evidencing "commitment to a very focused set of concerns" (Clark, 1995: 510), and advocating these concerns in the political sphere. The most significant NGOs focus on the environment, developmental politics and human rights (Gorg and Hirsch, 1998: 602). Redistributive politics is not therefore the issue of highest importance for the large majority of NGOs. Finally, NGOs are often viewed as representatives of civil society, and indeed commonly "claim a certain legitimacy for their causes by virtue of popular representation" (Clark, 1995: 508).

Since they are generally not affiliated to states, the potential exists for NGOs to successfully execute transnational political campaigns. Individual NGOs may run nearly identical campaigns in a number of states simultaneously, as with Oxfam International's Education Now campaign (Oxfam International, 2000). Alternatively, various NGOs might build horizontal coalitions across states, as occurred before and during the Seattle WTO meeting (Foreign Policy, 2000). Such coalitions have been aided greatly by the increasing ease of communication over the internet (Economist, 1999c). Interestingly, then, it seems that improvements in communications technology have helped empower both transnational finance and transnational NGOs.

Coalitions of NGOs organising transnationally have already won a number of major political victories, and some of their successful campaigns have been in direct opposition to the interests of global finance. One of these was the movement against the OECD-negotiated Multilateral Agreement on Investment (MAI), which, if agreed upon, would have cemented certain rights of market access for international investors and consolidated the liberalisation of state controls on capital. Many NGOs specifically objected to its lack of consideration of social and environmental issues (Mabey, 1999: 65). Negotiations for the MAI had been going on in secret between finance ministries for some time when in 1996, the first details of the proposal were leaked (Mabey, 1999: 64). A broad-based NGO coalition soon emerged in opposition of the treaty, spearheaded by the US NGO Global Citizen and coordinated through the Internet (Foreign Policy, 2000). This movement was soon able to introduce environmental and social considerations into the negotiations, and eventually helped to end the talks altogether (Mabey, 1999: 61). It should be noted, though, that neither the proposal nor the movement have gone away, as attempts have been made to introduce the MAI into other intergovernmental fora (Public Citizen, 2000).

Another major NGO achievement has been the success of the International Campaign to Ban Landmines (ICBL). First formed in 1992 as a coalition of six NGOs seeking an international ban of landmines, the movement helped to place the landmine issue on the international agenda, and eventually witnessed the birth of a Mine Ban Treaty, which entered into force in March 1999. Notably, the ICBL received the 1997 Nobel Peace Prize for its efforts (ICBL, 2000).

Perhaps the most effective group of NGOs has been the environmental movement. Often these organisations share some of the same goals and opponents as the redistributive left; indeed, it has been noted that "many of the effective contemporary anti-capitalist voices... come from a Green rather than a socialist background" (Callinicos, 2000: 121). Certainly many environmental NGOs were part of the anti-MAI coalition, with some, such as Friends of the Earth, playing a leading role. Generally, the environmental movement has been highly successful in influencing state behaviour, including in intergovernmental contexts. For example, pressure from environmental NGOs, particularly in the United States Congress, assured that trade and environmental issues were linked for the first time in NAFTA (Baker Fox, 1995: 49). Similarly, NGOs strongly affected the negotiating positions of governments in the WTO meeting in Seattle, helping to lead to that conference's failure. American NGOs helped assure that "for the first time since the Second World War, the US was not pressing for an ambitious programme of trade liberalization" (Bayne, 2000: 143), instead focusing on labour and environmental standards. At the same time, environmental NGOs in Europe were particularly effective in hardening the EU's position on genetically modified food (Bayne, 2000: 138).

Other notable successes of the environmental movement include both the existence and the achievements of the Rio de Janeiro Earth Summit in 1992 and the Kyoto Conference on Climate Change in 1997, and more generally, the prominence of environmental issues on the global political agenda. Increasingly, the ideology of environmentalism informs policy debate and influences political outcomes even without the direct involvement of environmental lobbyists. NGOs have been successful at framing issues in environmental terms, with forestry, for example, now an issue of environmental conservation rather than simply economic production (Bernstein and Cashore, 2000: 82).

Moreover, environmental issues are more and more often perceived by policymakers, especially in the North, as issues of public interest rather than partisan politics, with environmental NGOs perceived to be speaking for civil society generally rather than for the politicised few (Fernando and Heston, 1997: 12).

NGOs and Transnational Finance

It is important to observe that although of transnational importance, the NGO-led political campaigns listed above have all been centred on states. The MAI was being negotiated between the governments of the OECD nations, and was thwarted through pressure upon those governments. The effective lobbying leading up to the NAFTA agreement and the WTO meeting in Seattle was executed through state channels. In addition, the Rio and Kyoto summits were fundamentally intergovernmental in nature. Indeed, most or all of the environmental NGOs' successes so far have come through work with states and/or international organisations, rather than outside the state and interstate systems in the multi-centric world of the market (Mol, 2000).

Yet it appears that today's NGOs are increasingly attempting to transcend the state system. Arthur Mol notes that many environmental NGOs are now trying to be "an independent 'third' force..., making alternating strategic alliances with state and market parties" (2000: 50). Indeed, NGOs may sometimes share common interests with market actors; insurance companies and environmental organisations, for example, are united in their concern about global warming, and thus both support climate change conventions (Newell and Paterson, 1998: 696). As well, many corporations, by agreeing to become 'environmentally friendly', receive a public boost in the form of the approval of NGOs. The World Wildlife Fund, for instance, allows such producers to display its distinctive panda logo. Janelle Diller confirms that "evidence that good corporate behaviour may enhance financial performance has tended to reinforce the moral imperatives for firms to act as 'good citizens'" (1999, par. 5).

However, transnational financial markets form a less straightforward target for NGOs. Unlike states or corporations, where particular authoritative actors may be lobbied, whether directly or indirectly, to take authoritative decisions, financial markets are in principle nonhierarchical institutions. These markets consist of a large number of buyers and sellers who are theoretically of equal status, and able to make transactions independently. Since each market actor makes transactions based on individual self-interest, there is no obvious 'general interest' to which to appeal. Admittedly, markets can be regulated by states, but investors can also move from state to state to evade and/or undermine regulations. The behaviour of financial markets may have political implications, but in theory, for campaigners trying to alter this behaviour, it is difficult to see where to begin exerting influence.

In practice, however, transnational financial markets may not be such egalitarian institutions. Instead, it seems that there has been a "centralization of investment decision making in the hands of a small number of financial actors" (Harmes, 1998: 99). Institutional investors, such as mutual funds, pension funds and insurance corporations, often control such large amounts of capital that they effectively constitute the global financial market by themselves. They now trade most bonds and equities (Economist, 1999b: 125), and so, in the words of the IMF, "the effective investor base is changing from a very large number of small investors to a very small number of large investors" (IMF, 1995, quoted in Harmes, 1998: 101). Individual investors often cede their investment decisions to institutions; in the United States, for example, more than 40% of household assets are managed by institutional investors (Economist, 1999a: 150).

Campaigning NGOs, increasingly understanding the importance of institutional investors in the international economy, are beginning to pursue these influential actors. Furthermore, NGOs have a strong source of leverage over the largest institutions. Since so many individuals now use investment vehicles such as mutual funds, institutional investors are more and more in the public eye, and now value the 'cleanliness' of their brand names as much as do large producers. This means that for NGOs, the "major financial institutions are readymade targets.... Boasting powerful brand names that they don't want sullied, they can be quite sensitive to pressure" (Gopinath, 2000: par. 5).

Most NGO pressure on institutional investors to date has focused on the corporations in which they invest, often by urging institutions not to channel money to 'bad' companies. For example, under pressure in 1997 from NGOs angry about an exploitative mining investment, ABN Amro Bank announced that it would only invest in mines which conformed to environmental and social guidelines. As well, institutional investors were urged to stay away from the PetroChina initial public offering, which then raised less money than expected. Most audaciously, the NGO Global Exchange is attempting to undermine the World Bank's authority by asking institutional investors to stop buying its AAA bonds (Gopinath, 2000).

NGOs have also been attempting to exploit institutional investors' power as large shareholders so as to change corporate behaviour. These campaigns have resulted in institutional investors sponsoring social resolutions in shareholder meetings, urging companies to improve environmental, human rights or labour standards. Diller confirms that "the most important sponsors of labour-related resolutions are indeed institutional investors, including insurance companies, pension funds, church funds, union funds, local authority funds and also fund managers" (1999: par. 19).

Some investment funds have even been designed as 'socially responsible funds', explicitly formed either to avoid investment in unethical companies or to take shareholder action. The shareholder-action funds sometimes work in tandem with NGOs to change corporate behaviour, and in the UK, control more than one billion pounds in assets in various institutions (Lewis and Mackenzie, 2000: 217). Funds that invest only in ethical companies are generally less profitable investments than the market norm, but they attract investors nonetheless, presenting people with reasons to choose a fund other than simple economic self-interest. Indeed, it has been demonstrated that investors with pro-environmental attitudes are willing to sustain small losses to invest in environmentally sound corporations (Mackenzie and Lewis, 1999: 439).

If NGO campaigns continue to be successful, and the increasing 'good behaviour' of institutional investors and ethical funds trickles down through the financial markets, it is possible that the environmental and social norms that these movements have helped to entrench in much of Western society and politics may also be entrenched in the marketplace.

For example, the institutional investor Friends Provident has adopted a philosophy of social responsibility for its fifteen billion pounds in assets, even claiming that "good corporate practice on human rights, child labour and environmental pollution is good for society, but it's also good for shareholders"

(Financial Times, 25). As well, new UK government regulations are to force institutional investors to "state the extent to which social, environmental and ethical considerations are taken into account in their investment policy" (Financial Times, 25), giving NGOs a further weapon with which to pressure funds to invest ethically. With ethical investment potentially on its way to becoming a financial market norm, then perhaps in the future, states and corporations will not only have to implement financial orthodoxy so as to attract large-scale investment, but assure their 'environmental orthodoxy' and 'human rights orthodoxy' as well.

The Contrarian: Are NGOs Playing Both Sides of the Human Rights Abuse Debate?

Non-governmental organisations are scrambling to come up with a new strategy following the release of the interim UN report on human rights abuses, says Jon Entine When Harvard's John Ruggie was tapped by UN secretary-general Kofi Annan to examine corporate responsibility for human rights violations, he promised to address "whether multinational firms should be the direct bearer of international human rights obligations - and, if so, what those standards should be". That's exactly what he's done.

In a rebuke of NGOs' key position, Ruggie found no precedent for "hard" international laws except for war crimes. Corporations can play some role in "weak governance zones", he wrote, but "the debate about business and human rights would be far less pressing if all governments faithfully executed their own laws and fulfilled their international obligations".

That conclusion fell far short of the demands of Amnesty International, Oxfam and other NGOs. They blame most environmental exploitation, plundering militias, and child labour on the complicity of rapacious "transnationals". Corporations "engage in irresponsible and dangerous actions," says Kathryn Mulvey of Corporate Accountability.

States or Chief Executives?

So, corporations are the bad guys, right? Not exactly. If NGOs have their way, we'll soon be deputising chief executives.

Since 2003, with the release of the UN Norms for Business, while bashing multinationals, NGOs have been demanding these same corporate desperadoes be held responsible for cleaning up messes in places where they are often holding on by their fingernails. This paradoxical NGO position runs "counter to the general structure of international law, which, for good reason, places the responsibility for enduring good governance and respect for human rights on states," says Maurice Mendelson, University of London professor emeritus of international law. Adam Greene, a corporate responsibility expert with the US Council for International Business, agrees. "NGOs vastly over estimate the independence and power of multinationals," he says. "No states, particularly corrupt ones, are about to allow corporations to enforce laws that they are loathe to enforce themselves." Greene points to the recent appropriations of multinational energy operations in Latin America. It began in Venezuela with a gradual nationalisation process under leftwing populist president Hugo Chávez. On 1 May, Bolivian president Evo Morales nationalised the nation's oil fields, defiantly declaring: "Foreign companies will not be able to steal from Bolivia [any longer]." Weeks later, Ecuador's Alfredo Palacio followed suit, seizing Occidental Petroleum's one-billion-euro oil operation, the country's largest foreign investment.

This played well with NGOs that label nationalisations the rightful comeuppance for energy companies, but the reality is more complicated. In communities where Oxy spent millions of euros building schools, clinics, community centres, and sanitation facilities, backed eco-tourism projects, and provided grants for students and teachers, the beer has not been flowing so freely. In the long term, Ecuador will pay a price. Direct foreign investments are on hold because the potential rewards are too meagre to compensate for political risks. Non-governmental organisations are scrambling to come up with a new strategy following the release of the interim UN report on human rights abuses, says Jon Entine.

Corporate Limits

What, then, is the responsibility of corporations? Corporations with a conscience that leave abusive countries may do more harm than good. Some corporations that resisted demands to leave South Africa came to be considered heroes because they guaranteed jobs and benefits to black workers in defiance of the white government, while boycott supporters cut and ran. In Burma, recently, Hilton Head bowed to international pressure and abandoned its properties. That has devastated its loyal workforce, raising concerns whether their rights would have been better protected by toughing it out.

NGOs remain hopeful that, in his final report, Ruggie will call for universally recognised standards and effective accountability mechanisms, says Alessandra Masci of Amnesty International. Addressing abuses requires an inside and outside strategy. Uniform standards would provide ammunition against dysfunctional tyrants.

But NGOs would be wise to embrace the reality that corporations are no substitute for civil stability. You can't expect to bash Corporate World, celebrate when populist leaders abrogate treaties and free trade agreements, and yet demand that these same corporations be held accountable for misdeeds that flow directly from decades of government corruption.

How Web of Activists Gives Coke Problems in India

Amit Srivastava doesn't own a car or a house. He runs a nonprofit, activist organization in California that has only one full-time employee -- himself. But he has been helping shake up one of the world's biggest corporations, Coca-Cola Co., thousands of miles away in India.

Speaking on a tour of U.S. college campuses in April, he accused Coke of egregious offenses in India: stealing water, poisoning land and selling drinks laced with dangerous pesticides. "It is destroying lives, it is destroying livelihoods and it is destroying communities all across India," the pony-tailed, 39-year-old college dropout told dozens of students at Smith College in Northampton, Mass. "That is the story of Coca-Cola in India."

Coca-Cola, which considers India a crucial element in its plans for global growth, wasn't invited to Smith to tell its version of the story. But the Atlanta-based soft-drinks giant is well aware of Mr. Srivastava's activities. Coke acknowledges he is a central figure in a burgeoning global campaign by nonprofits -- commonly known abroad as nongovernmental organizations, or NGOs -- that has cost it millions of dollars in lost sales and legal fees in India, and growing damage to its reputation elsewhere.

Mr. Srivastava and the NGOs have flagged some serious issues, such as Coke's onetime practice of giving away waste material to local farmers that some studies later showed contained toxic materials. But amid the heated rhetoric, there have been some dubious claims as well. Mr. Srivastava, for example, has compared Coke's environmental practices to the industrial accident at Bhopal, which killed thousands.

Amid the NGOs' campaign, Coca-Cola has been forced to fight legal and legislative battles all across India -- including challenging a court order in the northern state of Rajasthan that would require soft-drink makers to list pesticide residues on their labels. The order was prompted by laboratory tests of soft drinks by a New Delhi-based NGO. The company says the levels are safe.

In the southern state of Kerala, local officials shut down a $16 million Coke bottling plant in March 2004 over still-unproven claims by local residents and Indian activists that it drained and polluted local water supplies. The company has been trying ever since to regain the plant's license, fighting a case that has gone all the way to India's Supreme Court. But even if Coke prevails, the company hasn't yet said whether it will reopen the plant.

Now Mr. Srivastava is rallying college students in the U.S. and Europe to take up the NGOs' cause. Under pressure from student protesters, at least a half-dozen colleges have decided not to renew contracts with Coke or boycott it, and other campuses are considering similar actions. Schools that have banned Coca-Cola products include Bard College in New York, Carleton College in Minnesota, Oberlin College in Ohio and two colleges in Ireland.

Even though he lives in Northern California, Mr. Srivastava has emerged as a key figure in Coke's travails in India. Activists inside and outside the country say he plays an important role in coordinating the activities of far-flung protesters on the subcontinent, and that he has become the point-man for communicating their cause to the outside world. That a one-man NGO armed with just a laptop computer, a Web site and a telephone calling card can, with his allies, influence a huge multinational corporation illustrates the role social activists can play in a world that's going increasingly online.

"The moral high ground seems to be anyone with a Web site," complains David Cox, Coke's Hong Kong-based communications director for Asia, who has spent months in India trying to combat the NGOs' allegations with little apparent success.

Mr. Srivastava and numerous NGOs both inside and outside India accuse Coke, among other "crimes," of sucking local Indian communities dry through excessive pumping. But the water allegations remain unproven. Kerala's highest court rejected such claims in April, noting that wells there continued to dry up last summer, months after the local Coke plant stopped operating. And a scientific study previously requested by the court found that while the plant had "aggravated the water scarcity situation," the "most significant factor" was a lack of rainfall. The NGOs respond that Coke shouldn't be locating bottling plants in drought stricken areas. From Coke's point of view, Mr. Srivastava and other activists "are making false environmental allegations against us to further an antiglobalization agenda," says Mr. Cox.

The dispute in India does raise questions about Coke's waste-disposal practices there. Coke officials acknowledge, for example, that they violated their own global safety standards by failing to conduct any toxicity tests on a dump site used by its biggest plant in India until after a Wall Street Journal reporter visited it in March.

Meanwhile, near the holy city of Varanasi in northeastern India, a local water official blames a Coke plant -- which has been the scene of many protests by NGOs and local residents -- for polluting groundwater by releasing wastewater into surrounding land. A Coke official confirms there had been a drainage problem with treated wastewater several years ago but says the company built a long pipeline to correct it.

Mr. Srivastava, whose father is a management professor in India, was born in the U.S. and grew up in India. He dropped out of Southern Illinois University after becoming more interested in activism than formal education.

In 2002, while working at Corp Watch, a nonprofit corporate watchdog based in Oakland, Calif., he commissioned an article for one of the group's Web sites about a protest outside a Coke bottling plant in a poor tribal area in Kerala. Local residents accused Coke of extracting so much water that their wells dried up or yielded brackish, undrinkable water. Coke, which says it uses about four liters of water to produce a one-liter bottle of soft-drink, blames the problems on area drought conditions.

The article, which appeared on a Web site called Corp Watch India that Mr. Srivastava oversaw, proved popular. The NGO followed up with a "fax action" in which Web-site visitors were urged to send a fax to Coke via the Internet, demanding that it close the Kerala plant. More than 1,400 people responded, according to Corp Watch, although it says many faxes didn't arrive because of technical problems.

In 2003, Corp Watch ran into financial problems. Mr. Srivastava lost his job but quickly launched his own NGO, called Global Resistance. He was allowed to take Corp Watch India with him, wrapping it into a new site called the India Resource Center.

The new site initially focused on various issues in India, including outsourcing and globalization. But the controversy over Coca-Cola soon began to dominate as Mr. Srivastava learned of growing protests in different parts of India and saw a need to try to bring them global attention. "It took on a life of its own," he says.

Today, the Web site, www.indiaresource.org, serves as a global platform for local activists and protesters throughout India and draws about 20,000 visitors a month, according to tracking numbers on the Web site. In contrast, a Coke Web site designed to counter NGO allegations, www.cokefacts.org, draws just 800 visitors a month, Coke officials say. Mr. Srivastava also has resumed the "fax action," relaying more than 9,000 faxes to Coke's headquarters to date, he says. In addition to frequent campus speeches, he says he's also advising potential investors who hope to launch a London-based hedge fund that would bet against the share price of Coke, among other companies, according to two other people involved in the planning. A portion of any profits would be donated to activist groups, these people said.

Activists throughout India credit Mr. Srivastava with helping to link them together. Protesters in the southern state of Kerala said that when they tried to email other activists in Varanasi, in the north, they found they couldn't communicate because they spoke different languages. Both turned to Mr. Srivastava, who became an intermediary to coordinate their efforts. Now they can help each other plan their protests for maximum impact.

"He has such enormous resources," says R. Ajayan, a Kerala activist. "We don't have a Web site or a communications system. Whenever we have a protest, we have no way to publicize it -- he's doing all this."

When he isn't traveling around the U.S. or India, Mr. Srivastava operates his NGO from a house he shares with friends in El Cerrito, Calif. He says he draws no salary but covers his expenses mainly through modest fund raising.

Global Resistance, which had a budget last year of $60,000, is supported by several private foundations interested in globalization and water issues, including the Unitarian Universalist Veatch Program at Shelter Rock in Manhasset, N.Y. The Unitarian Church social-action fund has given him $45,000 to date, according to its grant administrator. Global Resistance maintains its tax-free status through Community Networking Resources Inc., an Albuquerque, N.M., nonprofit that handles its finances. Mr. Srivastava is the only full-time employee; there's a part-time Web-site editor in New Delhi. "We've been able to survive, barely," the activist says. "I have good friends who keep me going."

Controversy overseas isn't new to Coca-Cola, whose revenue last year totaled $22 billion. In 1999, quality-control problems in Europe sparked a widespread consumer scare and prompted governments to pull Coke products from shelves. The company also has been dogged in recent years by claims by U.S. activists and local union officials that it was complicit in the murder and harassment of union leaders and workers in Colombia. The company denies the claims.

In the wake of the European problems, Coke has tried to respond to critics more quickly and forcefully. Lately, it sends teams of executives to college campuses to rebut charges. But the company isn't always invited. In April, the Union Theological Seminary in New York banned the sale of Coke products on campus because of "considerable evidence" of human-rights violations and environmental damage abroad. A seminary spokeswoman says company officials weren't "invited to present their side." The decision to ban Coke was made by the seminary's president on the recommendation of the school's institutional and community affairs committee.

The president of the seminary, which has only about 300 students, later did extend an invitation to the company. Coke sent six representatives, including four from Atlanta. Mr. Srivastava says his travel schedule didn't permit him to attend. The spokeswoman says the school will re-evaluate its ban in the fall.

For years, Coke was India's leading soft drink. In 1977, the company left after a new government ordered it to dilute its stake in its Indian unit and turn over Coke's secret formula. The company returned in 1993 when the government began trying to attract foreign investment. Coke quickly gained a lead in the market by buying up popular local brands, including Thums Up soda. Its products are now produced in 76 bottling plants and officials say India is one of its fastest growing markets. But the continuing allegations by NGOs -- over excessive water use, pesticides, pollution and waste disposal -- have taken their toll. During a conference call with analysts in April, Mary Minnick, who had been president of Coke's Asia division and now heads global marketing, innovation and strategy, called India a "work in progress" and noted the company still was feeling "the residual effects of the unfounded pesticide scare in 2003."

That scare occurred after the Center for Science and Environment, a New Delhi-based NGO, issued a report on lab tests of a dozen local Coca-Cola and PepsiCo Inc. soft drinks. The tests showed they contained pesticide and insecticide levels of between 11 times and 70 times the maximum set by the European Union for drinking water. Coke's product sales plummeted by as much as 40 percent.

Coke and Pepsi, which together hold about a 95 percent market share of soft-drink sales in India, disputed the lab results and say their products are safe. But an Indian parliamentary committee last year backed up CSE's findings and a government-appointed committee is now trying to develop the world's first pesticide standards for soft drinks. Coke and PepsiCo oppose the move, arguing, among other things, that lab tests aren't reliable enough to detect minute traces of pesticides in complex drinks like soda.

Coke's Mr. Cox accuses Sunita Narain, CSE's director, of "brandjacking," using Coke's brand name to draw attention to her campaign against pesticides. Ms. Narain says CSE's study of pesticide residues in soft drinks was a natural follow-up to a previous study it did on bottled water. "It's the arrogance of Coke that makes it believe that we were targeting it," she says.

To further publicize the pesticide issue, some NGOs last year began spreading stories online and to the news media of Indian farmers who had begun spraying Coke on their crops as a pesticide. "Things grow better with Coke," read a headline in Britain's Guardian newspaper. But Mr. Srivastava admits the whole thing was a publicity stunt by local activists and farmers, and it's unclear how many farmers participated. "We played it up as well, obviously," he says.

The controversy in India has been marked by other outlandish or misleading claims. At a recent appearance at the University of Michigan, which has been debating whether to renew its contract with Coke, Mr. Srivastava compared the possible long-term health effects of some of Coke's environmental practices in India to the devastating 1984 gas leak at a Union Carbide plant in Bhopal. "Twenty years from now we can have another Bhopal," he said. Coke officials dismiss the analogy as absurd.

A Boston-based nonprofit called Corporate Accountability International posted on its Web site a "Coca-Cola fact sheet."

It suggested that as a result of Coke's extraction of water in Kerala, "Water riots and water-related murders are now an everyday occurrence as water becomes scarcer."

But there are no reports of daily water-related murders and riots in Kerala. Asked to back up the claim, Patty Linn, the group's campaign director, said after checking that she couldn't. The group later removed the statement from the "fact sheet."

Coke also has been selective with its information. On the Web site of Coke's India unit, under a section called "Facts on Kerala," there's a document that disputes allegations that plant officials there distributed dangerous waste material to local farmers to use as fertilizer. The company acknowledges that until 2003 it had given away sludge -- a byproduct of water- and sugar-treatment processes, and bottle- and equipment-cleaning operations -- but maintains it was safe. "Numerous reports since the commissioning of the plant, and as recently as December 2003, have confirmed that the levels of heavy metal traces are within the (Kerala state) Pollution Control Board norms for classification as non-hazardous," Coke's Web site states. But the document doesn't mention two other government studies of the Kerala waste material, including one by India's highest environmental regulatory authority. The study found that the material contained high enough levels of cadmium, a highly toxic metal, to deem it hazardous.

Harry J. Ott, Atlanta-based director of Coke's global water resources center, says the company didn't mention the other studies because he and other officials questioned the validity of one of them and didn't know the basis of the other. But, he added, "I guess we could show there were tests by other agencies that indicated that there were higher than acceptable levels."

At Coke's largest bottling plant in India, a sprawling, modern factory at Dasna, near New Delhi, sludge is stored in a large concrete tub out back. More than 440 pounds are produced a day and treated with micro-organisms at the plant, according to plant officials.

A plant official said the sludge was disposed of about 8 miles away and that it would be difficult to get there. But the site actually is about half a mile away, within sight of the plant, and on a small empty tract owned by a local landowner.

The owner, Shekhawat Ali, said he willingly uses the material for landfill and accepts it free. He said Coke has been dumping it twice a month for two years and that he hopes someday to build a factory on the site.

Noting that India has no authorized dump sites for nonhazardous industrial waste, Mukul Kumar, Coca-Cola's environmental manager for India, said, "This is one of the designated options that helps him and the government and us." The company also said in a prepared statement that the site complies with its "biosolids disposal standards and practices which provide absolutely safe procedures."

But those standards require Coke to conduct annual soil testing at its waste sites to ensure that the waste isn't hazardous or polluting the area. Asked for copies of those tests, Coke officials produced eight -- all of which were done days after the Journal reporter visited the site in March.

"I will tell you right now that they were not following the company standards to the limit like they were supposed to," says Mr. Ott, the Coke water-resources official who acknowledged that tests should have been performed much earlier. Kari Bjorhus, a Coke spokeswoman, added that "the good news" was that the tests showed the soil samples weren't hazardous.

Mr. Srivastava and other activists vow to continue their anti-Coke campaign until the company shuts down three controversial plants in India and pays compensation to local communities that suffered pollution or loss of water, among other demands. Mr. Srivastava refuses to even sit down with Coke officials, despite repeated invitations from Mr. Ott. "There's no space for dialogue right now," the activist says.

From the Streets to the Inner Sanctum

Activists have come a long way since the violent protests of 1999. Now companies and trade policymakers are giving them a place at the table. Unhappy over the World Trade Organization's refusal to discuss contentious labor issues at its

1999 meeting in Seattle, activist Mike Waghorne joined tens of thousands of protesters on the streets. The demonstrations, which turned violent, sparked anti-globalization protests around the world. Nearly six years later, Waghorne is still unhappy with the Geneva-based trade group. But now he can voice his displeasure from a much more comfortable perch.

Waghorne was among 70 outsiders given the chance to grill three candidates last month for the position of WTO director general. It marked the first time in the organization's 10-year history that activists were allowed to have input in the selection process, an event that Waghorne, an officer with labor coalition Public Services International, described as "civil" and a far cry from the fireworks he had expected.

Once relegated to the streets and hallways, social and environmental activists like Waghorne are finding these days that businesses and trade officials are receptive to their concerns. Activists are prompting changes in corporate practices or trade policy, in some cases partnering with their former targets. Representatives of Amnesty International and other groups were even invited into the proceedings of the World Economic Forum last month in Davos, Switzerland.

"In the old days, it was complete lunacy. There was a moat and a castle, and we were serfs," said Mark Ritchie, president of the Institute for Agriculture and Trade Policy, an organizer of the WTO candidates forum. "It is totally different now. We're not inside, but at least we're visiting from other realms of the kingdom."

The effects have been wide- ranging. Organizations including anti-poverty group Oxfam International and consumer group Public Citizen have helped push once-secretive agencies, including the World Bank, to open up their meetings, publish documents on their websites and respond to concerns about the social and environmental effects of their activities.

Greenpeace International persuaded refrigerator maker Whirlpool Corp. to use environmentally friendly insulation. Under pressure from activists, Home Depot Inc. and Lowe's Cos. agreed to stop buying lumber from Canada's environmentally sensitive Great Bear rain forest. Gap Inc. and

Nike Inc. have collaborated with labor advocates to clean up sweatshops in Cambodia. Prodded by consumer activists, Dell Inc. and Hewlett-Packard Co. are working with consumer groups to step up recycling of computers and cut down on toxic waste. And activists are collaborating with Procter & Gamble Co. and Coca-Cola Co., to name two, to hasten the acceptance of codes of conduct and other measures designed to boost socially responsible corporate behavior. "When we first started working on codes of conduct back in the 1990s, this was kind of like way out there," said Sister Ruth Rosenbaum, founder of the Center for Reflection, Education and Action, an anti-poverty group based in Hartford, Conn. "Now, it is absolutely normal for a company to have a code of conduct."

Activists haven't abandoned their old-fashioned methods of protest, such as street demonstrations and boycotts. But through the years they have adopted new tactics. "Protests are just one tool in the tool kit," said John Passacantando, executive director of Greenpeace USA. "As the threat intensifies, we are pushing ourselves to be smarter, to use new tools to be able to put pressure on these companies in a number of countries simultaneously."

Aided by the Internet, activists can swiftly spread the word about alleged corporate misdeeds and enlist help from like-minded people in other countries. They have become more adept at fundraising; some organizations that once ran on a shoestring have large and global staffs, replete with lawyers, researchers and Web masters.

Many have expanded their use of financial tools - buying company shares and pressing for shareholder resolutions, for example - honed during the fight against companies doing business in apartheid-era South Africa in the 1970s and '80s. Efforts in this arena have gained credibility because grass-roots activist organizations have joined forces with more powerful corporate governance watchdogs like the California Public Employees' Retirement System, the nation's largest public pension fund.

What's behind the change? Public opinion, for one thing. Nongovernmental organizations, as citizen activist groups are often called, rank as the most trusted institutions in the United

States, Europe, Latin America and much of Asia, according to the Edelman Trust Barometer, a survey of 1,500 global opinion leaders by public relations firm Edelman. The biggest jump was in the U.S., where the "trust ratings" of NGOs soared to 55% in 2005 from 36% in 2001.

At the same time, public regard for corporate executives and government officials has fallen, according to the survey, which was released at this year's World Economic Forum. Tarred by corporate scandals, chief executives and financial officers are viewed as credible sources by only 3 of 10 opinion leaders in the U.S., Europe and Japan.Now, by teaming with onetime adversaries in the environmental or labor movements, companies are hoping "to borrow some credibility from the NGOs," said Richard Edelman, president of Chicago-based Edelman.

In addition, feaı on the part of corporations that a failure to police themselves could lead to rigorous government regulations has led to voluntary initiatives. Responding to accusations that they exploited poor workers abroad and sullied the environment with their discards, Dell, Hewlett-Packard and IBM Corp. agreed last year to adhere to an electronics industry code of conduct designed to improve the labor and environmental standards of their supplier factories.

In another example, De Beers Group, the British-South African diamond giant, has gone from villain to model of social responsibility, in large part because of a relationship it developed with two of its loudest critics: London-based Global Witness and activist group Partnership Africa Canada. In the 1990s, those groups targeted De Beers as part of a campaign to stop the smuggling of diamonds used by rebel groups to fund violent conflicts in Africa. After the issue was taken up by the United Nations, De Beers agreed to participate in an authentication program that tracks stones from their source.

Andrew Bone, a De Beers spokesman, said that effort not only had boosted the company's image - prompting praise from U.N. Secretary-General Kofi Annan - but also had reduced the trade in so-called conflict diamonds. "One of the things we learned and realized quickly was the need to engage with NGOs instead of walking away and saying, 'It's not our problem,'

Bone said. Not everyone, however, is enamored of activist groups' influence. Gary Hufbauer, an economist with the Institute for International Economics, contends that the true agenda of some activists is to stop development and trade liberalization, not to improve the economy. Activists still complain about the lack of openness of the World Bank, he said, "even though the quantity of information is substantially more than a decade ago. I think there's no limit" to their demands.

Often, activists' efforts fall short of their goals. Labor advocates trying to improve working conditions in apparel factories, for instance, have failed to persuade Wal-Mart Stores Inc. to open its supplier network to public scrutiny or allow independent auditors into its factories.

But on balance, activists and their causes appear to be gaining increased traction in business and trade. That was apparent at the annual meeting of the World Economic Forum, long viewed as a club for the rich and powerful and often the scene of violent protests. Although there were small demonstrations outside this year's meeting, representatives of about 50 NGOs were inside the conference, buttonholing heads of state and CEOs.

The crowded Davos itinerary of Irene Khan, secretary-general of Amnesty International, included an appearance on a panel with the chief executive of oil giant BP and private meetings with the prime minister of Pakistan, the president of Georgia and the chief executive of machinery maker Caterpillar Inc. She was focusing on poverty and women's issues. "What makes a difference is our ability to dialogue with them in a setting like Davos," she said. "It's not across a barrier, and it's not confrontational."

Business/NGO Partnerships – What's the Payback?

Here's a look at some high profile cases of business/NGO partnerships and the strategic benefits and challenges for both sides.

When Greenpeace shared a platform with Shell at the Johannesburg Summit, the contrast with the classic notion of business/NGO confrontation could not have been starker. A decade earlier, one of the oil giant's redundant platforms (such as Brent Spar) would have been the only kind to have interested the campaign group.

Johannesburg was the Partnership summit. It was built on the premise that governments cannot achieve sustainability on their own, that businesses can be part of the solution, and that NGOs have at least as good an idea what the solution is as anybody else. The business world is also formally engaged in pursuing the UN's Millennium Development Goals.

The joint call by Greenpeace and the World Business Council for Sustainable Development for action on climate change symbolized the growing feeling on both sides that NGOs working with businesses can often achieve more than by attacking from the outside. Many campaigners are still suspicious, and even those working with business reserve the right to criticize. But many partnerships were launched in Johannesburg; many more have flowered since -- from BAT on biodiversity to Coca-Cola on HIV/Aids.

The attractions are obvious, but so are the dangers. Most significant, perhaps, is the danger that the concept is used simply to get businesses to stump up money, which is more like taxation than partnership. Even within a more meaningful relationship, companies risk wasting time and money, and possibly divulging sensitive information which could be misused. NGOs risk reputational damage if a partnership goes wrong, and wasting scarce resources if the desired outcomes are not achieved. The risks can be worth it, of course. For businesses, an NGO can bring knowledge and expertise, but also credibility and reputational gains -- "look how great we are; we're working with WWF/Rainforest Network etc." For an NGO, business brings money, but more substantially a chance to change the way that particular business, and possibly a whole industry, operates.

That highlights a key difference between a true partnership and a conventional project alliance. A shallow alliance can be little different to conventional philanthropy, with a company providing money to back an NGO project, like Nike's recent donation of $275,000 to fund a micro-enterprise program run by the China Foundation for Poverty Alleviation and Mercy Corps. There's nothing wrong with such alliances, of course.

They can make a difference, on some level at least. But it is perhaps glorifying the relationship to call it a partnership. It's not exactly a one-night stand, but it's not marriage either.

Building Lasting Relations

A deeper partnership implies a medium-term relationship, with both parties contributing skills, resources and expertise, and sharing the risks. It should help the business achieve something it otherwise couldn't, and the NGO should get a change of business practice, not just project funding. The relationships between the Rainforest Alliance and companies such as Chiquita are good examples. And they can involve NGOs which are otherwise fierce anti-business campaigners, as you can see in the UK venture between Greenpeace and Innogy to create the Juice wind power brand, which recently began to feed power generated by a huge offshore wind farm into the grid. In this case, Greenpeace has helped provide a marketing channel but also to lobby for planning permission for the site. And the risks to Greenpeace were demonstrated when its partner was taken over by the German group RWE -- which operates nuclear power stations in Germany. The campaign group also came a cropper in its anti-GM food alliance with the Iceland supermarket chain, when Iceland's management (and opposition to genetic modification) changed.

These deep partnerships are few and far between, according to Seb Beloe, director of research and advocacy at the consultancy SustainAbility, which last year published a study* on the future of NGOs. "Many partnerships are not really partnerships, just loose relationships or traditional sponsorship," he says. But he is convinced that there is huge potential, and that NGOs are increasingly interested. "NGOs are beginning to think more strategically about how to engage with companies. In some there is a sense that if you are helping a company be more commercially successful, that devalues what you are doing. But a new breed of NGOs are emerging which want to help companies to make money because they realize that has to happen or companies are not going to be interested." Unlike some campaigning organizations, WWF has long recognized that it is possible to work with business without losing independence or the capacity to criticize. Its work with Unilever to create the Marine Stewardship Council is one of the leading examples of effective partnership. It created something new, which has achieved an independent existence and is helping to make a difference. More recently, a five-year alliance has been formed with HSBC is more like conventional funding. The bank's cash will finance work on protecting freshwater habitats. Of course HSBC is not immune from NGO's criticisms, and WWF got it in the neck last year from some fellow campaigners for getting into bed with cement company Lafarge, whose attempt to develop a quarry in Scotland was opposed by many NGOs (including WWF).

Dax Lovegrove, WWF UK's company relations manager, says it's a matter of judgement. "You can't always work with the cleanest companies, and there's no point just preaching to the converted. As long as your partners are willing to accept challenging targets, they are the ones you should be working with."

The nature of business/NGO links is evolving fast. Increasingly they bring together one or more businesses with one or more NGOs, possibly also including government agencies. For example, Hewlett Packard has helped to build a new public-private consortium in Uganda to provide microfinance, involving organizations as diverse as ACCION International, Freedom from Hunger, and the Grameen Foundation, and with some funding from the U.S. Agency for International Development.

The World Business Council for Sustainable Development (WBCSD) has been midwife to some of the most significant alliances which have built consensus in some of the most difficult industries. The International Institute for Environment and Development (IIED) brokered agreements in forestry and mining with groups of companies brought together by WBCSD. The mining initiative resulted in the creation of the International Council on Mining and Metals to take forward a sustainability strategy in the form of the Toronto Declaration.

The Nordic Partnership is another interesting example of these multi-member partnerships. Born shortly before the Johannesburg summit, it brings together leading Scandinavian companies with WWF and the Danish think-tank Mandag

Morgen. Novo Nordisk and Volvo Car Corporation are the main corporate sponsors. Other corporate participants include Procter & Gamble, consultancies ERM and Cowi, the engineering group ITT Flygt and food manufacturer Danisco. The partnership aims to stimulate sustainable development. "By collective action, we aim to catalyze a new type of business culture," it says.

One early outcome of its work is a report** on business/ NGO partnerships, published in January, which concludes that even in inclusive Scandinavia, progress has been slow. Michael Brinch Pedersen, the Partnership's managing director, says: "Despite a stated willingness to engage in partnerships, the practice of partnering in the Nordic region is still at a very early stage." The report identifies ambitious targets, including "shared lobbying." It says such joint pressure could be a more effective way to get points across, but while that may be true, it is difficult to think of many companies and NGOs which could find much common ground to lobby on.

Risks of Partnerships and Engagement

The Nordic report also sees several dangers when companies and NGOs get into bed with each other. NGOs risk jeopardizing their legitimacy. Businesses risk wasting resources. But there are also risks for the partnership -- that the business simply reaps the reputational reward without making serious efforts to achieve progress. That could backfire on both partners, the report says: "For business, it's undeniable that partnering with NGOs has positive effects on their image. However, if this benefit is misused and not underscored by a willingness to actually work with NGOs towards shared goals, it will quickly lose its value, as NGOs credibility diminishes, along with that of business."

The odds are probably stacked against this kind of partnership really achieving dramatic changes rather than superficial success. But if both sides go about it in the right way, significant gains can be achieved, as the RMC, Starbucks and FedEx cases demonstrate. SustainAbility identified some key success factors:

- o The company must be serious about changing its behavior, and should be able to drive change in its own sector and across the business community more generally.

- o The NGO must be able to maintain clear accountability to its own key stakeholders, and must maintain its independence from the business partner.
- o Each partner needs to benefit directly, and to understand the other's benefits.
- o The "rules of engagement" need to be clearly agreed at the outset.
- o Individual participants must be sufficiently senior to have their organization's mandate and be able to take difficult decisions without constantly having to refer back.
- o The people involved must trust each other.

The difficulty of achieving all those conditions explains why effective partnerships are few and far between. But if it works, companies prepared to take the risk can benefit in more ways than simply enhancing their reputations as good corporate citizens. They can also learn in ways which help them avoid or reduce risks, seize new market opportunities, and stimulate innovation.

> *"Some more enlightened companies can see quite a lot of potential in partnerships, if they have the capacity to run them effectively," Beloe says. But he has a warning for NGOs which shy away from the risks of being "contaminated" by getting too close to the corporate world. "If they don't exploit these opportunities they may become less relevant."*

Organizations such as Pact, the U.S.-based organization with a history of capacity building, and the International Business Leaders Forum, are working hard to make sure that does not happen. They have collaborated to develop NGO understanding of and confidence in business partnerships in several countries. Pact has also developed skills in understanding which businesses and NGOs are capable of making partnerships work. Its successes include working with Coca-Cola in Indonesia to transform libraries into youth learning centers, with Chevron in Angola to build local business and civil society, and with Citibank on microfinance in Vietnam. Like so many initiatives, though, most such projects essentially use the business partner solely to provide funding, and perhaps other resources. Deepening the relationship to challenge and change business practices, or work jointly to change government policies, seems to be more difficult -- but if it works it should also be more rewarding.

NGOs: More than Flower Power

When Global Exchange decided to make Starbucks sell "fair trade" coffee, the nongovernmental organization campaigning for more thoughtful and fairer ways of running the world economy planned dramatic demonstrations outside the chain's outlets nationwide. Within days of the first televised protest, Starbucks executives were visiting the group in San Francisco to discuss how they could offer consumers coffee made from beans grown under more humane conditions, and sold at more remunerative prices for poverty-stricken growers.

Today, Global Exchange and Starbucks work together to make "fair trade" a reality. The deal is one in what a new report on the future of NGOs calls "early tremors" that "represent warning signs of seismic shifts" in the way increasingly powerful NGOs are operating.

With a turnover approaching $1 trillion a year, according to one study, and a reservoir of public trust much deeper than either governments or business enjoys, the international NGO sector could become "amongst the most influential institutions of the 21st century," in the words of John Elkington, coauthor of the study published by SustainAbility, a British consultancy company. And signs indicate that many leaders in the field are "moving beyond a culture of criticism to one of engagement with business and other partners in a search for solutions" says Gavin Power, a spokesman for the UN Global Compact, which helped draw up the report. But the shift, spurred by recognition of the power of market forces, is risky, the study warns. NGOs that have earned international credibility as watchdogs could be in danger of becoming lapdogs.

Businesses that have concentrated on the short-term bottom line have now to focus on long-term prospects. Both sides have to ally themselves with people they once treated as enemies. "We had to psychologically shift gears" in discussions with Starbucks, recalls Kevin Danaher, a cofounder of Global Exchange. Instead of confronting a corporation, and shaming it, "we were saying 'We want to help you.' "

The rewards are tempting, both for NGOs to inculcate their human values in the business world, and companies looking to grow their economic value. "Successful companies plan for the long haul," says Mokhethi Moshoeshoe, who runs the African Institute of Corporate Citizenship in Johannesburg. "If you are not acceptable in the communities where you operate, your business will fail and shareholders will not be happy."

SustainAbility's report, "The 21st Century NGO: In the Market for Change," points to cases where NGO cooperation with business has had mutual benefit. Amnesty International's section in Norway helped train employees of Statoil to spot and resolve human rights issues in the oil company's third-world operations, for example. In the Canadian province of Alberta, energy companies and NGOs work from the outset of every project on limiting environmental damage, giving NGOs a decisive say in planning, while the companies have an easier time with regulatory authorities.

"Greenpeace is a company's best ally," said John Passacantando, an official with the NGO at a business conference last year. The group can help "bring companies into port before the storm." NGOs that set themselves the task of civilizing capitalism through markets seek to hold that system in check in a world where globalization is weakening the grip of governmental regulation. Raymond van Ermen, who once lobbied European Union officials for stricter environmental safeguards, found the process "long and difficult." Though regulations are still needed, he says, the European Partners for the Environment, a firm he runs from Brussels, sets up "a fast track to influence the market" by working directly with business leaders,trade unions, and NGO activists. "In the last two or three years, we have seen impressive changes in the way stakeholders can influence the business agenda," he says.

A similar trend is evident in the way antiglobalization protesters - so violently visible in Seattle or Genoa - are shifting their approach to promote "alternative globalization." Rather than demanding an end to this historical process, they are seeking to shape it by globalizing labor rights and high environmental standards. But government regulations are still important to sanction companies that don't take the ethical bait NGO's offer, say some NGO activists, and noisy campaigns have a place alongside quiet persuasion.

The prospect of a public campaign can be just what a company needs to heed an NGO's complaints, says Mr. Danaher. "We tell them we know how to make their lives miserable but we'd rather not," he explains. "If they want us to go bother some other company, they just have to do the right thing." And NGO negotiators in suits find their job easier if they seem to be struggling to make their voice of reason heard over the cacophony of protest in the street. "Inside or outside, we are all on the same side," Danaher says.

Beyond the carrot-and-stick tactics that Danaher employs, the nature of NGOs' long-term relationship with corporations is at stake. In many cases, says Mr. Moshoeshoe, that relationship goes little further than philanthropy. Huge companies that treat workers appallingly and devastate the environment "outsource their conscience," he scoffs, by donating money to NGOs.

"Our work is to make the business case for corporate social responsibility - if a business is to be sustainable it needs to integrate social and environmental issues into its structure," he says. That attitude is gaining ground, says Seb Beloe, a coauthor of the report. Ratings agencies are springing up that measure companies' financial performance as well as a "triple bottom line," which takes account of their social and environmental record, as well as their profit margins. Though only a few hundred companies have drawn up "triple bottom lines" so far, that is "massively more than a few years ago," he says.

And on the other side of the activist-corporation divide, a matching change of mood points to some new directions. "Instead of just railing at capitalism," advocates Danaher, "let's see if we can't use some market savvy."

Dot-com Exiles Turn Up at New Charities

Philanthropy-watchers hail entrepreneurial prowess of ex-high-tech execs, but say many have much to learn Entrepreneurial zeal carried Tiffany Brown far during the dotcom bonanza, eventually landing her a job developing websites for a business-solutions firm called Organic.com. But when the economic downturn led Organic to scrap her position in 2001, she decided to redirect the energy she had poured into reinventing business into a nonprofit organization that aimed to deliver Web access to people in Africa. With the technology industry in the doldrums, many former "dotcommers" like Ms. Brown are enlisting in the nonprofit world. It's the newest wrinkle in nonprofit management - and it is grabbing the interest of many of those who monitor the universe of nonprofits.

Executives with experience in the Internet business have reinvigorated many nonprofits with fresh thinking and new philanthropic approaches. But experts are also concerned by questionable or failed charities managed by dot-commers who may lack the necessary experience, altruistic values, or understanding of nonprofit regulations. No one knows how many former technology executives have emerged in the land of nonprofits. But the Management Center, a San Francisco firm that trains nonprofit managers, says that as many as a quarter of its programs are filled with former high-tech and dotcom executives. That figure is consistent with a random sampling of nonprofits the Monitor surveyed using data provided by GuideStar, a leading source of nonprofit information. That research found 17 of 100 nonprofits formed since 2000 had former technology executives as top directors.

In high-tech hubs like San Francisco; Boston; and Austin, Texas; the occurrence was even more significant. The chief reason for the trend: The three-year economic downturn has flooded the market with talent that typically bypassed nonprofit work. Many entrepreneurs, tired of technology's struggles, have seen an opportunity to start anew in the nonprofit sector. "They've done their stint in technology and are ready to get out of the cutthroat environment and do something that has a real impact," says Matt O'Grady, the Management Center's associate director.

Earlier this month, Kevin Hartberg of Fort Collins, Colo., created the nonprofit Northern Colorado Idealabs. The firm hopes to draw businesses to the region by showcasing the area's business-friendliness. Before starting Idealabs, Mr. Hartberg ran his own technology firm called Critical Dimensions. Mr. Hartberg says that he hopes many dotcom qualities will serve him well. "You learn how to be aggressive and decisive," he says. "And you also learn a very different management style."

Success with merging the worlds of quick-minded dotcommers and often slow-moving nonprofits has been mixed, but Mr. O'Grady says those who prevail often have previous nonprofit involvement. "If they've volunteered or served on a nonprofit board, their success rate is much higher." Ultimately, boards of directors and donors want managers who know the culture and intricacies of working with nonprofits. For Deborah Sheldon, being laid off from IBM, where she marketed to dotcommers, allowed her to reassess her goals and return to more philanthropic endeavors. But the change wasn't without sacrifice. "I had to learn everything all over again. IBM had a very different culture from my nonprofit and that was a hard change.... [But] I think I'm having a positive impact on my community," says Ms. Sheldon, who is now an executive at CyberSkills, a Burlington, Vt., nonprofit that trains job seekers to use the Internet. "I also took a better than 50 percent pay cut." Nonprofits are learning a lot from technology executives, according to Paul Light, a senior fellow at the Brookings Institution and a professor of public service at New York University. "Their style is aggressive, intense, and very focused on outcomes and deliverables," he says. "Nonprofits are quickly adapting and learning the new language." Mr. Light says that new approach has helped nonprofits better communicate with today's donors, who appear increasingly focused on a nonprofit's community impact.

Sheldon joined an existing nonprofit, but others have ventured off to start their own. That's vexing many industry watchers, who are concerned about a start-up management team's experience and understanding of nonprofit regulations. Take Idea Village, a New Orleans organization that helps build small businesses by offering them consulting services, funding, and business-development training. "We started this as a for-profit entity and raised over $1 million," says Timothy Williamson, its founder. "But we quickly realized there were a number of advantages to being a nonprofit, including access to community funding," he says. That's where he may run into trouble. Lack of understanding the financial-management issues is the No. 1 shortcoming for technology executives entering the nonprofit world, according to the Management Center's O'Grady.

"Understanding tax laws and fundraising regulations is ... where many are coming up short," he says. Such a gap helped cause the demise of Joko Club, a nonprofit that hoped to bring the Internet to Africa, says Ms. Brown. The firm opened its doors in 2001 and closed a year later. "It's not easy to start a nonprofit, and we had some big goals," says Ms. Brown. "Ultimately, the funders of the project decided to dramatically scale back the project." Brown is now doing freelance consulting work. Having lofty goals is the way most dot-commers run into trouble, says NYU's Light. "Don't expect to snap and get results immediately - you won't solve the world's problems overnight," he cautions high-tech executives making the leap. But Light believes dot-commers will have a positive impact on the nonprofit world. "As arrogant as dot-commers may seem, they are worth listening to," he says. "They'll bring a new discipline and entrepreneurial approach that the industry can really use."

Verifying a Nonprofit's Credentials

Unsure about the validity of a given nonprofit? The Federal Trade Commission and GuideStar, a nonprofit information provider, have compiled a checklist for donors examining charities.

Verify an Organization's Charitable Status

If a charity is not on the GuideStar website (www.guidestar.org), ask to see its letter of determination or, if it is faith based, its official listing in a directory for its denomination.

Get the Cold, Hard Facts

A reputable organization will define its mission and programs clearly, have measurable goals, and use concrete criteria to describe its achievements. Avoid charities that won't share information. Ethical charities are willing to discuss their programs and finances.

Avoid charities that pressure you.

Reputable nonprofits don't use pressure tactics and are willing to provide literature or direct you to a website discussing their activities.

Trust your instincts.

If, after going through the previous steps, you still have doubts about an organization, don't contribute to it. Find another nonprofit that does the same kind of work and with which you feel comfortable, and then make your donation.

Has the American Enterprise Institute Lost Contact with Reality?

The American Enterprise Institute (AEI) has a problem. It is loaded with corporate money, full of rich fellowships for Washington, D.C. influence peddlers, masquerading as conservatives, who wallow in plush offices figuring out how to assure that big corporations rule the U.S. and the rest of the world. During the past twenty-two years, the AEI, their nearby corporate patrons, their allied trade associations and corporate "think tanks" have, in effect, taken over the executive branch, the Congress and promoted the judgeships of right-wing corporate lawyers demanding another salary increase. The Clinton administration hardly slowed their stride. In fact one high official of the U.S. Chamber of Commerce told me that they loved the Clinton government. Why not, under Clinton they got corporate-managed trade called NAFTA and WTO, laws furthering media, telecommunications, agribusiness, banking, brokerage and insurance industry concentration, weak to nonexistent regulation, a chronic softness on corporate crimes against pensioners and small investors, and a pathetically indifferent consumer and labor policy - to name a few surrenders.

What's left to do? How does the AEI keep its corporate supremacists writing those big checks? How to avoid institutional ennui? Why, go after the liberal or progressive non-governmental associations (NGO's). Describe them as a collage of Goliaths running an all-points wrecking machine over government and business. Open a theater of the absurd.

On Wednesday, June 11, 2003 the AEI held such a forum on what to do about this burgeoning civic menace, as they contrive it. Speaker after speaker weighed in with their strained fulminations. The room was full, of course, with AEI partisans nodding in agreement. These are the affluent ones who cavil against living wages by janitors who clean their offices, farm workers who harvest their food and hospital workers who care for their parents. These are the fully health-insured comforted ones who assail pleas for universal health insurance for over 45 million American children and adults and those who have contempt for the environmental groups that care about stopping toxic polluters in poorer areas of the country, while living in shrubbered suburbs far from the incinerators and waste dumps. Here was speaker, Jon Entine of Miami University, describing "capitalism's trojan horse: reasonable people should be concerned about the growing influence of the social investment community, and its emerging partnership with NGOs, most of which share a knee jerk demonization of corporations and free markets. Its leaders are products of the activist community, yet they are different and more dangerous."

Whoa! Trying to persuade shareholders to press for more corporate responsibility, in the midst of a corporate crime wave by the managers, is somehow subversive in his mind. How dare the social investment community advise its clients about corporate misbehavior and urge the owners (shareholders) to exercise more control over their own companies.

Nothing quite captures AEI's intent better than the official AEI statement announcing the conference. Some of its words bear quoting: "NGOs have created their own rules and regulations and demanded that governments and corporations abide by those rules. Many nations' legal systems encourage NGOs to use the courts - or the specter of the courts - to compel compliance."

"Politicians and corporate ledgers are often forced to respond to the NGO media machine, and the resources of taxpayers and shareholders are used in support of ends they did not intend to sanction. The extraordinary growth of advocacy NGOs in liberal democracies has the potential to undermine the sovereignty of constitutional democracies, as well as the effectiveness of credible NGOs."

Has AEI lost contact with reality? This is what democracy is all about - advocating, petitioning, suing, lobbying and urging power centers like government and business to do better. AEI has its own positions, together with its corporate allies doing all this and much more with corporate campaign cash and economic power ultimatums. Somehow, citizen groups, that have no governmental power - either in fact or by purchase - have become a threat to "constitutional democracies." Has the AEI read our nation's Bill of Rights? What they are condemning, with vague, ironic regulatory nostrums proposed against dissenting citizen groups, is democracy itself. What the AEIstas prefer is plutocracy.

These corporate think tanks have spent too much time talking to themselves in too comfortable sinecures. They are afflicted by what George Will called "pitiless abstractions" (in a column against anti-air bag interests). They need to visit factories, foundries, mines, hospitals, prisons, slums, trailer parks and small farms for some sensitivity training. Maybe alleviating their chronic empirical starvation will tap some residual humanity that places people before corporations. They might remember that two hundred years ago, the early corporations in New England were chartered by state legislatures to be our servants, not our masters.

Bringing the War Home: Right Wing Think Tank Turns Wrath on NGOs

Having led the charge to war in Iraq, the American Enterprise Institute (AEI), an influential think tank close to the Bush administration, has added a new target: international nongovernmental organizations (NGOs). AEI and its partner in the project, the Federalist Society for Law and Public Policy Studies, are setting their sights on those groups with a "progressive" or "liberal" agenda that favors "global governance" and other notions that are also promoted by the United Nations and other multilateral agencies.

The two organizations announced June 11th that they are launching a new website (www.NGOWatch.org) to expose the funding, operations, and agendas of international NGOs, and particularly their alleged efforts to constrain U.S. freedom of action in international affairs and influence the behavior of corporations abroad. The organizations are especially alarmed by what they see as the naiveté of the Bush administration and corporations that provide NGOs with funding and other support. "In many cases, naive corporate reformers, within corporations and in government, are welcoming them," complained John Entine, an AEI fellow.

To mark the site's launch, AEI, which is funded mainly by major corporations and right-wing foundations, also held an all-day conference entitled NGOs: The Growing Power of an Un-elected Few, which featured a series of presentations depicting NGOs as a growing and largely unaccountable threat to the Bush administration's foreign policy goals and free-market capitalism around the world. The conference was co-sponsored by the right-wing Australian think tank, the Institute of Public Affairs (IPA).

"NGOs have created their own rules and regulations and demanded that governments and corporations abide by those rules," according to conference organizers. "Politicians and corporate leaders are often forced to respond to the NGO media machine, and the resources of taxpayers and shareholders are used in support of ends they did not sanction. The extraordinary growth of advocacy NGOs in liberal democracies has the potential to undermine the sovereignty of constitutional democracies, as well as the effectiveness of credible NGOs," they added.

Both the website launch and Wednesday's conference might normally be dismissed as a pep rally of a far right obsessed with left-wing and European conspiracies to impose world government on the United States and destroy capitalism. But the fact that no less than 42 senior administration foreign policy and justice officials have been recruited from AEI and the Federalists and that AEI "fellows" include such prominent figures as Lynne Cheney (the vice president's spouse), former UN Ambassador Jeanne Kirkpatrick, and the influential Iraq hawk and former chairman of the Pentagon's Defense Policy Board, Richard Perle, suggests that Wednesday's events may herald a much more antagonistic attitude toward NGOs on the part of the government.

Global Governance a "Stalinist Concept"

The conference was also held on the heels of harshly critical remarks late last month by Andrew Natsios, the director of the U.S. Agency for International Development (USAID), which often contracts with NGOs for relief and development work. Natsios reportedly charged that NGOs receiving USAID funding for projects in Afghanistan and elsewhere were not giving sufficient credit to the U.S. government as the source of the aid. His remarks coincided with moves by USAID to use more private contractors, instead of NGOs, for work in Iraq and other countries, and to impose stricter rules regarding contacts between NGOs working on USAID projects and the press that would reduce their independence. In that context, according to one international NGO official who asked not to be identified, the AEI conference could be seen as part of a troublesome pattern. "There are a number of things we're seeing that we want to be sure are nothing more than coincidence," he said.

The general message at Wednesday's conference was that while NGOs like Amnesty International, CARE, Oxfam, and Friends of the Earth have performed valuable work in promoting human rights, development, and environmental protection, their general policies, particularly at the international level, may be inimical to U.S. interests and free-market principles.

According to George Washington University political science professor Jarol Manheim, international NGOs are pursuing "a new and pervasive form of conflict" against multinational corporations, which he calls "Biz-War," the title of his forthcoming book. NGOs, for example, work with like-minded institutional investors, such as union- and church-based pension funds, to sponsor shareholder resolutions demanding that corporations adopt more environment--or human rights--friendly policies. Such efforts, he said, should be seen as "part of a larger, anti-corporate campaign," which includes consumer boycotts and other efforts to influence corporate behavior. Companies are increasingly engaging in joint projects with NGOs, using them as consultants, or even hiring former NGO officials to protect themselves against negative publicity.

This was echoed by John Entine, an AEI adjunct fellow, who called the "social investing" movement, a "wolf in sheep's clothing" and argued that "anti-free market NGOs under the guise of corporate reform are extending their reach into the boardrooms of corporations." Cornell University government professor Jeremy Rabkin was particularly contemptuous of corporations that tried to establish good relations with NGOs by, for example, working on joint projects or contributing money or other kinds of support. "Why are NGOs in a position to confer legitimacy?" he asked. "A lot of this is a kind of protection racket."

On the political front, international NGOs, which in recent years led the fight for the global ban on anti-personnel mines, the Kyoto Protocol to fight global warming, and the treaty establishing the International Criminal Court, are pursuing a "liberal internationalist" vision that "wants to constrain the United States," said American University law professor Kenneth Anderson.

The groups prefer a world order based on "global governance" and the rule of international law to one that is based on "democratic sovereignty," where nation-states whose governments are subject to the vote of the people are the highest authority. In this quest, they are aided by UN agencies, which see in international NGOs and the global civil society they claim to represent an "alternative form of legitimacy beyond democracy," Anderson said.

"If you think about it, of course this is a left-wing program," added Rabkin. "The whole enterprise of global governance is going to appeal more to the parties of the left ... If it is global, it is anti-national," he said, at one point noting that the original notion of a nongovernmental organization was a "Stalinist concept."

US Conservatives Take Aim at NGOs

While non-governmental organizations (NGOs) such as Amnesty International, Greenpeace, and Oxfam have made significant contributions to human rights, the environment, and development, they are using their growing prominence and power to pursue a "liberal" agenda at the international level that threatens U.S. sovereignty and free-market capitalism. That was the message delivered by a series of speakers at an all-day conference, "Nongovernmental Organizations: The Growing Power of an Unelected Few," Wednesday sponsored by the American Enterprise Institute (AEI), a Washington think tank that has been particularly influential with the Bush administration. "NGOs have created their own rules and regulations and demanded that governments and corporations abide by those rules," according to AEI and the conference co-sponsor, the rightist Institute of Public Affairs of Australia. "Politicians and corporate leaders are often forced to respond to the NGO media machine, and the resources of taxpayers and shareholders are used in support of ends they did not sanction." "The extraordinary growth of advocacy NGOs in liberal democracies has the potential to undermine the sovereignty of constitutional democracies, as well as the effectiveness of credible NGOs," they warned.

To shed more light on NGOs, AEI announced the launch of a new website, NGOWatch.org (www.ngowatch.org), that will provide information about their operations, funding sources and political agendas. Brian Hook of the Federalist Society for Law and Public Policy Studies, which is co-sponsoring the site, said it will cover those NGOs "with the most influence in international affairs." NGOs, which have proliferated at the local level since the 1980s--particularly in developing countries--have become major players at the United Nations and other multilateral agencies, such as the World Bank, which had traditionally dealt only with governments. Several thousand NGOs now enjoy "consultative status" at the UN, which entitles them to participate in some debates, while their image as representatives of "global civil society" has endowed them with a moral and political legitimacy, which they have used as leverage in dealing with the other major global actors, governments and corporations. But, unlike corporations and governments, they are largely unregulated, and their internal processes often lack transparency and accountability, according to their critics and even to many NGOs themselves. Indeed, a

UN commission on civil society chaired by former Brazilian President Henrique Cardoso is expected to recommend the adoption of guidelines or other mechanisms to ensure that NGOs recognized by the UN are transparent and accountable.

To the groups who gathered at AEI Wednesday, however, international NGOs raise concerns that go far beyond transparency and accountability. To them, the international NGOs are pursuing a leftist or "liberal" agenda that favors "global governance" and other notions that are also promoted by the United Nations and other multilateral agencies. "This is inherently a project that is tilted to the left," according to Cornell University government professor Jeremy Rabkin, who argued that NGOs are using the multilateral system to try to regulate corporations and governments. "NGOs want to be players. They want to be regulators," agreed IPA's Gary Johns. He cited NGO lobbying for the adoption of codes of conduct for multinational corporations. "Before long, you have a degree of regulation that no one thought was possible."

In fact, according to George Washington University political science professor Jarol Manheim, international NGOs are pursuing "a new and pervasive form of conflict" against corporations which he calls "Biz-war," the title of his forthcoming book. NGOs, for example, work with sympathetic institutional investors, such as union and church-based pension funds, to sponsor shareholder resolutions demanding that corporations adopt more environment- or human-rights-friendly policies. Such efforts, he said, should be seen as "part of a larger, anti-corporate campaign." This was echoed by John Entine, an AEI adjunct fellow, who called the "social investing" movement, as it is called, a "wolf in sheep's clothing. "Anti-free market NGOs under the guise of corporate reform are extending their reach into the boardrooms of corporations," he said. "In many cases, naive corporate reformers, within corporations and in government, are welcoming them."

Moreover, the strategy is working. "Big shareholders are getting embarrassed to be associated with some companies," said Manheim, who noted that companies are increasingly using NGOs as consultants or even hiring former NGO officials to protect themselves against negative publicity or consumer boycotts. On the global political front, international NGOs, which led the fight for the global ban on anti-personnel mines, the Kyoto Protocol to curb greenhouse-gas emissions, and the treaty establishing the International Criminal Court (ICC), are pursuing a "liberal internationalist" vision that is very much at odds with that of the Bush administration, according to American University law professor Kenneth Anderson.

These efforts are intended in part to further a world order based on "global governance" and the rule of international law, rather than one based on the sovereignty of democratic nation states. The leaders of international NGOs are part of a culture that "wants to constrain the United States" and whose ideas about world order "are not congenial to the ideas of this administration," according to Anderson.

Several speakers praised the work of NGOs in providing services and humanitarian aid to needy people in developing countries but stressed that, at the international policy level, much of what they did actually hurt the intended beneficiaries. Roger Bate, director of Africa Fighting Malaria, cited NGOs' opposition to the use of DDT to fight malaria and to the delivery of genetically-modified maize in southern Africa as examples of policies which amounted to "eco-imperialism" and showed a "callous disregard for human life." "NGOs definitely provide benefits in the short run, but in the long run, their influence is almost always malign," he said. Mike Nahan, IPA's executive director, charged that international NGOs supported secession movements in East Timor and Aceh, Indonesia; put Papua New Guinea "on the road to bankruptcy" by forcing out the mining industry; and is "destroying civil society in many of these countries."

DEMOCRACY AT THE BARRICADES

Heads of state were besieged in July in Genoa. They talked trade and money inside a guarded, if luxurious, compound, while outside the Italian carabinieri confronted demonstrators, only a few of whom were violent. Results: news footage of handshakes and governmental agreements, their details already forgotten - and of an unwarranted death, 600 injuries, beatings and frustration. The next talks will be in the safe enclave of

Qatar. After the disgrace of Genoa, multinationals and European and international institutions targeted by "anti-globalisers" have a recurrent problem: how to discredit, weaken, manipulate and, if possible, annihilate the international citizens' movement which has disturbed the gatherings of the masters of the universe since Seattle. Police retaliation and direct repression are the most obvious weapons in the anti-anti-globaliser armoury. This April spring in Quebec smelled of tear gas: the official figure for the number of canisters fired against anti-FTAA (Free Trade Area of the Americas) demonstrators was 4,707 - "excessive" according to a committee set up by the government of Quebec. Asked by doctors about chemical components and propulsion agents, the authorities professed ignorance: "We only do testing in terms of how effective the gas is on people".

In Europe, too, the use of force and manipulation has reached new extremes. In Gothenburg, during the demonstrations at the summit meeting of heads of state and government of the European Union in June, the Swedish police used live ammunition. In Barcelona, on 22 June, where forums and demonstrations went ahead although the World Bank had retreated from holding its new economics conference, plain clothes police infiltrated the end of the march, vandalised property and attacked uniformed officers to provoke them into violent reprisals against demonstrators and journalists.

In Genoa, the Italian police went further: one dead, more than 600 injured, hundreds of arbitrary arrests and a real political plot. There is evidence of complicity between the authorities and gangs of Black Block agents provocateurs that damaged parts of the city.

But force seems to have little effect, so the authorities are resorting to legal harassment. A leading member of the Ruckus Society, known for its training sessions in non-violence to prepare for occasions like Seattle, was picked up on the streets of Philadelphia the day after demonstrations at the Republican Party convention. He was questioned for six hours by an officer who cheerfully admitted that he had orders to "dump a bunch of shit on his booking papers", indicted on 13 counts and (unprecedented for such minor offences) required to put up bail of $ 1m.

Wrongful arrest, intimidation and ill-treatment of detainees, and closing meetings "as a preventive measure", are common wherever opponents of globalisation meet. For evidence, visit one of the independent, decentralised Indymedia websites that are causing headaches in Washington. On the day of the big demonstration in Quebec, FBI and US secret service agents appeared at the Indymedia office in Seattle with court orders requiring it to disclose the names and email addresses of everyone who had visited the site in the previous 48 hours - several thousand people. This was in flagrant breach of rights guaranteed under the US constitution. In Genoa, on the night of 21-22 July, carabinieri raided the alternative media centre without a warrant, beat and arrested people, and claimed they were looking for evidence of infiltration by "rioters".

In Europe too, governments have no compunction about taking liberties with the law. In December 2000 an attempt was made to reduce the scale of the demonstrations against liberal policies pursued by the EU. At a European Council meeting in Nice, 1,500 Italian nationals were held at the Franco-Italian border although they had valid tickets and passports. In January 2001 Swiss authorities blocked all access roads to Davos, transforming the region into a military stronghold. The Italian government suspended the Schengen agreement for four days in a vain attempt to prevent demonstrators from other countries congregating in Genoa.

The Backlash

There is a serious ideological backlash, too. How can the powers regroup after a fiasco like Seattle? The first ploy is to accuse opponents of being "enemies of the poor", a ploy used by London's Financial Times and The Economist, and by Mike Moore, director-general of the World Trade Organisation, who said in Geneva "these protesters make me want to vomit". Paul Krugman, economist at the Massachusetts Institute of Technology and media darling, added: "The anti-globalisation movement already has a remarkable track record of hurting the very people and causes it claims to champion." Of the demonstrators in Geneva, he said: "Whatever their intentions, they were doing their best to make the poor even poorer".

The theme was taken up on the eve of Genoa by President George W Bush, in a statement to Le Monde: "The demonstrators are condemning people to poverty". In its first issue after Seattle, The Economist tried a second argument. Faced with the success of the NGOs, it claimed that they "represented a dangerous shift of power to unelected and unaccountable special interest groups". The alleged lack of legitimacy of the "anti-globalisers" has been a constant complaint in business circles since the publication of the Geneva Business Declaration in September 1998, an outcome of a dialogue organised by Helmut Maucher, then president of the International Chamber of Commerce (also chairman and managing director of Nestlé and president of the Round Table of European industrialists) and the UN secretary-general.

The declaration said that: "Activist pressure groups should place emphasis on legitimising themselves. Where this does not happen, rules establishing their rights and responsibilities should be considered. Business is accustomed to working with trade unions, consumer organisations and other representative groups that are responsible, credible, transparent and accountable, and consequently command respect. What we question is the proliferation of activist groups that do not accept these self-disciplinary criteria."

The third ploy is to repeat that the protesters don't know what they are talking about, to label them and their organisations "opportunist" or "alarmist". Their ideas and opinions are described as "disinformation", "blatant lies" and "nonsense". Thomas Friedman of the New York Times says opponents of neo-liberalism are "despicable [and] deserve a slap in the face". The Financial Times, mildly threatening, says that if the advance of globalisation's foes is to be halted, "now is the time to draw a line in the sand". But what happens if the "self-discipline" is not forthcoming, if no-one takes any notice of the "line in the sand" and the opposition continues to "talk nonsense"? A great many people are considering this.

In the Middle of the Desert

In March 2000 the Cordell Hull Institute in Washington, a pro-free-trade think-tank, ran a seminar "After Seattle:

restoring momentum in the WTO". Of the 50 participants - senior civil servants, ministers, advisers to big firms, ambassadors - only two represented NGOs. One, scandalised by the proceedings, posted an account of them on the internet. The meeting had been less concerned with the WTO than with finding ways to silence the opposition. Cecil Parkinson, who had been British minister for trade in the cabinet of Margaret Thatcher, began by saying they must never have another WTO meeting on US soil as it was far too easy to organise protests there. Clayton Yeutter, former US secretary of agriculture, agreed. They should choose a place where "security could be assured" and give little advance notice to "keep the protesters off balance".

The Brazilian foreign minister favoured holding the next meeting "in the middle of the desert" - more or less what will happen in November when the WTO conference meets in Qatar - or "on a cruise ship". In fact, the G8 summit in 2002 will be held in a nearly inaccessible place in the Canadian Rockies. To general applause, he then passionately defended child labour: children in Brazil helped their families by earning a few reales hauling bags of coal from depot to steelworks. A senior US civil servant suggested they should "give the NGOs some other sandbox to play in": they could be told to take their concerns to the International Labour Organisation, which has no powers. Another senior US civil servant, keen to "delegitimise the NGOs", suggested persuading the foundations that fund them to turn off the tap. That would force them to back down.

And whatever the real reasons, the most important American foundations are changing their approach. According to reliable sources - who prefer to remain anonymous - think-tanks and organisations opposed to globalisation are beginning to be denied resources. Also, and unusually, the presidents of major foundations are personally monitoring allocations of funds by their programme managers in cases where, in the past, they have funded groups in the Seattle constellation. The Ford and Rockefeller foundations now favour think-tanks like the Economic Strategy Institute, whose president is a former adviser to Ronald Reagan and whose list of donors reads like a Who's Who of US transnational corporations.

Electronic surveillance is another powerful business weapon. The eWatch company illustrates capitalism's ability to profit from anything, including the activities of those who question its supremacy. This subsidiary of a public relations company offers to monitor everything on the net about its corporate subscribers, checking not only the media, but also a database of 15,000 online public discussion groups and 40,000 newsgroups. For an annual fee of $3,600-$16,200, "you can monitor the competition, government regulators, activists, opposition groups, and anything else that impacts your business". Cheap at the price.

Such tactics are not expected. And maybe they prove that the opponents of corporate-led globalisation are making a real impact - why otherwise would the masters of the universe bother with them? But that is to underestimate the importance international capital attaches to this battle. Its hatred of democracy has never been so clearly displayed. It must, by fair means or foul, establish the legitimacy of its domination before any more shocks. (From this point of view, the elections of Bush and of Silvio Berlusconi are heaven-sent.) Social movements have to watch their step now, especially since Genoa. They are entering a minefield.

Charity Finds that US Food Aid for Africa Hurts Instead of Helps

CARE, one of the world's biggest charities, is walking away from about $45 million a year in federal funding, saying American food aid is not only plagued with inefficiencies, but may hurt some of the very poor people it aims to help. Its decision, which has deeply divided the world of food aid, is focused on the practice of selling tons of American farm products in African countries that in some cases compete with the crops of struggling local farmers. "If someone wants to help you, they shouldn't do it by destroying the very thing that they're trying to promote," said George Odo, a CARE official who grew disillusioned with the practice while supervising the sale of American wheat and vegetable oil in Nairobi.

Under the system, the U.S. government buys the goods from American agribusiness, ships them overseas on mostly

American-flagged carriers and then donates the goods to the aid groups. The groups sell the products in poor countries and use the money to fund their anti-poverty programs there. As Congress considers a new farm bill, neither the Bush administration nor representatives are looking to undo the practice, known as "monetization." In fact, some of the nonprofit groups say it has worked well and are pressing for sharp increases in the tonnage of American food shipped for sale and distribution to support development programs.

The Christian charity World Vision and 14 other groups say that CARE is mistaken, that the system works because it keeps hard currency in poor countries, can help prevent food price spikes in them and does not hurt their farmers. But criticism of the practice is growing. Former President Jimmy Carter, whose Atlanta-based Carter Center uses private money to help African farmers be more productive, says a flawed food aid system has survived partly because the charities that get money from it defend it. Agribusiness and shipping interest groups have tremendous political clout, but charitable groups are influential, too, Carter said, because "they speak from the standpoint of angels." "The farm bloc is powerful, but when you add these benevolent organizations, the totality of that has blocked change in the system," said Carter, who is also a Georgia farmer.

Some charities that champion monetization bristle at such suggestions. And their allies in Congress say that maritime and agribusiness interests are essential allies for programs to aid the hungry. "Sure it's self-interest if staying in business to help the hungry is self-interested," said Avram Guroff, a senior vice president at ACDI/VOCA, which ranked sixth in monetization sales last year. "We're not lining our pockets."

But Peter Matlon, an agricultural economist based in Nairobi and a managing director of the Rockefeller Foundation, said converting American commodities into cash for development was a case of "the tail wagging the dog," with domestic farm policies in the United States shaping hunger-fighting methods abroad. "The NGOs have been ignoring this evidence for years that there's a negative impact on the prices farmers receive," said Matlon, who is involved in a $150 million effort financed by the Rockefeller and Bill and Melinda Gates foundations to increase the productivity of African farmers. The Government Accountability Office, the non-partisan, investigative arm of Congress, also concluded this year that the system was "inherently inefficient." CARE and Catholic Relief - who rank first and second in money raised through monetization - say they recover only 70 to 80 percent of what the United States paid for the commodities and shipping. But while Catholic Relief Services and Save the Children, which ranked fifth last year in such sales, agree with CARE that the system is inefficient, they also say they will not stop converting American food into money unless Congress replaces the lost revenues with cash. They help a lot of poor people with the money, they say.

The experiences of Walter Otieno, a grizzled Kenyan farmer in mud-stained pants, illustrate the paradoxes of paying for rural development through sales of American farm goods. Over the years, he had watched four of his 12 children die of measles, which is more often fatal for the malnourished. He has had difficulty growing enough to feed his family. "My children were skinny and their skin was dull," he said. Then last year he began growing a small patch of sunflowers on a hill sloping down to Lake Victoria with help from a program that CARE finances through the sale of American farm goods here. A CARE extension worker, Rosemary Ogala, has taught him and dozens of farmers in his group where to buy sunflower seed, when to plant it, how to space the rows and when to harvest.

CARE has also connected them to a ready market: the Kenyan company Bidco Oil Refineries, whose managers say they could more than quintuple the amount of sunflower seed they buy from Kenyan farmers to process into vegetable oil. The profit Otieno earned from the crop rescued his family from dire poverty. Now, with his new earnings, he plays with his sons and daughters, plump on eggs and milk, at the family's general store, a tiny shack stocked with goods financed by the sunflower sales. "Our lives have changed," he said. The question is whether small-scale sunflower farmers like Otieno would have done better if nonprofit groups had not sold tons of American crude soybean oil, a competing product, to the same

Kenyan company that purchased Otieno's meager crop. CARE and some other experts say the answer is a clear yes.

In 2003, Bidco bought almost 9,000 metric tons of crude soybean oil sold to the United States by Bunge, the agribusiness giant. Altogether that year, Bunge sold the United States 15,180 metric tons of oil for resale by the nonprofits in Kenya. American law requires aid groups to establish that such sales will not discourage production by local farmers, but some critics say it is a conflict of interest to ask nonprofit groups to select experts to make this determination.

In this case, the nonprofit organizations hired a consultant who advised them in 2003 that they could safely sell up to 38,000 metric tons of vegetable oil in Kenya, which mostly depends on imports. That amount, about 10 percent of the country's consumption, was "negligible," he said. But Odo of CARE disagreed, saying in a memo that "the truth is that the subsidized importation from the U.S. reduces the growth in the local market." Ultimately, CARE's decision to phase out such sales evolved from a senior manager's change of heart. Daniel Maxwell, a professor of nutrition at Tufts University, was a food security adviser for CARE in Nairobi who saw sales of American food as an imperfect, but useful way to raise money.

He knew firsthand, however, how risky it was to manage projects financed in fluctuating commodities markets. When prices sank, CARE had too little money and was sometimes forced to lay off workers. Maxwell also strongly suspected that buyers offered too little for the farm goods, knowing they were dealing with aid workers who were novices in commodities trading. As he and Christopher Barrett, an agricultural economist at Cornell University, researched a book, "Food Aid After Fifty Years," his doubts deepened. "Not only was it a pain the neck," he said, "but there were potentially serious knock on effects that would be damaging to farmers and trade."

In 2004, Maxwell and Barrett made the case against the practice at CARE headquarters in Atlanta. They recalled that the senior vice president, Patrick Carey, who has since died, cautioned them that leaving the system would be like "an act of partial suicide" for the nonprofits. Nonetheless, by 2009 CARE will end almost all of its participation in such projects across the developing world. It will try to raise money to replace the lost revenues from philanthropies and other donors, and by making its own aid programs profitable. One of those programs could be seen in action one recent afternoon in the Kenyan village of Poche. CARE has helped local women bypass local middlemen to sell pineapples at better prices in big supermarkets in Nairobi, 10 hours away by road.

One woman, Doreen Amimo, a 52-year-old grandmother, has seen her weekly earnings rise to $18 from $11. She can now afford to feed and clothe an orphaned niece and nephew. "And I never lack sugar in the house," she said, "and we can have tea and milk every morning!"

These farmers are selling their fruit to a small company, Vegcare, that CARE and a Kenyan company started with an investment of $170,000 in 2005. Vegcare advises farmers on how to grow pineapples that meet supermarket standards, buys them and trucks them to a wholesaler in Nairobi that supplies Nakumatt, a Kenyan supermarket chain.

CARE's idea is that a profitable business is more likely than a charitable venture to survive when foreign aid runs out. CARE managers here say they hope its renunciation of most of the money from commodity sales will free it to candidly address the flaws in the American strategy to combat world hunger. "What's happened to humanitarian organizations over the years is that a lot of us have become contractors on behalf of the government," said Odo of CARE. "That's sad but true. It compromised our ability to speak up when things went wrong."

Chances of Achieving MDGs "Slim" Without Civil Society

Global civil society leaders called on non-governmental organisations (NGOs) Thursday to use both international channels and their muscle on the ground for applying pressure on governments to achieve the Millennium Development Goals (MDGs).

The Civil Society Development Forum also heard that the global picture for progress towards the MDGs is uneven, with sub-Saharan Africa and western Asia set to miss most of the targets -- despite there being enough money to achieve the goals. All regions, including sub-Saharan Africa, are on track to achieve full primary school enrolment (goal two). But sub-Saharan Africa will, on average, not be able to halve the proportion of people living on less than a dollar a day, or halve the number suffering from hunger by 2015, said Nikhil Seth, director of the division for support and co-ordination at the United Nations Economic and Social Council (ECOSOC). In western Asia poverty rates have doubled over the past few years, while half the population of the whole of the developing world still has no access to sanitation. No progress has been made with reducing the number of underweight children, said Seth. Inequality both within and between countries is growing, stressed Salil Shetty, director of the United Nations Millennium Campaign. Certain countries have shown progress, however, with Tanzania, Rwanda, Mozambique and Bangladesh set to meet many of the goals.

Some 500 delegates from NGOs from across the world have gathered in Geneva, Switzerland, for the Civil Society Development Forum which has been arranged by CONGO, or the Conference of Non-governmental Organisations in Consultative Relationship with the United Nations. The United Nations Millennium Campaign co-hosts the event. The results of the forum will be conveyed to the annual high-level meeting of ECOSOC taking place later this year. The focus of the forum is also to mobilise NGOs to promote goals one and eight. Goal one concerns eradicating poverty and hunger, and goal eight creating a global partnership for development.

"Without civil society as the driving force behind the MDGs, the chances are very slim that we will reach the MDGs," said CONGO President Renate Bloem in her opening address. "Together we should pursue the vision that respect for human rights and human development go hand in hand." The systematic and active participation of NGOs is essential to hold government accountable for progress with the MDGs, said Dalius Cekuolis, ECOSOC president. He told delegates about the recent reforms at ECOSOC which allow for involvement of NGOs in development policies at the international level. ECOSOC will hold a Development Co-operation Forum next year, where development policies will be reviewed. NGOs should also use the offices of the U.N. based in their own countries to advocate for issues of concern, said Kumi Naidoo, secretary general of CIVICUS, a global non-governmental organisation representing civil society.

He reminded delegates that the MDGs were minimal goals. At the time of the drafting of the MDGs activists were also worried that while the goals which developing countries had to fulfil (one to seven) had target dates, goal eight -- which developed countries had to fulfil -- had no deadlines, said Naidoo. This was especially worrying against the background of the "compliance deficit" that the U.N. system suffers from, he said. Many goals have been set and missed in the past. Part of the problem is the lack of political will, which is especially important when it comes to financing, said Sergei Ordzhonikidze, director general of the U.N. office in Geneva.

According to Shetty, success in working towards the goals is determined by whether MDGs are given high priority by political leaders, whether policies and budgets are in place, and whether donors come to the table, offering assistance such as debt cancellation -- and more and better quality aid. Speakers emphasised that enough money is available globally to finance the MDG processes. The current global expenditure of 1.2 trillion dollars on arms far exceeds the global spending on development, Sergei Ordzhonikidze pointed out.

Economic growth has globally been the highest ever in the past 50 years, so there is a question about where the resulting wealth is going, said Roberto Bissio, executive director of the NGO Social Watch. There are some 12 million individuals who each have more than one million dollars in offshore investments, totalling 12 trillion dollars. Calculations showed that if the interest on this money was taxed even at a minimal level, more money could be raised than was necessary to fund the achievement of the MDGs, said Bissio.

Strength in Numbers for Globalization's Critics

Environmentalists, churches, trade unions -- globalization's opponents have many faces. But they have one thing in common: They want to limit the power of corporations and make sure people have a greater say.

Maria Mies was in Seattle in 1999 as ten thousands of demonstrators marched through the streets chanting the slogans "No globalization without participation" and "The world is not for sale." Trade unions, church groups, environmentalists, women's movements and third world groups protested against a new round of liberalization of world trade. A retired sociology professor and member of the organization Attac, which is critical of globalization, Mies said she was aware of the many faces of the anti-globalization movement. "There were alsc poor people, farmers and (blue-collar) workers who took part spontaneously," she said. "There were indeed different groups, but they all were fed up and knew what they didn't want anymore."

The movement considers the promise that globalization will bring the world peace, equality, freedom and prosperity to be a lie. They believe that poor countries in particular suffer from corporations' pursuit of growth and are forced into poverty and dependency.

Opponents of globalization say companies scale down social achievements, such as minimum wages and occupational health and safety, using the argument that they must remain internationally competitive. Opposition groups demand guarantees for people's right to self-determination and for minimum of social standards and want to change international trade agreements to favor developing countries.

More say for the People

Mies said democracy is globalization's first victim, adding that the movement's central demand for people to become more involved in political decisions has remained unchanged. "That's no longer possible in a globalized world controlled by multinational corporations," said Mies. "National laws cannot simply be tossed aside when a few companies lobby Brussels."

Political scientist Claus Leggewie said those opposed to globalization could be divided into five groups. In his book "Die Globalisierung und ihre Gegner" (Globalization and its Critics), he separated the groups into five subsets: Leftists and radical leftists are interested in social justice and want to develop a different societal system; the academic left has taken up some ideas from the ecological movement and engages in a certain amount of Marxist criticism; reformers from the business world favor employing a social democratic approach to tame capitalism; globalization critics grounded in religion link to the churches' traditions of social reform; and right-wing opponents to globalization put the stress on the nation state

Heterogeneity has Advantages

In addition to large organizations, such as Attac, Greenpeace, trade unions and churches, innumerable smaller local and regional groups are also part of the struggle, but the varying currents united by one movement isn't problematic, according to Leggewie.

"A movement is characterized precisely by a high level of heterogeneity and loose connections," he said, adding that it allows the movement to distribute various tasks. The groups aiming for reform had their target audiences just as the radical and militant groups that organize protests did.

Churches made opponents of globalization capable of action by providing financing, infrastructure and organizational skills needed by a movement low on resources before trade unions or political parties get involved, Leggewie said. Despite their different perspectives, the groups must see their work as being interrelated, according to Mies.

No progress could be made if economic factors are viewed as being unconnected to the environment issues, she said. Leggewie, however, said the movement could already chalk up a huge success. "Worldwide, there's no one anymore who pursues globalization as it was in the 1990s," he said. "All of the criticism that is warranted is mainstream today -- such as criticism of the ecological consequences of unfettered globalization."

Securing Autonomy, Retaking the Initiative

South American social movements face an unprecedented panorama: the majority of governments on the continent define themselves as progressive or on the left. This is a reality which these same movements contributed to shaping and which can either help them to grow or block their development.

Indeed, seven of the ten South American countries have governments which claim affinity with the social movements.

This new scenario is having such an impact on the movements that they can no longer continue working as before. In broad outlines, there are two notable differences from the previous period. On the one hand, the contradiction between neo-liberal governments and social movements no longer takes first place. The growing polarization between new governments and the old right, now renewed with new issues and slogans, tends to displace the movements from their previous prominence.

In Venezuela and Bolivia the right is able to mobilize important sectors of the population, and in the latter case raises autonomy proposals that serve as an excellent playing field to bring together their societies. Something similar could happen in Ecuador when Rafael Correa takes office on January 15. In Argentina, the right is regrouping to block the advance of the human rights cause and was able to organize an important strike in the agricultural sector against Nestor Kirchner's policy for that area. In Brazil, the excuse for the electoral mobilization of the right was corruption.

The novelty is that the right is able to bring together segments of the middle classes and sometimes to take to the streets with hundreds of thousands of sympathizers. In these circumstances, not only are the movements and their demands displaced, but they are also forced to rally in support of governments with which they are often only partly in agreement.

On the other hand, a new relationship is emerging between the forces which make up progressive and left-wing governments and the popular sectors which form the social base of the movements. These are complex relations which are beginning to be built, almost everywhere, on the basis of previous policies focused against poverty. In general, there are two "models" in use on the continent.

The one being implemented in Ecuador, and to a certain extent in Bolivia, appears to be centred on "strengthening social organizations", which were assigned - starting with the creation of PRODEPINE (Development Project for Indian and Black Peoples of Ecuador) in the mid-1990's - the task of designing and implementing their own welfare programs. These programs have profoundly damaged the movements. In Ecuador, they were at the point of provoking a split in the Confederation of Indigenous Nationalities of Ecuador (CONAIE) and succeeded in weakening it considerably.

In Brazil, Argentina and Uruguay, the policies on poverty being implemented by progressive governments have taken a qualitative step forward compared to previous programs, all of them financed and promoted by the World Bank, as in the previous case (Ecuador). In a strict sense, we can no longer talk of "focused" policies, given that in Brazil they cover 25% of the population and in Argentina and Uruguay somewhere between 10 and 20%. In reality we are facing a reconfiguration of relations between the state and the popular sectors, different from the one which developed during the period of the welfare state.

The result is that these policies affect the capacity for action by the movements -- of the organized poor -- and further, tend to bring into question their own autonomy, gained during the period of hard and fast neo-liberalism. Two facts are at the base of this weakening effect: social subsidies generate client - and therefore, vertical - relations between the "social" ministries and the masses of unorganized poor, which now appear less inclined to mobilize. In parallel, many leaders of the movements move into lower-level jobs in the progressive governments, distancing themselves from their organizations or even placing them in a subordinate relation to the governments for which they work.

Faced with this new scenario, there is little use in insisting on repeating what until now has produced results. Recognizing the changes is the first step towards moving out of the current state of weakness. Insisting on strengthening autonomy (cultural, political, and material) appears essential for facing the current difficulties. On our continent, in addition to the Zapatistas, the landless of Brazil are those who have developed the clearest analysis. They did not hesitate to mobilize in support of Lula in the second round of elections, with the object of cutting off the right. But now they have launched a campaign of mobilizations and propaganda, knowing that without pressure from below Lula will not move a finger to implement agrarian reform. Although it is necessary, returning to the streets cannot solve all problems. As the coordinator of MST (Movement of the Landless Workers), Joao Pedro Stedile, points out, it is necessary to study, analyze and comprehend the new realities that are being born under these governments.

And finally, it appears indispensable to establish new relations between the organized sectors and the unorganized from below. Without that, it will not be possible to retake the initiative. But we still do not known precisely how, nor with whom, nor where. Everything points to the belts of poverty around the big cities being the scenario of future revolts. The landless are betting on the hip hop movement - on the poor black youth. In Buenos Aires, there are glimpses of new relations among the youth that mobilized in the pickets, the young poor influenced by underground music, and the Paraguayan and Bolivian immigrants. In any case, in these districts satanized by the powers-that-be - even the progressive powers - there is a world of potential which could feed new movements.

"Global Poverty or Global Justice?"

A quite new journal called GLOBALIZATIONS, edited by Barry K. Gills, a professor of International Relations at Newcastle University, recently published a special issue titled Global Poverty or Global Justice? [Volume 3, No.2, June 2006] The response has been such that Routledge, the journal's publisher, will now re-issue it in book form. Barry Gills, a young Fellow of TNI in the late 1980s and early 1990s, asked me for a preface to the volume, to appear later this year. He has graciously accepted that it appear on my TNI site prior to publication. We both hope this will encourage readers to look for the book later on and acquire it - I can vouch that it is well worth it.

The decision to publish as a book the Special Issue on "Global Poverty or Global Justice?" of the journal Globalizations is well-taken. With the exception of climate change, surely no question could be of such great import for our common future. This collection of articles deserves a broad audience and the present volume will help it to find one.

Rather, however, than indulging in the usual prefacer's routine noting that "A argues B and X demonstrates Y", giving each contributor deserved - certainly in the present case - praise; I want to tackle in my own way the issue that none of us, in these pages or elsewhere, can grasp in its entirety. The varieties of global injustice are too numerous, its victims too diverse, its perpetrators too devious for comprehensiveness. The title, however, "Global poverty or global justice?" asks the right question, assumes we have a choice between alternatives, and implies that sane people could not possibly want to choose global poverty.

I fear they could, they do. Consider the following: "All for ourselves and nothing for other people seems, in every age of the world, to have been the vile maxim of the masters of mankind". (1) This was the view of Adam Smith, who had no illusions about capitalism. He goes on to explain how, in his own time, such an outwardly sane person preferred a pair of diamond shoe-buckles, or any other frivolous and useless thing, to the upkeep of a thousand men for a year. The masters of mankind have consistently opted for other peoples' poverty over justice and, in our own age, they are suddenly able to do so on a global scale.

We must consequently revise our philosophical scale as well. From Plato's Republic onwards, until quite recently, the pursuit of justice was seen as a task for the polis, a discrete and homogenous community; or, later, for nation-States, but certainly not for an entity so vague as "the world". How could "the world" possibly undertake such a mission? Using what tools? What laws? What democracy? This is the new question a miscellaneous collection of geographically separated, vastly dissimilar people, with little money and none of the attributes of the masters of mankind, are, in a courageous - perhaps foolhardy - manner, attempting to answer. They have become part of a worldwide assembly with indistinct borders, a movement usually called [at least in English-speaking countries] the "global justice movement". This name is at once intuitive and innovative: time will tell if it is also hopelessly utopian. Whatever their dreams, this may well be the case, although the title of this book and the contributions it contains leave the question open and imply that they - that we - have a chance. From now on, I shall say "we".

The notion of justice surely encompasses such concepts as equity, equality, fairness, rewards and punishments, the proper satisfaction of human needs and so on. But for justice to exist in real human communities, there must above all be laws and the means to enforce them. Not for nothing are the law courts, in Latin-based languages, called "palaces of justice". Without reliable law, every struggle for human emancipation would be a Sisyphean task; every case of individual or collective victimhood would require a fresh start and the stone to be pushed up the mountain would grow heavier each time. A movement which hopes for justice yet cannot impose upon others the legitimacy, in the strongest legal sense of the word, of its objectives in the longer term is bound for disappointment and sooner or later for failure.

The quest for global justice thus demands global legitimacy and global law. Where are these to be found? Some brave texts, such as the Universal Declaration of Human Rights, are like beacons guiding us, but unenforceable. The more cynical, like Jeane Kirkpatrick, refer to this instrument as "a letter to Santa Claus". Actually existing global institutions such as the World Bank, International Monetary Fund and World Trade Organisation will never lead to global justice and can indeed be empirically shown to create its direct opposite. Present global rules are, on the whole, those of the unbridled free market or of military power in which wealth and might substitute for right. The longer such institutions remain in charge and such rules in force, the more deeply entrenched global injustice will necessarily become.

Furthermore, no entity one might call a global "people", as in "we the people", can be presently identified to oppose these institutions and the present rules in a coherent and unified way. During the past two centuries, in some nations, fairness and equality have visibly improved because popular struggles and elected governments, at least nominally "of the people, by the people, for the people", have instated them, but we are far from such achievements on a global scale.

We are far from them because we have no international democratic processes, machinery or institutions to work with. Even limited democracy and popular participation in the making and enforcing of law come to a brutal halt at national boundaries. While this state of affairs is not, to say the least, conducive to the establishment of global justice, it is extremely convenient for the present masters of mankind. Its laws and institutions suit their needs, and place the free-market economy on the ruler's throne. "Freedom" is not what anyone's democratic Founding Fathers understood by the word but rather the freedom of capital to go where it wants when it wants, to produce, buy and sell wherever it wants and to do so with the fewest constraints possible imposed by labour laws and social conventions.

This neo-liberal road is leading humanity into a wasteland. Rather than continuing to seek fairness where it is not to be found, or worse still, giving up, let us attempt to look at the problem of global justice in a fresh way. The global justice movement has at least a few good cards in its hand. For one thing, it is encouraging that a large body of scholarly work on "globalization" and "global systems" is being assembled; this volume is one example. Many of those contributing to this corpus honour the philosophical tradition which holds that thinking requires first and foremost saying No. "Posing the negative", challenging the received wisdom, advancing the dialectic has never been more urgent.

Nor is it that difficult. Myriad proof is virtually staring honest scholars in the face. Whether they concentrate on the public or the private actors in the global system, they can find an overwhelming embarrassment of riches. International governance rules are mostly set by the institutions one is tempted to call the Terrible Triplets - Bank, Fund, WTO - almost entirely in the interests of their most powerful members. When confronted, they often react by changing the names rather than the substance of their policies so that, for example, the failed HIPC - for Highly Indebted Poor Countries - initiative becomes the Poverty Reduction Strategy Papers; or the usual trade negotiations are labelled the Doha "Development" Round.

Despite the best efforts of these formal institutions, common or garden capitalist activities of transnational corporations and financial markets do, if anything, more damage than they do. Our present global system, based on turbo-capital and neo-liberal, Washington Consensus, free-market rules is engendering one human disaster after another. Without insisting on too many numbers, since a preface is not the best place for these, let us nonetheless cast a cursory glance at a sampling of the data.

We may take the case of debt, often identified by social movements as the most glaring of all global injustices. By 1980, the South was already seriously indebted with debt stocks amounting to $540 billion. Twenty-five years later, in 2004, the stocks had increased to $2.600 billion, nearly five times as much. Meanwhile, over the same twenty five years, these indebted countries had reimbursed $5.300 billion, almost ten times what they owed in 1980. Magic! From another perspective, we may note that after the Second World War, the United States provided war-torn Europe with the Marshall Plan, about $90 billion in today's currency. The South's reimbursements to the North have, over a quarter-century, provided the creditors with 59 Marshall Plans.

Perhaps debt's most inherently revolting aspect is that people who had no role in accumulating the debts are now called upon to make enormous sacrifices to reimburse them. Borrowed money rarely reached the poor; a fair proportion of it went straight to private accounts in Northern banks. Yet now, for example, even Sub-Saharan Africa, the poorest part of the world, continues to supply its creditors with $28.000 a minute. The global justice movement concentrated for a time on debt cancellation and was making headway, but the stonewalling of rich countries and institutions has continued and few countries have so far benefited. What the history of anti-debt struggles tell us that there is no level of human suffering which, in and of itself, will cause policies to be changed.

Nor were huge debt-service outflows compensated by aid, investment or other incoming funds. The net South-to-North transfer in 2004 was about $270 billion; it would have been much greater had the sums sent home by immigrants not figured in the totals. Pakistan's most lucrative export is people - remittances make up the major part of its foreign exchange; in the Philippines twenty-five million families rely on their emigrant members for survival. The calculations concerning net transfers in the North's favour do not include the yearly loss of tens of thousands of skilled workers moving from South to North in search of a better life. Poor people and poor countries often count on exports of one, two or three commodities for their foreign exchange but the rich countries, through prohibitive import duties, deny them the possibility of processing these. In the 20 years from 1980 to 2000, the price of sugar fell by 77 %, cocoa by 71%, coffee by 64%. Given that the average annual subsidy to a United States cotton farmer is about $100.000, one can calculate that, in terms of GDP per capita, a Malian cotton farmer would need about a hundred years to equal a single year of the Northerner's income from his subsidy alone. The Malian is also prevented from earning a fair return on his crop since US subsidies depress world cotton prices by at least a quarter.

What of the apparently legitimate activities of financial markets, whose currency speculators and leveraged merger and acquisition artists, working for the major banks and brokerage houses, are simply doing their jobs? The International Labour Organisation tallies ninety-five countries that suffered economic and financial crises between 1990 and 2003 alone. Many of these were caused by speculative attacks against their currencies and included the imposition of much higher interest rates and sharp devaluations, ruining businesses and reducing peoples' salaries, savings, pensions, etc. by at least a third.

More recently, and for good reason, the concept of ecological justice has entered the language. Present global rules and practices have even managed to increase the frequency and severity of natural disasters which one might think, erroneously, were evenly distributed. Once more, poor countries and poor people in rich ones, are disproportionately vulnerable. According to the ILO, "natural", weather-related disasters in the early years of our millennium are running at twice the rates of the mid-1990s; with some 600 million people [a great many of them poor farmers] affected by these events in 2002.

This was triple the average number of victims during the previous decade. Whereas the rich emit the greenhouse gasses that advance global warming; the poor take the consequences. Ecological neglect and over-exploitation of the environment increased the devastating impact of the Asian tsunami; Hurricane Katrina hit the poor unable to flee....one could go on and on.

Presumably, however, readers of this book will have their own collection of figures, of horror stories and the proper tools to add to them. None of us really needs any further proof of injustice because we are not wilfully ignoring the evidence. What we, and above all the people most affected need is some good news about official steps taken towards justice. Here, we risk further disappointment.

The standard panaceas proffered by the conventional wisdom, notably growth and trade, are not working. The Center for Economic and Policy Research [CEPR] in Washington has carried out pioneering work showing that neo-liberal policies practiced and imposed by both public and private institutions are not contributing to growth, which has notably slowed since 1980, the very moment when neo-liberal policies began to take hold. Nor is it wise to place one's hopes in trade as today's major importers are likely to reduce their purchases drastically.

The masters of mankind periodically gather to deplore the effects of poverty and injustice while remaining quite comfortable with their causes. The G-8 stops even talking about debt once the pressure is off. The achievement of the modest objectives of the Millennium Development Goals set in 2000 to be reached by 2015 will now require, we are reliably informed, over a hundred years.

The victims of injustice, particularly though not exclusively in the South, and their allies everywhere must change their future for themselves as the rich are not going to do it for them. The global justice movement, especially the scholars that count themselves part of it, can help by continuing to expose the policies that lead inexorably to poverty, and show why they do not and cannot work. Faced with well-financed neo-liberal propaganda, progressive researchers and teachers must impose their own legitimacy. It is also possible, though not always effective, to demonstrate why justice is in the interests of everyone, even of the masters of mankind.

Beyond these obvious steps, the global justice movement should take comfort in its very newness. Many would date its existence, even if several precursor moments could be cited, from the battle of Seattle against the WTO in late 1999. In historical terms, this is nothing, an instant. Hopeful signs exist all around us. Alliances are becoming easier to form as more and more groups recognise how they are being harmed by present policies. The internet works for us more than for our adversaries, reduces the costs of organising and provides alternative sources of information. Previously isolated struggles - for example, the "water wars" in Bolivia, and elsewhere - are providing templates for others and inspiring similar efforts to reclaim public water worldwide.

Every month seems to bring a new, at least mildly progressive, government in Latin America. Over a hundred governments have accepted the principle of international taxation and some have made a modest start by taxing airplane tickets; opening the way for a future global fiscal policy. The failures of established international institutions are harder and harder to hide and the legitimacy of elites is less and less recognised. Imperial wars no longer succeed and resistance to them, whatever its ambiguities, is increasing. In spite of setbacks, there are more democratic governments in the world than two decades ago and people who have tasted democracy do not willingly give it up. These can help to lay the foundations for international democracy.

As the manifold oppressions of global poverty grow, so do the hopes for global justice. A sense of acute urgency must accompany them. Undoubtedly every generation sees the problems of its own age as demanding urgent solutions - think of the people who fought against slavery or who saw the rise of fascism in the 1930s. In all such times, and ours is one, neutrality is blindness; impartiality between perpetrators and victims of injustice cowardly. Let us thank the authors in this volume and the editor, Barry Gills, for being both visionary and brave.

6

Promises and Actions of the NGOs

Those whom you push down will chain you down, Those whom you leave behind will pull you behind, The more you envelop them under darkness of ignorance, The more distant will your own welfare be, "Disgraced", Rabindranath Tagore

Last year, the Global Call to Action against Poverty (GCAP) established four key policy demands: debt cancellation, trade justice, a major increase in the quantity and quality of aid and national accountability - focusing mainly on accountability of national governments with regard to realising the Millenium Development Goals (MDGs).

In this context, several civil society coalitions have produced MDG shadow reports alongside those of National Governments which were prepared for the United Nations World Summit in September 2005. The civil society reports, which were produced in an exemplary consultative manner, have observed amongst others things that many National MDG Reports had failed to consult with civil society organisations which deal directly with communities. In addition, most of them utilized government statistics, which in many instances do not fully reflect the nature of the reality. In so doing, many governments have overstated their achievements with regard to the MDGs. For example the South-African MDG report while focusing on MDGs 3 and 4, on empowering women and on education, failed to note the number of girls dropping out of school due to pregnancies, financial factors etc. and only focused on the increase in numbers of those who started school (South Africa Civil Society Speaks report, issued by the Peoples' Budget Campaign and available at www.sangoco.org.za. Other interesting national reports include the Ugandan Report titled A Long Way to Go - Civil Society Perspectives on the progress and challenges of attaining the Millennium Development Goals (MDGs) in Uganda, (www.ngoforum.or.ug) and the Bangladesh People's Progress Report on MDGs (www.campebd.org).

International organisations such as Save the Children, CIDSE - and WEDO also produced focused monitoring tools and documents in the course of 2005. Using a child centred approach, Save the Children analysed the European Union's efforts to realise the MDGs. Their report makes key recommendations on achieving the MDGs at the EU level, including a series of "quick wins". CIDSE produced Europe: a true global partner for development (http://www.cidse.org/), which reports on the European Progress towards Millennium Development Goal 8. WEDO in their report "Women's Empowerment, Gender Equality and the Millennium Development Goals" (www.wedo.org,) describes the Millennium Development Goals, their connection to women's equality and strategies to ensure that they include a gender perspective.

One basic issue on which all these civil society groups involved in development and poverty alleviation agree, is the necessity and importance of facts and reliable statistics as a basis for any advocacy campaign. But why should CSOs be involved in monitoring? As Roberto Bissio, Social Watch Director, says: these initiatives "are not intended as pure research but are used to interpolate authorities and help shape better pro-poor and pro-women policies". Indeed monitoring helps:

* to improve on research and policy advocacy, and inform mobilisation
* to make National Governments fully accountable and transparent in the use of public resources
* to actively involve civil society, particularly poor and? excluded groups, in the formulation of national development priorities, policies and plans.

And what exactly should we be monitoring? Only the MDGs? As Brian Pratt from INTRAC writes: "Commitment to the MDGs is no doubt worthy. However, we need to be wary of allowing them to be used as an excuse for avoiding difficult political issues, and ignoring the very real complexity of human development in its widest understanding. Development cannot, and should not, be reduced to simple physical and technical indicators and we should question the real motives of those organisations and donors who adopt such methods. (...). We need to ensure that we maintain a vision of social justice, gender equity, and human development that relates to more than just the MDGs."

ActionAid International with its "As if people matter" global report in 2005, attempted to look further than just the MDGs, including in its analysis a human rights and gender based approach.

Finally, how should we monitor, so as to avoid reinventing the wheel? Certainly we should take advantage of some of the existing tools and networks, such as the Social Watch network established over 10 years ago. Social Watch's report 2005, available online at www.socialwatch.org/en/portada.htm, titled Roars and Whispers: gender and poverty: promises vs. action, provides a very comprehensive account of the state of poverty and gender equality globally and, more specifically, in 50 countries. Social Watch has actively followed up the fulfillment of internationally agreed commitments on poverty eradication and gender equality. Furthermore, they have developed tools such as the "Basic Capabilities Index" (perhaps the real alternative to the politically-accepted UNDP Human Development Index) as well as the "Gender Equity Index" to assist in this effort.

Two other monitoring initiatives are emerging and being developed that deserve our attention: the "African Monitor" initiative and the "European Aid Watching".

The "African Monitor" initiative , calls for an authentic African platform for making Africa's voice heard on Africa's needs. The African Monitor observes that the momentum in support of tangible and lasting change (which has been further fuelled by extensive advocacy efforts), is largely rooted in, and reflects the perspectives of, the global north. What is missing is a complementary and comprehensive contribution from Africa itself. The proposal for an African Monitor is designed to meet this need and so provide significant added weight to the call for poverty to be tackled. The promises of 2005 (which include a doubling of aid by 2010, and significant further debt cancellation) need to be implemented efficiently and effectively.

A second interesting initiative is the "European Aid Watching". A number of national European NGOs and Networks have decided to come together in 2006 to improve collective monitoring of European (bilateral and multilateral) aid spending. Indeed, if the commitments made in 2005 are acted upon, we will be witnessing the largest expansion of ODA since its establishment in 1960. European member states will be at the forefront of this, having pledged to increase their ODA by $38.3 million a year by 2010. This would result in Europeans collectively being the biggest givers of ODA, accounting for just over 60% of total overseas development assistance. This initiative has received acclaimed support from various civil society organisations. European Aid Watching will produce a joint NGO advocacy report to be launched in Brussels in April 2006.

While the world is growing richer, the poor are getting even poorer. Without a major shift in present trends, even the minimum targets agreed by the Heads of State and government at the Millennium Summit in 2000 will not be met. Therefore, we must listen to the people's voice, counter the official statistics where they don't reflect the reality and continually raise our concerns so as to bring about real and lasting change.

Keeping the Focus on Geneva

Last year, we were less than fifteen, but at this year's WTO July General Council meeting more than 300 civil society representatives were present in Geneva. Public debates, workshops, meetings, street mobilizations and actions were organized and joined by various groups from different parts of the world. Without doubt, what was happening at the counter event -- known as the "General Council of People"-- was a lot more exciting than the talk inside the WTO. More importantly, while inside the WTO, government negotiators and corporate lobbyists could not agree on the formulae to open up markets and carve-up trade profits, outside the WTO an unambiguous common position on the WTO has emerged among trade activists and social movements. This can be summed up as "no deal is better than bad deal". For most people, it is now obvious that in the current context of negotiations the only possible deal that the WTO could produce at the end of this year in Hong Kong is a bad deal. This convergence of analysis and understanding among activists is crucial for a strong campaign in the run up to Hong Kong. Still, there are a lot of challenges ahead of us.

Right after the WTO summer break, a very intense negotiation is anticipated and it seems that Geneva is going to be centre stage. During the last Trade Negotiation Committee (TNC) meeting, the chairperson called for all members to focus their energies on Geneva. This of course implies a central role for the WTO secretariat right at the moment when former EU trade commissioner Pascal Lamy takes over the helm. However, this in no way guarantees a more transparent and fairer negotiation process. Not only has the WTO secretariat never challenged the legitimacy of untransparent practices, such as the green rooms, mini-ministerials, and the use of the WTO facilities by corporations (to lobby governments), it often legitimizes, even facilitates, such processes. Undoubtedly, the green room process is going to be intense in the coming months and a mini-ministerial is reportedly scheduled in town before the October General Council.

All Eyes on Geneva in October

Northern governments are determined to squeeze developing countries for the most profit possible for their transnational corporations in this round. In order to achieve that, they need to establish a narrow framework for further negotiations as soon as possible, in which October will be a critical moment. On the part of the civil society, we also know that it is imperative to concentrate our efforts on Geneva this October. We were more than three hundred in July, but it will take much more than that to make a difference. Clearly, a lot more people must be in Geneva this time around. This means much more work needs to be done to mobilise the Genevois and the Swiss, and activists and movements from nearby regions and countries. But numbers are not the only crucial factor. Also key to the success of the October people's event is the broad representation of people from various sectors and from different parts of the world, particularly from the South. One of the good aspects of July mobilisation was that we had an interesting representation from social movements and NGOs from the South, but we must, and can, do better than that. Of course, to make it possible, more financial support is needed, but it is also important for trade activists in the South to understand the important of coming to Geneva, and realize that their contribution here is vital.

Linking to the Local Campaigns

Apart from the public events and mobilisations, the interaction with key countries delegations in Geneva is strategically important and the possibility of having civil society representatives from the same country as the officials with whom we meet leads to a more meaningful interaction and creates a sense of accountability with the government delegates. While we had interesting meeting with a number of missions in July, some were not ready to spare the time. This may be even more evident in October when many ministers are likely to be in town. That means we should be ready to employ new, innovative ways to get the messages through, in case a normal rendezvous is ignored.

There is a real danger of Geneva-based NGOs becoming detached from the work at the grassroots and national levels if there is not enough exchange and interaction. The General Council of People at the end of July was partly an attempt to bridge and create more synergy between the work in Geneva and campaigns in different countries and regions. However, in order to achieve complementary and coherent work, an event in itself is far from sufficient. The involvement of national campaigners and social movements in the preparation process for the mobilization and related activities in Geneva is vital. The inputs from national campaigns into the building up of arguments and debates in Geneva were lacking in July. This means there is much more that could be done in reaching-out and reaching-in between Geneva and beyond.

This does not mean that Geneva should become the centre of gravity in the people's campaign against trade liberalization.

On the contrary; the aim of mobilising in Geneva is to make the WTO and its corporate-oriented trade agenda irrelevant to people's lives, and this can only be achieved by ensuring that our campaigns at different levels support and strengthen each other.

People Power Rattling Politics of Latin America

First came the indignation, then the street protests and the disapproving comments from foreign countries. It culminated last Sunday with an estimated 1.2 million Mexicans marching silently through center of the capital. But President Vicente Fox moved to defuse the political crisis Wednesday night by accepting the resignation of his attorney general, who had been leading the criminal case against popular Mexico City Mayor and 2006 presidential hopeful Andrés Manuel López Obrador.

Chalk up another victory for Latin American people power. In the 1990s, what politicians feared most was apathy. But lately, Latin Americans from Mexico City to Quito, Ecuador - much like the citizens of Ukraine and Lebanon - have been taking to the streets in unprecedented numbers. Civic protest is emerging as an increasingly effective - if controversial - political tool. The power of the megaphone has been amplified by new organizing technologies: e-mail, Internet chat rooms, and text messages make it easier to contact, inspire, and bring people together quickly. The pro-López Obrador rally in Mexico City Sunday, for example, was coordinated via e-mail, with smaller protests in Los Angeles, Madrid, Rio de Janeiro, and Paris. The ever-larger demonstrations are mostly peaceful, usually self-controlled, always televised - and more often than not successful. "This is something new, if only in terms of the breadth, strength, and frequency of these movements lately," says Laura Carlsen, Mexico representative for International Relations Center, a civic-advocacy group. "Latin America's populations are increasingly looking for options and have decreasing patience with the promises of the past ... especially economic ones."

Seeds of a Protest

Yesterday, Elena Poniatowska, one of Mexico's best-known contemporary writers, awoke with a smile. Mr. López Obrador had turned up a month ago on her doorstep in a faded colonial neighborhood and asked for help. The leftist politician was in trouble. He needed a team, he explained, to help coordinate demonstrations, and he wanted her, an author who has dedicated her life to capturing the voices of Mexico, on it.

She signed up, spending her days planning with market hawkers, union workers, the unemployed, and university students. They created signs and they thought big. Sunday's rally was one of the largest protests ever seen in this city. "We were, in our own way, very loud," says Poniatowska with a smile. "And I think we have changed the situation."

Fox did not mention López Obrador or the protests in his speech Wednesday. But, he said, "As head of state, my duty is to promote national unity. My administration will not stop anybody from running in the next federal elections." Fox had previously said López Obrador should face charges for ignoring a 2001 court order to stop building a road on private land to a hospital. Earlier this month, Mexico's congress voted to strip López Obrador of the immunity his office provides. A conviction in the land case would have made a presidential bid illegal.

A similar story of public outrage spun out earlier this month in Ecuador, where people took to the streets chanting and banging pots and pans - and demanding the resignation of President Lucio Gutiérrez, who had illegally dissolved the Supreme Court. Within a few days, the president fled the country. "The demonstrations got bigger and bigger. The whole city seemed to be out on the streets and the process took over," says César Montúfar, executive director of Participación Ciudadana, a Quito civic organization involved in the recent protests in Ecuador. "In a country with weak institutions and illegitimate and corrupt leaders, citizens became actors in the only way they could."

Riordan Roett, director of the Latin American Studies Program at the Johns Hopkins School of Advanced International Studies (SAIS) in Washington, sees the phenomenon as a "redefinition of civil society," able today to stand up to traditional elites. "Ten to 15 years ago, many of these countries were just coming out from under dictatorial rule and civil society was weak and disorganized, and it took a while for civil society to restructure itself," says Mr. Roett. "Today, their high expectations have been disappointed, and the people are saying ...we are democratic and independent and we. can assert ourselves."

Since 1990, 10 South American leaders have had to step down before their terms ended, many eased out by mass protests against them, according to the Argentine think tank Nueva Mayoria. A popular uprising brought down Bolivian President Gonzalo Sanchez de Lozada in 2003, and then almost toppled his replacement, President Carlos Mesa, earlier this year; Peru and Argentina have all seen their governments fall, with angry crowds thronging the capital. In Ecuador, Mr. Gutiérrez is the third president in a decade to be forced from office. And Haiti has seen several elected leaders brought down by mass protests.

In Nicaragua, President Enrique Bolaños put the Army on standby Tuesday night after two weeks of sometimes violent street protests against bus-fare hikes. Rival politicians are calling on him to resolve the crisis or resign.

The Latin Difference

Mass marches are, of course, not exclusive to Latin America. From Kiev to Hong Kong to Beirut, demonstrators have been pushing governments. But analysts say that the waves of public protest in Latin America illustrate a coincidence in the democratic development of the continent: the weakening of authoritarian regimes and the growing self-assurance of the people - including, in the case in Bolivia, the indigenous.

Governments and militaries, to start, are far more reluctant than in the past to repress demonstrators, says Poniatowska. She is best known for her book "La Noche de Tlatelolco," about the Army's massacre of student activists in Mexico City in 1968. "That was a very different time," she says.

Marta Lagos, an economist and pollster in Chile, says, "This is all a very healthy thing. People have an idea what real democracy is, and they know they don't have it quite yet. They want governments that represent them and they will go out to the streets to get that."

But some observers see the phenomenon as negative. They say the protests may prevent democratic institutions from carrying out their functions, thus undermining judicial independence and the rule of law. "This is not constructive participation," argues Vinay Jawahar at the Inter-American Dialogue in Washington. "It is hard to argue that this sort of instability is good for a country." Mr. Jawahar calls the argument that people have no other recourse "opportunistic." "The idea that as soon as people are unhappy with the performance of a president they can remove him means that legitimacy begins to rely on popularity, and it is dangerous when the two are confused."

But back in Mexico, the diminutive 72-year-old Poniatowska is not worried about such risks. It's 8 a.m. Thursday and she is listening to Fox's speech on the radio. Interior Secretary Santiago Creel, the presumptive presidential candidate from Fox's party is talking about "putting the López Obrador case to one side and getting on with our work." Poniatowska is satisfied, for the moment, that her work is done.

The Ethical Revolution Sweeping through the World's Sweatshops

They are the global brands that have raked in multimillion-pound profits on the back of sweatshop labor in developing countries. But after a decade of denying any wrongdoing, companies such as Nike and Gap are now admitting that their workers have been exploited and abused, and have pledged to improve the conditions of the millions of people who are paid a few pence a day to make their top-selling goods. The wholesale reform is being hailed as a victory for anti-sweatshop campaigners who just a few years ago were being derided and dismissed by the big brand names. With consumers becoming increasingly concerned with "ethical shopping", activists say firms are realizing that being linked with sweatshop labor can lead to a dip rather than a rise in profits.

This week, for the first time, Nike published details of the 700 factories that make its goods in an effort to create more "transparency" for customers. The company pledged to set up a task force to ensure that its codes of conduct on pay, hours and conditions are complied with. Extraordinarily, Phil Knight, the founder and chairman of Nike, also admitted that the firm had failed to respond to previous allegations of exploitation, and disclosed that a quarter of its factories were still not meeting minimum standards. Just two years ago, Nike aggressively defended a court case in which it was accused by activists of lying and making misleading claims about its working practices in a corporate and social responsibility report. The company eventually donated $2m (£1.1m) to the American Fair Labor Association as part of an out of court settlement.

The clothing company Gap made a similar declaration a few months ago when it published a shocking "social responsibility" report that revealed terrible working conditions in its factories in Mexico, China, Russia and India. Gap cancelled contracts with 136 factories after the report disclosed details of child labor, the virtual slavery of workers and working weeks in excess of 80 hours. Levi Strauss, the jeans company, is now being praised by anti-sweatshop campaigners for working with unions and activists to improve conditions in its factories, when just a few years ago it was accused of a "two fingers" attitude towards allegations of exploitation.

Mick Duncan, the founder and secretary of the campaign group No Sweat, said: "When the protests and campaigns first started 10 years ago, the companies were really bullish - they either completely denied there was a problem or adopted a 'so what?' attitude. The real change we have seen in the last year or so is that they are putting their hands up to it and admitting that they have got a problem. "There is a still long way to go but we are beginning to see real movement on this issue."

Campaigners have changed their tactics in recent years, from backing boycotts and protesting outside city stores, to playing companies at their own game and then working with them to improve conditions. The protests started in America in the 1990s, when Levi Strauss moved its operations from California to factories in Mexico. But the campaigns were run by the big American unions and their attitude was more protectionist than focused on the plight of foreign workers. Then in the mid 1990s, students became involved, staging protests on behalf of Mexican workers and supporting strikes and attempts to organize local unions. When No Sweat was established, it decided not to back boycott campaigns. Mr Duncan said: "Boycotts just meant that people don't buy the goods, companies close down factories and people lose their jobs. What we have switched to doing is working on the ground with the workers and local unions, and working with the companies to improve conditions and pay." Activists have also used slick poster campaigns and detailed research to raise awareness among consumers of the issue. Sam Maher, of the protest group Labor Behind The Label, said: "These companies are obsessed with branding and spend millions of pounds on advertising to get a very particular image of their products across. By raising awareness of sweatshop labor, that really tarnished the brands, and hit these companies where they hurt."

Having been "fobbed off" in the late 1990s by companies issuing codes of conduct, which were then routinely broken, activists have now piled pressure on the companies to raise monitoring standards and ensure compliance. And in the David and Goliath battle of the small activists against big business, even the companies themselves are admitting defeat. Hans Faber, the senior manager in corporate communications for Nike Europe, said: "There have been problems in the past and we admit that, and one of our weaknesses was that we thought we could sort these out on our own. We are now working with NGOs and governments, and the campaigners, to make sure standards are raised, because we care about the people who work for us, and of course our customers."

But concerns remain over the continued abuse of garment workers around the world - 70 per cent of them are women, particularly with the ending in January this year of the World Trade Organization's multi-fibre agreement. The MFA was established in the 1970s and set international quotas for textiles, in an effort to protect the industries of countries with higher manufacturing costs from a flood of cheaper foreign imports. Campaigners are worried that the scrapping of the agreement will lead to a huge shift in manufacturing to countries with the cheapest costs but the worst record on working conditions, such as China. And despite some companies' repentance and reforms, other top-name brands are still using sweatshops. Among those on the target list of campaigners are Tommy Hilfiger, Umbro and Fila.

People Power Gets to G7

Nelson Mandela, 86, needed no support when he walked up to address thousands at Trafalgar Square in London Thursday. He had the support of a cheering crowd, and of one of the most powerful movements ever to gather against world poverty.

Mandela spoke at Trafalgar Square -- London's traditional venue for people to make a political statement -- on the eve of the meeting Friday and Saturday of finance ministers from the G7 countries (the United States, Canada, Britain, France, Germany, Italy and Japan). He was carrying a message for that meeting, and succeeded before it began.

Steps to counter poverty are already set to dominate the G7 meeting. Traditionally G7 finance ministers are more given to talk of exchange rates and macro multinational issues. What Mandela says counts, and behind Mandela spoke about 220 British civil society groups who invited him to the Trafalgar Square rally. The British groups came together late last year in a campaign 'Make Poverty History'.

"Many of us realised that 2005 is going to be an important year to campaign against poverty," Lysbeth Holdoway from Oxfam who has been working with the Make Poverty History campaign told IPS Thursday. This year Britain has presidency of G8 (which includes also Russia) and will have presidency of the European Union (EU) in the second half of the year. "So we have come together this year in UK and around the world to put pressure on governments to act," she said. The British movement is tied internationally into the Global Campaign for Action Against Poverty.

Mandela was invited to Trafalgar Square "because he is such an important leader, and we know that if he came people would have to take action," Holdoway said. The immediate result was that civil society, backed by all major trade unions and the Church of England, has managed at least in substantial measure to set the agenda for a G7 finance ministers' meeting.

"As you know, I recently formally announced my retirement from public life and should really not be here," Mandela said. "However, as long as poverty, injustice and gross inequality persist in our world, none of us can truly rest." Mandela linked the new civil society campaign with his own campaign against apartheid. "The Global Campaign for Action Against Poverty can take its place as a public movement alongside the movement to abolish slavery and the international solidarity against apartheid," he said.

Mandela told the wildly cheering crowd: "I can never thank the people of Britain enough for their support through those days of the struggle against apartheid. . . . Through your will and passion, you assisted in consigning that evil system forever to history. But in this new century, millions of people in the world's poorest countries remain imprisoned, enslaved, and in chains. They are trapped in the prison of poverty. It is time to set them free." There was more than emotion to Mandela's appeal. "The steps that are needed from the developed nations are clear," he said. "The first is ensuring trade justice. The second is an end to the debt crisis for the poorest countries. The third is to deliver much more aid and make sure it is of the highest quality."

Mandela said finally: "I say to all those (G7) leaders: do not look the other way; do not hesitate. Recognise that the world is hungry for action, not words. Act with courage and vision." Mandela was due to take his message directly to the ministers at a meeting with them Friday. The task will not be easy, Mandela said. "But not to do this would be a crime against humanity, against which I ask all humanity now to rise up."

The Mandela-civil society cocktail was made considerably stronger with support from Britain's chancellor of the exchequer (finance minister) Gordon Brown. Brown wants the ministers to extend a freeze on debt repayment by the tsunami-hit countries, and to take decisions to write off the debt of the poorest nations. At the least Brown wants about 40 billion dollars owed by the poorest countries, most of them in Africa, to be completely written off. He is also looking for radical decisions on more fair trade rules and for a doubling of developmental aid.

Members of the Make Poverty History campaign point out that 2.8 billion people around the world live in poverty, and that 30,000 die from poverty- related causes every day.

Britain last hosted the G8 meeting in Birmingham in 1998. An estimated 70,000 people came together then to form a human chain around the city centre to demand cancellation of unpayable debt. This time the civil society groups who brought those people together are a stronger force -- with stronger allies.

More than 1,000 NGOs Launch

More than 1,000 NGOs, backed by Brazil's president, launched a global campaign to press world leaders to halve poverty within 10 years. The non-governmental organizations issued their ambitious appeal for worldwide mobilization against poverty on the sidelines of the World Social Forum in the southern Brazilian city of Porto Alegre. The groups urged people around the world to press for adherence to the UN Millennium Development Goals, which aim to cut poverty by half by 2015.

Brazilian President Luiz Inacio Lula da Silva, a left-leaning former trade union leader, hailed the new campaign. "The global campaign has a vision and a profile to which we can adhere as president of Brazil and as leader of an emerging nation that has been able to put in the forefront of international concern something other than war and fighting terrorism," he said. "For the first time, the Forum takes upon itself the task of making a priority of an issue such as poverty," Lula told some 15,000 people, many of them from his Workers Party.

But about 100 people jeered Lula, who has faced mounting criticism from his erstwhile staunch supporters who claim he has strayed from his leftist past to maintain the South American country on a pro free-market track. Following his appearance at the event, Lula headed to Switzerland to attend the Davos summit of the world's political, financial and business heavyweights. Many participants at the WSF see the gathering in the Swiss Alps as a celebration of the crass capitalism they oppose.

In Porto Alegre, the NGOs urged "world citizens" to wear white ribbons around their wrists to show their support for the anti-poverty campaign, which they said would be backed by publicity spots featuring personalities such as former US President Bill Clinton, UN Secretary General Kofi Annan, and rockers Bono and Lenny Kravitz. "We citizens must press governments, multilateral organizations and companies to assume their responsibilities to eradicate the shameful scourge of poverty," said Candido Grzybowski, one of the organizers of the forum.

John Samuel, of the Consultative Group to Assist the Poorest -- a consortium of 28 private and public donor agencies -- likened the ravages of poverty to those wrought by the December 26 tidal waves that killed 280,000 people in south Asia. Samuel, who recently surveyed the devastation in India, decried what he called "a silent tsunami in Africa, in Congo, in Rwanda" and in Asia, where "millions of children die of hunger." In their appeal, the NGOs called for "justice in trade relations, debt eradication, a real increase of official development aid, and national public policies to eliminate poverty that must be democratic, transparent and controled by citizens."

Development aid organizations, including Oxfam and Caritas, as well as trade unions were key in launching the "white ribbon campaign." Guy Ryder, of the International Confederation of Free Trade Unions, said the campaign was crucial at a time when one out of six children works instead of going to school and a record 185 million people worldwide have no job. "This appeal should reach all the way to Davos," said Ryder.

Where Have all the Protesters Gone?

Far fewer than the usual number of protesters were on the streets when the World Bank and the IMF met for their annual conclave in Washington on October 2-3. While many observers interpret this as evidence that the anti-globalization movement is on the wane, that may not necessarily be the case.

Consider the parable about a man who looks for his keys under the streetlights instead of where he lost them. Asked why, he said, "Because it's easier to see where the light is better." The resistance to globalization may be found by shedding light not only on demonstrations in Washington, but by also looking beyond those public displays. What Prime Minister Tony Blair derided as the "traveling circus" of anti-globalization is not fading out; it's simply adapting to the post-9/11 phase of globalization. But is it really anti-globalization? Just as with the debate over the word "terrorism," in defining anti-globalization, the power of language matters. Language conjures up meanings and images, and accordingly, the vocabulary varies according to the positions of the strong and the weak. Recall that during the apartheid era, South Africa's white redoubt and President Ronald Reagan alike called the imprisoned Nelson Mandela a terrorist, but he later received the Nobel Peace Prize.

Similarly, the idiom anti-globalization, deployed by star columnists and celebrity economists in the West, pigeonholes diverse actions. The difficulty is that it slots a wide variety of stances on globalization in two boxes: for and against. This over-simplification obscures myriad complaints about globalization and the debates over ways to engage, not evade, it.

Moreover, the use of the prefix anti- defines the resistance solely as a negation and, thus, the term eliminates the idea of the creation of positive alternatives. Many critics resist not because they are against aspects of globalization such as increased access to innovative technologies, more information, and new knowledge. Rather, without entertaining fantasies about a make-believe world, they are trying to imagine possibilities for a just world, an alter-globalization.

Now, the main sites of the conflict over globalization are no longer fortified meetings of international economic summits. So, too, the strategy of protest no longer centers on counter-summits at the Battles of Seattle. More often, the issue is framed as the conflict over the efforts to secure economic globalization by military means. This debate is largely about "global empire."

The global justice movement, heterogeneous networks without a hierarchy of leaders, is merging with the peace movement. They see President George W. Bush, aided by his squad of advisors, as the commander-in-chief of militarized globalization. While the campaign against corporate power and the powerful international economic institutions continues, a prime target of protest is US military interventions that would safeguard globalization.

Another site of contesting globalization can be found in practices of everyday life, certainly a more subtle and latent form of resistance. My students at Ritsumeikan University in Kyoto prepared a paper on "The Resistance to Genetically Modified Foods in Japan." Strikingly, the students' incisive research shows that, despite the absence of conspicuous confrontations over globalization in Japan, there is substantial and highly varied resistance to it. In a country that has not experienced large-scale protests against globalization, the government supported the biotechnology industry's efforts to redesign plants using genes from other organisms, including different species. Opposition came not from head-on street demonstrations, but from consumers, especially the Consumers Union of Japan, and dairy farmers. Not stridently voiced, their apprehension reflects uncertainty over safety, the ethical question of tampering with nature, and media coverage and advertisements regarding genetically modified foods. Certain Japanese food companies felt obliged to address public concerns through either official pronouncements or altered policies. For example, Taishi Food Industry stated that "we never use GM [genetically modified] crops as raw materials." Similarly, Kikkoman, Japan's largest soy sauce company, changed the soybeans in its "marudaizu" series and labeled its nongenetically modified products. A second team of student researchers prepared a paper on "WTO and Farming Product (Rice)," which details another quiet form of resistance. Not surprisingly, Japanese rice growers oppose opening to the global market because they do not want to face stiff international competition. Also, they perceive open markets as a threat to their identity, connections to nature, and cultural and spiritual heritage, of which rice is a principal part. Competition from overseas and mechanized technology endangers family farming, as well as the life-ways and values attendant to it.

For many Japanese consumers, the taste of foreign rice is unappealing. They fear that the pesticides applied in countries with little regulation present health risks. At bottom, the issues regarding governmental policy and the WTO's promotion of free trade are seen as matters of cultural dignity, food security, and environmental protection. Without making big noise, their resistance meshed several forms, some of them different from the Western varieties. Yet another site of resistance to globalization is within people's mindsets. In Washington, in April 2002, a colleague, 12 graduate students, and I interviewed 243 participants at a rally sponsored by the organization Mobilization for Global Justice. We administered our questionnaire consisting of 25 items about participation in protests, attitudes toward globalization, and the strategies of the global justice movement. When asked the most important reason for protesting globalization, only 6 percent of the interviewees said "to abolish the international financial institutions." The largest single response was to oppose US foreign policy. The majority of those interviewed regarded the US government as an active, interventionist agent of globalization. Queried about violence, nearly two-thirds of the interviewees ruled it out, while only four percent strongly agreed that violence is a legitimate strategy. A large plurality of those surveyed disapproved of violence under any circumstances, invoking the names of Mahatma Gandhi or Martin Luther King, Jr., or a religion to justify their position.

In our survey of changing attitudes, we found that those who resist globalization do not reject it or adopt an across-the-board anti-globalization stance. Although core international economic institutions are seen as problematic, the resistance embraces the gains of globalization.

The agenda has shifted to what can be done to harness globalization so that its benefits are inclusive and its processes are more transparent, participatory, and democratic. The emphasis is on formulating concrete, affirmative proposals. To develop them, there are infrastructures, such as the San Francisco-based International Forum on Globalization. Also, since 2001, the World Social Forum has brought together representatives of social movements from several countries. Meeting in Porto Alegre, Brazil, and then in Mumbai, India, participants think about ways to enact alternatives to neoliberal globalization and have established regional forums.

Increasingly, the protest over the dark side of globalization may be found both within and outside governments and intergovernmental organizations. Chaired by the foreign ministers of a northern and a southern country, Finland and Tanzania, the Helsinki Process on Globalisation and Democracy is assembling leading globalization actors and activists to develop and implement ideas for equitable human security. The key to removing the blinkers is to turn on the high and low beams. The task is to illuminate not only the street theater that dramatizes the harsh side of globalization, but also the other stages where new forms of resistance and novel opportunities may be found.

A Milestone in the Global Struggle Against Injustice and War

We are assembled here in Beirut at a critical moment. It is a moment marked by crosscurrents: In Iraq, the US gets deeper and deeper into a Vietnam-style quagmire, with the number of American soldiers killed since the March 20, 2003 invasion passing the 1,000 mark in the first week of September. Yet in Palestine, the Zionist Wall continues to be built at the rate of a kilometer a day. A year ago, on September 14, 2003, some of us in this hall were in Cancun, Mexico, dancing with joy at the Convention Center as we celebrated the collapse of the Fifth Ministerial Meeting of the World Trade Organization. Today, the WTO, the supreme institution of corporate-driven globalization, is back on its feet with the adoption last month of the Geneva Framework Document designed to speed up the economic disarmament of developing countries.

In New York a few weeks back, we saw massive repudiation of George W. Bush and his pro-war policies by over 500,000 people that marched in the streets of New York. Yet, today, polls show that the same George Bush has a 10 per cent lead over John Kerry in the lead-up to elections the results of which will have a massive impact on the fate of the world in the next few years. The future, comrades, is in the balance, as we meet in this historic city, with its glorious history of resistance to Israeli aggression and American intervention. As you know, many more people wanted to come to Beirut to be with us. The size, breadth, and diversity of our assembly here today underline the strength, the power of our movement. It would be useful to briefly review our history over the last decade to gain an appreciation of where we are today.

March from Marginalization

Less than 10 years ago, our movement was marginalized. The founding of the WTO in 1995 seemed to signal that globalization was the wave of the future, and that those who opposed it were destined to suffer the same fate as the Luddites that fought against the introduction of machines during the industrial revolution. Globalization was going to bring prosperity in its wake, and how could one oppose the promise of the greatest good for the greatest number that the transnational corporations, guided by the invisible hand of the market, were going to shower the world? But the movement stood firm in the face of the scorn of the establishment during the 1990's, when the boom in the world's mightiest capitalist engine-the US economy-appeared to be destined to go on and on. It was steadfast in its prediction that, driven by the logic of corporate profitability, the liberalization and deregulation of trade and finance would bring about crises, widen inequalities within and across countries, and increase global poverty.

The Asian financial crisis in 1997 provided sudden, savage proof of the destabilizing impact of eliminating controls from the flow of global capital. Indeed, what could be more savage than the fact that the crisis would bring 1 million people in Thailand and 22 million people in Indonesia below the poverty line in the space of a few weeks in the fateful summer of 1997?

The Asian financial crisis was one of those momentous events that removed the scales from people's eyes and enabled them see cold, brutal realities. And one of those realities was the fact that the free market policies that the International Monetary Fund and the World Bank imposed on some 100 developing and transitional economies had induced, in all but a handful of them, not a virtuous circle of growth, prosperity, and equality but a vicious cycle of economic stagnation, poverty, and inequality. The year 2001 brought us not only Sept. 11. 2001 was also the year of reckoning for free-market fundamentalism-the year that the Argentine economy, the poster boy of neoliberal economics, crashed, while in the United States, the contradictions of finance-driven, deregulated global capitalism wiped out $4.6 trillion in investor wealth-half of the US' gross domestic product-and inaugurated a period of stagnation and rising unemployment from which the world's central capitalist economy has not recovered till today.

As global capitalism moved from crisis to crisis, people organized in the streets, in work places, in the political arena to counter its destructive logic. In December 1999, massive street resistance by over 50,000 demonstrators combined with a revolt of the developing governments inside the Seattle convention center to bring down the third ministerial of the WTO. Global protests also eroded the legitimacy of the IMF and the World Bank, the two other pillars of global economic governance, albeit in less dramatic fashion. Anti-neoliberal mass movements brought new governments to power in Venezuela, Argentina, Brazil, Ecuador, and Bolivia. The fifth ministerial meeting in Cancun, an event associated in many people's minds with the altruistic suicide of the Korean farmer Lee Kyung-Hae at the barricades, became Seattle II. And, in November last year, in Miami, the same alliance of civil society and developing country governments forced Washington to retreat from the neoliberal program of radical liberalization of trade, finance, and investment that it had threatened to impose in the western hemisphere via the Free Trade Area of the Americas (FTAA).

Fighting against Empire

The fight for global justice and equity has been one thrust of our movement. The other has been the struggle against militarism and war. For the movement against imperial intervention, the 1980's and 1990's were not good decades. National liberation struggles retreated, lost momentum, or were compromised in many parts of the world. Of course, there were exceptions, as in South Africa, where the ANC came to power; Palestine, where the first Intifadah handed Israel a political and military defeat; Lebanon, from where the US fled in 1983 after 241 American Marines perished in the bombing of their base located just a few kilometers away from here, and from where the Israelis were gradually squeezed out over the next decade; and, not to forget, Somalia, where the destruction of a US Ranger unit in Mogadishu forced the Clinton administration to terminate its military intervention in October 1993. The ideologues of globalization promoted the illusion that accelerated globalization would bring about the reign of "perpetual peace." In contrast, our movement warned that as globalization proceeded, its economically and socially destabilizing effects would multiply conflicts and insecurities. Driven by corporate logic, globalization, we warned, would herald an era of aggressive imperialism that would seek to batter down opposition, seize control of natural resources, and secure markets. We were proved right, but it took us some time to gain our bearings.

We were still too disoriented by the events of September 11, 2001, and by the internal politics of Afghanistan to enable us to respond effectively to the US invasion of that country. But it was soon clear that the so-called War against Terror was simply an excuse for implementing a quest for Absolute Military Supremacy or, in Pentagon jargon, "Full Spectrum Dominance."

In late 2002 and early 2003, the movement finally swung into action, becoming a global force for justice and peace that mobilized tens of millions of people throughout the world on Feb. 15, 2003, against the planned invasion of Iraq. We did not succeed in stopping the American and British invasion, but we have surely contributed to delegitimizing the Occupation and made it increasingly difficult for invaders that have brazenly violated international law and many rules of the Geneva Convention to remain in Iraq. The New York Times, on the occasion of the Feb. 15, 2003, march, said that there are only two superpowers left in the world today, the United States and global civil society. Let me add that I have no doubt that the forces of justice and peace will prevail over the contemporary incarnation of empire, blood, terror, and greed that is the USA.

Bibliography

Aptekar, Lewis. *Street children of Cali,* Durham, Duke University Press,1988.

Gabriel, Marie Cruz: *Children of the street,* New York, Penguin Books, 1994.

Global Policy Forum: *NGOs and the United Nations,* New York, Global Policy Forum, 1999.

Harold K. Jacobson: *Networks of Interdependence: international organizations and the global political system,* New York, Knopf, 1984.

John Boli and George Thomas: *Constructing World Culture: International Nongovernmental Organizations Since 1875,* Stanford, Stanford University Press, 1999.

John Ehrenberg: *Civil Society: The Critical History of an Idea,* New York, New York University Press, 1998.

Marcos Arruda: *NGOs and the World Bank: Is It Possible to Collaborate Critically?,* Rio de Janeiro: PACS, 1995.

Paul J. Nelson: *The World Bank and NGOs: The Limits of Apolitical Development,* New York, St. Martin's Press, 1995.

Peter Willetts: *Pressure Groups in the Global System,* London, Francis Pinter, 1982

Thomas G. Weiss & Leon Gordenker: *NGOs, the UN & Global Governance,* Boulder, Lynne Riener, 1996.

Thomas Princen and Matthias Finger: *Environmental NGOs in World Politics,* London, Routledge, 1994.

Yolanda N. Kakabadse and Sarah Burns: *Movers and Shapers: NGOs in International Affairs,* Washington DC, World Resources Institute, 1994.

Index

A

Adoption, 23, 29, 89, 151, 254, 298.
Architecture, 139, 158.
Association, 10, 11, 18, 62, 110, 131, 180, 289.
Atmosphere, 41, 44, 53, 54, 55, 56, 57, 75, 80, 81, 82, 83, 98, 121.

B

Business, 3, 24, 36, 66, 67, 133, 134, 142, 143, 168, 172, 176, 185, 192, 208, 210, 211, 221, 222, 233, 235, 236, 237, 238, 239, 240, 241, 242, 243, 244, 245, 246, 248, 249, 258, 260, 261, 264, 268, 290, 293.

C

Communication, 1, 5, 16, 55, 215.
Concentration, 53, 56, 57, 60, 83, 168, 247.
Construction, 7, 22, 42, 43, 44, 49, 50, 52, 53, 77, 78, 80, 85, 86, 88, 97, 110, 112, 113, 195, 199.
Contribution, 54, 80, 113, 131, 137, 193, 281, 284.
Criticisms, 238.

D

Departments, 9, 13, 14, 34, 35, 39, 40, 114, 120, 188.

E

Economics, 116, 129, 171, 235, 256, 299.
Ecosystem, 1, 20, 91, 98, 99, 100.
Employment, 46, 142.

F

Financial Institutions, 127, 128, 131, 136, 137, 148, 167, 168, 169, 171, 173, 219, 297.

G

Global Compact, 241.
Global Warming, 218, 252, 276.

H

Human Rights NGOs, 188.

I

Industry, 2, 24, 31, 32, 37, 42, 43, 44, 47, 52, 53, 54, 55, 57, 58, 61, 62, 65, 66, 92, 97, 147, 160, 161, 234, 236, 244,. 245, 246, 247, 255, 296.
Infrastructure, 154, 179, 180, 186, 268.

Insurance, 22, 218, 219, 220, 247, 248.
Investment, 40, 73, 102, 125, 134, 147, 149, 154, 155, 156, 159, 170, 178, 216, 219, 220, 221, 222, 228, 248, 264, 275, 300.

L

Laws, 4, 23, 32, 39, 42, 49, 89, 92, 100, 101, 102, 103, 105, 106, 113, 127, 157, 170, 194, 196, 198, 199, 200, 201, 202, 210, 221, 222, 246, 247, 267, 272, 273, 274.

M

Management, 13, 15, 18, 20, 32, 33, 34, 35, 36, 37, 42, 50, 51, 52, 66, 72, 89, 90, 95, 96, 97, 99, 113, 159, 165, 185, 226, 237, 244, 245, 246.
Manufacturing, 43, 44, 77, 290.

N

Nuclear Power, 74, 77, 78, 86, 237.

O

Observations, 55, 56, 63.
Operations, 73, 74, 122, 138, 139, 143, 144, 145, 147, 165, 172, 179, 182, 187, 189, 191, 215, 222, 230, 242, 250, 253, 289.
Ownership, 141, 154, 178, 179.

P

Partnerships, 122, 235, 236, 237, 238, 239, 240.
Performance, 128, 142, 181, 218, 243, 288.
Politicians, 248, 250, 253, 285, 287.
Politics, 3, 159, 215, 217, 220, 285, 301.
Property, 76, 79, 87, 103, 104, 105, 256.
Proteins, 83.

R

Renewable Energy, 147.
Revolution, 40, 288, 299.

S

Security, 1, 15, 16, 64, 88, 132, 133, 134, 156, 167, 168, 169, 171, 176, 177, 178, 185, 259, 263, 296, 298.

T

Technology, 2, 18, 45, 47, 215, 244, 245, 246, 257, 296.
Traditions, 268.
Transportation, 19, 43, 45, 47, 56, 81, 82, 176.

V

Ventilation, 57.

W

Wars, 278.
Wind Power, 237.
Workshop, 114, 115, 117, 118.